Tax Cooperation in an Unjust World

Tax Cooperation in an Unjust World

ALLISON CHRISTIANS
LAURENS VAN APELDOORN

OXFORD
UNIVERSITY PRESS

OXFORD
UNIVERSITY PRESS

Great Clarendon Street, Oxford, OX2 6DP,
United Kingdom

Oxford University Press is a department of the University of Oxford. It furthers the University's objective of excellence in research, scholarship, and education by publishing worldwide. Oxford is a registered trade mark of Oxford University Press in the UK and in certain other countries

First Edition published in 2021

Impression: 1

Published in the United States of America by Oxford University Press
198 Madison Avenue, New York, NY 10016, United States of America

British Library Cataloguing in Publication Data

Data available

Library of Congress Control Number: 2021940613

ISBN 978–0–19–284867–3

DOI: 10.1093/oso/9780192848673.001.0001

Printed and bound by
CPI Group (UK) Ltd, Croydon, CR0 4YY

Transferred to digital printing 2022

Acknowledgements

This book is the culmination of several years of writing, presenting, and collaborating with colleagues, students, and friends across disciplines and professions and around the world. We wish to thank everyone who made useful suggestions over the years, including anonymous referees. We are grateful to the research assistance of our students, in particular Jodie Côté Marshall, Nicole Maylor, Andrew Medeiros, and Lily Maya Wang, and to all of the students and alumni with whom we have worked over the years, whose work and encouragement continue to inspire us. Our research was supported by grants from the Ford Foundation, the Social Sciences and Humanities Research Council of Canada, and the H. Heward Stikeman Tax Law Initiatives Fund at the Faculty of Law, McGill University.

Acknowledgements

Contents

Introduction

In this book we set out to demonstrate the key role that the international tax system plays in achieving justice. To do so, we first establish that the international tax system currently allows states with great wealth to claim more than they are justifiably entitled to from the global economy. We then demonstrate that this status quo both facilitates and feeds off continued human suffering, and therefore violates even minimal conceptions of international distributive justice. Finally, we explain how this situation of ongoing injustice can be addressed through existing institutions and processes and show that a fairer international tax system could be achieved with incremental yet effective adaptation, that is, without requiring radical reform or a new world tax order.

In making these claims, the book connects theories about tax policy largely from the legal and economics literature to theories of international justice from philosophical literature. As with any interdisciplinary effort, doing so risks alienating both camps. We hope we have muted this risk by showing that foundational commitments of widely accepted conceptions of international justice are reflected in existing tax policy, even if norms and processes do not fully reflect those underlying principles.

Two main observations motivate the book: first, that there are extreme conditions of injustice in the world today; and, second, that the international tax system currently contributes to this injustice but is capable of altering course.

It is short work to demonstrate the first point. Popular media and academic writing continuously document the ongoing suffering of peoples all over the world despite the presence of vast wealth, much of which derives from cooperation among nations, which has allowed global investment to multiply over the past century. The Sustainable Development Goals, unanimously adopted by the 193 member states of the United Nations in 2015, clearly demonstrate the global scope of unmet needs and attendant injustices visited upon the world's most vulnerable populations.[1] The COVID-19 pandemic threw these existing

[1] UN, *Transforming Our World: The 2030 Agenda for Sustainable Development* (United Nations 2015).

Tax Cooperation in an Unjust World. Allison Christians and Laurens van Apeldoorn, Oxford University Press.
 DOI: 10.1093/oso/9780192848673.003.0001

problems into sharp relief even as it dramatically increased their scope and magnitude.

There is broad agreement among the main intergovernmental institutions—the United Nations, the Organisation for Economic Co-operation and Development (OECD), the International Monetary Fund (IMF), and the World Bank—that tax revenues are key to resolving these injustices.[2] All of these institutions, together with countless nongovernmental organizations, are working on strategies to 'mobilize' revenues to meet the demands of the Sustainable Development Goals.[3] The problems are well documented and well known, and the proposed solutions always involve directing money to the right programs and initiatives, often through multilateral cooperative efforts.[4]

The real work of this book is to demonstrate the second point: that conventional tax norms and the institutions we have built to further them are both implicated in the problem and capable of delivering a solution. It is a more challenging task to demonstrate this because tax norms and institutions clash and cooperate through multiple interactions of domestic and international legal and quasi-legal institutions and actors, all of which have multiple interconnected economic, political, social, and cultural impacts in the world.[5] Any positive claims about this legal order risk errors of omission and commission given the sheer scope of the phenomenon being studied.[6] Likewise, any proposed change to a given legal rule or norm can have any number of possible economic effects involving any number of different people, with any number of social implications.

[2] UN, 'Addis Ababa Action Agenda: Monitoring Commitments and Actions' (2016); World Bank, 'Conference Report: Taxation and the Sustainable Development Goals' (23 April 2019) 9.

[3] World Bank, 'Domestic Resource Mobilization' (World Bank 2018); OECD, 'Global Outlook on Financing for Sustainable Development 2019' (2019).

[4] UN, 'Addis Ababa Action Agenda' (n 2).

[5] Yariv Brauner, 'An International Tax Regime in Crystallization' (2003) 56 Tax L Rev 259; Insop Pak, 'International Finance and State Sovereignty: Global Governance in the International Tax Regime' (2004) 10 Ann Surv Int'l & Comp L 165; Allison Christians 'Hard Law and Soft Law in International Taxation' (2007) 25 Wisc J Int'l L 325; Reuven Avi-Yonah, *International Tax as International Law: An Analysis of the International Tax Regime* (Cambridge University Press 2007) 1; Allison Christians, 'Networks, Norms, and National Tax Policy' (2010) 9 Wash U Glob Studies L Rev 1; Kerri Sadiq, 'The Inherent International Tax Regime and Its Constraints on Australia's Sovereignty' (2012) 31 U Queensland LJ 131; Terence C Halliday and Gregory Shaffer, *Transnational Legal Orders* (Cambridge University Press, 2015); João Marcus de Melo Rigoni 'The International Tax Regime in the Twenty-First Century: The Emergence of a Third Stage' (2017) 45 Intertax 3; Allison Christians, 'BEPS and the New International Tax Order' (2016) 1 BYU L Rev 603.

[6] Christina D Romer and David H Romer, 'The Macroeconomic Effects of Tax Changes: Estimates Based on a New Measure of Fiscal Shocks' (2010) 100 Am Econ Rev 763; William G Gale and Andrew A Samwick, 'Effects of Income Tax Changes on Economic Growth' (2016) Brookings <www.brookings.edu>.

Yet history teaches that reform becomes possible when serious problems come to light and receive adequate attention from policymakers. Significant reform of a number of key tax regimes is currently underway in multiple forms, most especially through the coordinating efforts of the OECD, long the world leader in international coordination on tax. In particular, since at least the mid 1990s, the OECD's work on harmful tax competition identified what in more recent years has become redefined as base erosion and profit shifting (BEPS), an issue that has rallied states both within and beyond the OECD membership to revisit some of the fundamental principles at stake. Given the massive revenue needs sparked by the pandemic, the attention of the world's policymakers to the challenge of BEPS will likely be stronger than ever in the years to come.

BEPS is roughly defined as the widespread availability of tax avoidance regimes and strategies that allow individuals and multinational enterprises, either facilitated by states or due to unintended mismatches between national tax systems, to shift profits into lower-tax jurisdictions and away from the places in which they really generate income.[7] These practices, the OECD warns, unfairly erode the tax bases of states, distort trade and investment patterns, and may 'hamper the application of progressive tax rates and the achievement of redistributive goals.'[8]

Together with the United Nations, the IMF, and the World Bank, the OECD has expressed the view that base erosion and profit shifting stand as major impediments to states raising the revenues they need to meet the aims identified within the Sustainable Development Goal framework.[9] The most recent focus of the OECD on this project has been an ambitious program of work to reconsider some of the most fundamental norms of taxation in the name of more fairly sharing the global profits arising from the digitalization of the economy.[10] That work continues apace and is likely to seed additional rounds of negotiation over the cooperative norms, rules, and institutions of taxation.

[7] OECD, *Action Plan on Base Erosion and Profit Shifting* (OECD Publishing 2013); OECD, *Harmful Tax Competition: An Emerging Global Issue* (OECD Publishing 1998).

[8] OECD, *Harmful Tax Competition* (n 7) 14.

[9] United Nations, 'Inter-agency Task Force on Financing for Development, Financing for Development: Progress and Prospects' (2018) <https://developmentfinance.un.org/sites/developmentfinance.un.org/files/Report_IATF_2018.pdf>; Trade and Development Board Intergovernmental Group of Experts on Financing for Development, 'Financing for Development: Issues in Domestic Public Resource Mobilization and International Development Cooperation' (2017) <unctad.org/meetings/en/SessionalDocuments/IGE_FfD_1st_session_Agreed_Policy%20_Recommendations.pdf> See also OECD, *Measuring Distance to the SDG Targets: An Assessment of Where OECD Countries Stand* (OECD Publishing 2017).

[10] OECD, *Base Erosion and Profit Shifting (BEPS) Action Plan Report on Addressing the Tax Challenges of the Digital Economy* (OECD Publishing 2015). The emphasis on fairness in this respect dates back to a 2001 framework agreement on the taxation of e-commerce, which is referenced in the 2015 Action Plan Report. OECD, *Taxation and Electronic Commerce-Implementing the Ottawa Framework Conditions* (OECD Publishing 2001).

All of these efforts are aimed at solving identified problems of fairness in taxation. Many of the problems we see being addressed in today's coordination efforts were brought to the fore by tax justice activism, which emerged following the 2008 global financial crisis when growing public concern about threats to social safety net programs rose sharply in relatively affluent states.[11] The current global public health crisis, which is simultaneously a global economic crisis and a humanitarian crisis in many parts of the world, significantly raises the stakes. Against the backdrop of the 2008 crisis, multiple media reports emerged of extremely low taxes paid on a worldwide basis by extremely visible and apparently profitable multinationals. Activists responded to that confluence of factors by launching successful tax justice campaigns to foment public ire in Europe and beyond, prompting European lawmakers to respond both in European institutional contexts as well as in the broader international community through the OECD.[12] Since then, tax justice advocates have continued their calls for reforms in the direction of increased corporate tax disclosure, while new urgency has developed around the rise of major digitalized business models with the likes of Amazon, Apple, Facebook, and Google at the forefront.

Central to the analysis of the problems identified as publicly unacceptable, and the solutions in the OECD-led initiatives in response, is the persistent normative question about which states are entitled to tax what, and the related question of which should prevail if more than one is entitled to tax. Answering these questions in normative terms is one of the main goals of this book; demonstrating the feasibility of moving closer to a more just tax system is the other.

Structure of the Book

Chapter 1 opens the discussion by introducing and examining the principle that states are entitled to the wealth generated within their territories and by their people, and the related principle of fair cooperation, which holds that states are entitled to share equally in the benefits of cooperation between them. The principles follow from a conception of international justice—widely, if implicitly accepted in international tax policy debates—that accepts the existence

[11] See, eg, '2011 Revisited: Charting the Year,' *The Economist*, 31 December 2011 <http://www.economist.com/node/21542191> accessed 12 April 2021.

[12] Allison Christians and Stephen Shay, *Assessing BEPS: Origins, Standards and Responses* (Int'l Fisc Assoc Cahier 102A, 2017).

of independent states of unequal affluence as morally justified and identifies only a limited set of principles as regulating their interactions. The chapter examines the meaning of the two principles assuming a just world, and then explains how national tax practices function as a means by which states share in the benefits of their cooperation with other states. An examination of prevailing tax norms and standards reveals that the entitlement and fair cooperation principles, while not always fully theorized, are nevertheless deeply embedded in the ways nations actually exercise their taxing powers. We conclude that the entitlement principle entails that states that host cross-border investment (commonly if imperfectly referred to as source states) are entitled to tax the income from such investment and moreover, given the principle of fair cooperation, they are entitled to an international tax system that enables them to exercise this entitlement.

Chapter 2 then presents a puzzle: even though there is broad agreement that source states are entitled to tax, many source states exercise this jurisdiction to a limited extent or not at all. The chapter offers two explanations: tax competition and international pressure, including through treaties and soft law. It examines how these two factors impede the fulfilment of the entitlement principle and result in an unequal sharing of the benefits from cooperation among states. We observe that the world now faces an extraordinary moment in which reform is actively under consideration at the multilateral level and multiple paths forward are currently possible. The language of fairness and justice appears within these dialogues, but we think that the underlying theories are currently underdeveloped and need to be both clarified and strengthened. As such, we conclude that this is an opportune moment to present our case for reforms for the reasons and in the ways we explore in the rest of the book.

Chapter 3 presents our first normative argument for international tax reform. The claim we make is that relatively affluent and well-ordered states have duties of assistance to help fulfil subsistence rights abroad, and that these duties directly impact the entitlement principle. The chapter sets out the duty of assistance and explains its relevance to taxation, analysing the implication that states' entitlement to the wealth of their territory is conditional on them having discharged their duty of assistance. It argues that until this duty is met, the gains arising from international investment of capital from states that do not suffer subsistence rights deficits into states that do should be seen as belonging to the latter until such time as subsistence rights can be met. Only then may states press their entitlement to the wealth of their territory and demand that the gains of international investment and production be shared among them.

Chapter 4 applies the claim made in Chapter 3 by examining the practical implications it holds for the design of international tax norms and standards. The main observation is that states suffering subsistence rights deficits are entitled to (at least) all the gains arising from cross-border investment originating from reasonably affluent states, until such time as these deficits are eliminated. In practice, this requires residence states to cede the right to tax in such a way that enables tax at source rather than discouraging it. The chapter examines a range of approaches residence states could take to achieve this result and concludes that given the feasibility and the lack of harm to relatively affluent states themselves in carrying out these policies, they can and must do so whenever their residents' cross-border investment flows interact with states suffering subsistence rights deficits.

Considering that there are those who would reasonably disagree with the principle that states have duties of assistance as described, Chapter 5 then revisits the implications of the entitlement and fair cooperation principles in an unjust world if one rejects the existence of such duties. The objective of this chapter is to show that, even then, the existence of subsistence rights deficits has significant implications for what states can rightfully claim as part of their entitlement. The chapter thus makes our second normative case for international tax reform. It does so by showing that even when states are not directly responsible for either the existence or rectification of subsistence rights deficits, this does not mean that they are entitled to all of the gain that is produced as a result of such deficits. In fact, they may be entitled to none of it, depending on the circumstances that produced the gains in question. The chapter establishes that subsistence rights deficits must be accounted for in determining what constitutes a fair sharing of benefits and burdens of investment among cooperating states.

Chapter 6 then applies the claim made in Chapter 5 by examining the practical implications it holds for the design of international tax norms and standards. This chapter explains in practical terms how subsistence rights deficits could be incorporated into conventional source tax rules in order to ensure that the principle of fair cooperation can be met. In doing so, it demonstrates that accounting for the cost of subsistence rights deficits is already possible (indeed, analogous practices already exist), so current practices could be moderately expanded to better reflect the normative imperative. We consider some of the likely objections and alternative policy prescriptions and conclude that our overall approach is not only normatively justified, it is also feasible because it is conceptually consistent with the current trajectory of multilateral tax cooperation efforts.

The book concludes with a call to action. The need to respond to moral claims upon the relatively affluent is urgent. It is unjust to remain complacent in the face of suffering from which those with the greatest resources financially benefit. Relatively affluent states should not continue to claim their own entitlements to wealth while denying the same to others that lack the ability to influence the relevant tax policy institutions and processes. The need for urgency is only confirmed, and the means for action furthered, by the ongoing efforts of the international community to redefine the international tax system to achieve more fairness among states. A reckoning with the parameters and implications of the entitlement principle and of fair cooperation must be seen as an urgent priority in this process, lest the mistakes of the past continue into the future.

1

Two Principles for Tax Cooperation

The goal of this first chapter is to lay the groundwork for the arguments that follow in the remainder of this book. We examine the role of taxation in securing justice in the context of a global economy characterized by international capital mobility. We proceed from a widely (though hardly universally) endorsed view of international justice that accepts the existence of independent states on the world stage under the so-called society-of-states model of international justice. On this model, associated most famously with John Rawls's *The Law of Peoples*, principles of international justice are geared towards securing the political autonomy of states—their ability to independently develop and sustain (minimally) just domestic institutions—which on the whole requires a policy of non-interference on the part of other states.[1] In this chapter, we start to consider the implications of this view for international tax cooperation by identifying two principles applicable to such cooperation in a world that is fully just.

We identify the purpose of cooperation on international taxation in terms of two complementary aims autonomous states have in a globalized economy: on the one hand the pursuit of national wealth through the facilitation of international capital mobility, and on the other hand the continued protection of their political autonomy. We argue that the first aim gives rise to fairness questions regarding the distribution of the benefits of this cooperation (the 'cooperative surplus') between the cooperating states. We suggest two principles of international justice applicable to resolve these fairness questions: what we will respectively call the entitlement principle and the equal benefit principle. We argue that the second aim requires that these principles be implemented in a way that allows states to remain politically autonomous, which in practice requires that they remain capable of pursuing income taxation. In the next chapter, we will consider some of the main obstacles to achieving these aims and the prospects for removing them.

[1] John Rawls, *The Law of Peoples, with The Idea of Public Reason Revisited* (Harvard University Press 1999).

Tax Cooperation in an Unjust World. Allison Christians and Laurens van Apeldoorn, Oxford University Press. © Allison Christians and Laurens van Apeldoorn 2021. DOI: 10.1093/oso/9780192848673.003.0002

1.1. International Justice

The vision of a fully just world, presented by those defending a society-of-states model of international justice, is a world in which states pursue their own ends within a framework of rules that guarantees the independence of each. In *Law of Peoples* (1999), John Rawls presents the most influential defence of such an account of international justice. He gives pride of place to the political autonomy of states (or 'peoples' as he calls them, for reasons that are not relevant here)[2] by which he means the ability to independently develop and sustain (minimally) just domestic institutions. Plausibly, such autonomy requires both being protected from interference by other states and being afforded a certain amount of effective control in securing policy outcomes.

Concerning the relevant policy outcomes, one may think first of the establishment of an effective legal system necessary for the realization of individual rights, but also of certain arrangements in the realm of health care, social security, and the domestic (re)distribution of wealth, among others necessary for a reasonable provision of the material needs of their populations.[3] The political autonomy of states must be achieved, Rawls argues, by the global implementation of a number of principles to regulate the actions of states broadly familiar from 'the history and usages of international law and practice.'[4] The key principles include the duty of non-intervention and territorial integrity, the duty to observe treaties and conventions, the prohibition of warfare other than for reasons of self-defence, and the duty to honour human rights.

Notably absent are principles of international justice requiring the redistribution of wealth between states of unequal affluence. It is true that Rawls accepts the existence of the so-called duty of assistance, to which we will return later in the book, which may require wealth transfers to what he calls burdened societies lacking political autonomy. However, international justice as Rawls understands it is compatible with significant global wealth inequality. For Rawls, principles of international justice answer the question of how states,

[2] See, Buchanan, 'Rawls's Law of Peoples: Rules for a Vanished Westphalian World' (2000) 110(4) Ethics 698–99.

[3] See Miriam Ronzoni, 'The Global Order: A Case of Background Injustice? A Practice-Dependent Account' (2009) 37(3) Phil & Pub Aff 229–56, at 248 for this development of Rawls's analysis of political autonomy, which is taken up by Dietsch in his work on tax competition. See Peter Dietsch, *Catching Capital: The Ethics of Tax Competition* (Oxford University Press 2015) 121–22. Dietsch puts this in terms of 'de facto', rather than 'de jure' sovereignty—sovereignty related to substantive policy space, rather than formal legislative authority. Buchanan, 'Vanished Westphalian World' (n 2) 702, emphasizes that for Rawls each state must be 'distributionally autonomous', which is to say that it 'can determine how wealth is distributed within its borders.'

[4] Rawls, *Law of Peoples* (n 1) 57.

as equal and independent members of the society of states, should interact and cooperate with one another. The principles both constitute states as independent actors and full members of the society of states (by attributing to them certain rights and powers) as well as regulate their international relations (by imposing certain obligations).

On this model, global economic integration, including the proliferation of international trade and capital mobility we see today, is the product of voluntary cooperation by states. States are conceived as being initially autarkic, having fully closed economies and allowing no economic relations between them. When states wish to take advantage of opportunities to cooperate for their mutual advantage, for instance by pursuing economic integration, they must coordinate relevant domestic rules and/or create and uphold international institutions that implement mutually agreed terms of accommodation and coordination.

The question arises whether international justice places demands on these actions. Are there any further principles of justice that apply to the various forms of voluntary cooperation between states? Some authors have answered this question in the negative. Thomas Nagel, for instance, argues that international treaties and conventions shaping economic globalization 'are "pure" contracts, and nothing guarantees the justice of their results', other than the requirement that states observe their agreements and mutually respect their political independence.[5] However, most defenders of the society-of-states model, Rawls among them, think that specific principles of international justice *do* apply to voluntary cooperation between states.[6] We agree with those authors and will argue for two: the equal benefit principle and the entitlement principle.

These principles apply to voluntary cooperation between states pursuing an augmentation of national wealth and concern the distribution of the benefits and burdens that result from their cooperation. It means that states, if they choose to cooperate for their mutual advantage, must structure their cooperation in a way that conforms to these principles. They must also continue to protect the political autonomy of each. This also applies to the terms of cooperation, as identified by means of these two principles. Cooperation between states must always be pursued in a way that is autonomy-preserving (that is to say, states must remain capable of securing for themselves minimally just

[5] Thomas Nagel, 'The Problem of Global Justice' (2005) 33(2) Phil & Pub Aff 141.

[6] Eg with respect to international taxation, specifically, these authors include Ronzoni, 'Global Order' (n 3) and Dietsch, *Catching Capital* (n 3).

domestic institutions). The political autonomy of states is, in other words, a limiting factor on the global rules they may create and the practices they may support in aid of their mutual advantage. As we shall see below, this has important implications for the design of fair international tax rules.

The Equal Benefit Principle

The equal benefit principle concerns the distribution of the (net) benefits of the cooperative surplus. It holds that *having undertaken to cooperate with each other, states are entitled to equally share in the (net) benefits produced by such cooperation.*

When states mutually enable economic activity across borders, the equal benefit principle requires that they must equally benefit from such cooperation—none can be required to be satisfied with fewer or no gains merely due to a lack of relative bargaining power.

Rawls alludes to such a principle when he notes that a full account of international justice should include 'standards of fairness for trade and other cooperative institutions.'[7] Rawls does not elaborate much on what these fair terms of cooperation might be, unfortunately. He suggests that cooperation between states must be 'to everyone's mutual advantage, at least in the longer run,'[8] which requires that it is 'suitably regulated by a fair background framework.'[9] David Miller argues that when states cooperate for their mutual advantage, 'the costs and benefits of co-operation should be fairly allocated, so that each party receives approximately the same net gain.'[10] Miller's proposal, in turn, has been further fleshed out by Aaron James, applying it specifically to the case of international trade in goods and services. He argues for what he calls the 'international relative gains principle,' which requires that the gains of trade be distributed equally between cooperating states.[11]

[7] Rawls, *Law of Peoples* (n 1). He also suggests that if cooperation between states has 'unjustified distributive effects' these would have to be corrected (Rawls, *Laws of Peoples* (n 1) 115).

[8] Rawls, *Law of Peoples* (n 1) 43.

[9] Rawls, *Law of Peoples* (n 1) 42: 'unless fair background conditions exist and are maintained over time from one generation to the next, market transactions will not remain fair, and unjustified inequalities among peoples [states] will gradually develop.'

[10] David Miller, 'National Responsibility and Global Justice' (2008) 11(4) Crit Rev Int'l Soc & Pol Phil 383–99, at 396–97; also D Miller, *National Responsibility and Global Justice* (Oxford University Press 2007) 76; D Miller, 'Fair Trade: What Does It Mean and Why Does it Matter?' (2017) 14(3) J Moral Phil 249–69, at 269.

[11] Aaron James, *Fairness in Practice: A Social Contract for a Global Economy* (Oxford University Press 2012) 18. Also Aaron James 'A Theory of Fairness in Trade' (2014) 1(2) Moral Phil & Pol; Aaron James, 'Fairness in Trade' in David Held and Pietro Maffettone (eds), *Global Political Theory Today* (Polity

James notes that international trade between private parties is only possible because states facilitate it. It is a practice fundamentally structured by the cooperation of trading states: it consists in the facilitation of, and reliance upon, a market within which individuals and companies transact across borders. The same holds true for cross-border investment. The relevant benefits of these practices (which international justice requires to be fairly allocated) are not the benefits accruing to the individual market participants but the benefits accruing to the states that facilitate their transactions.

States participate in a practice of market reliance by removing tariffs and other trade barriers on a reciprocal basis and by coordinating an international division of labour on mutually agreed terms. They thereby facilitate the creation of additional national income, income that would not have arisen but for their cooperative efforts. Since these gains cannot be attributed to the efforts of any one state but only to the efforts of all of them together, and since states must be considered as moral equals with symmetrical interests (namely the augmentation of their national wealth), James asserts that 'the default fair division is equality of gain in (endowment-adjusted) national income'.[12] From a moral perspective, the gains from trade are analogous to a windfall to which none of the trading nations has any special entitlement, and which must therefore be shared equally.

James agrees with Miller that the principle applies only to the distribution of the net gains of cooperation, that is, 'the benefits and burdens that international economic integration *creates*'.[13] This means that its application requires a determination of the gains of economic integration in relation to the counterfactual situation of national economic autarky. James renders his equal relative gains principle sensitive to pre-existing national endowments by requiring the equalization of endowment adjusted gains, such that wealthier and more developed states receive a greater share of the total (gross) surplus (since they would have been more productive than other states had no trade taken place).[14] The principle takes into account the opportunity costs of cooperation: since larger and wealthier states would have gained more in autarky than smaller and poorer states, they must receive a larger share of the gross gains from trade for the net gains to be equally distributed. The endowment

Press 2016). James defends the international relative gains principle as component of a 'practice dependent' account of justice.

[12] James, *Fairness in Practice* (n 11) 168.
[13] James, *Fairness in Practice* (n 11) 18.
[14] James, *Fairness in Practice* (n 11) 222.

adjustment proposed by James, in other words, does not apply to the *net*, but the gross, gains of cooperation—the net gains must be equally shared between the cooperating states.[15]

The Entitlement Principle

The equal benefit principle presupposes a commitment to what we call the entitlement principle. Briefly stated, the entitlement principle holds that *states have an entitlement to their 'national endowment,' that is, the wealth of their territory.*

The equal benefit principle presupposes that states have an entitlement to their national endowment in two respects. First, states are required only to equally share the cooperative surplus. This means that they are entitled to pre-existing endowments not produced through cooperation as well as to the gains arising from cooperation that can be considered the opportunity costs of such cooperation—gains the state would have produced in autarky by productively employing its national endowment locally. As Miller puts it, '[e]qual net benefit applies only to the surplus created by the co-operation. It leaves untouched inequalities that arise independently of it.'[16] The endowment adjustment, included in James's version of the equal benefit principle, is required on the basis of the entitlement principle: wealthier and more developed states receive a greater share of the total (gross) surplus created by international trade because they are, on the basis of the entitlement principle, entitled to the wealth they would have produced in autarky.

Second, states only have an entitlement to share (equally) in the cooperative surplus because in the production of that surplus they employ their respective national endowments to which they are entitled. If they did not have an entitlement to their pre-existing national endowments, it would be hard to explain why they should receive an equal share of the benefits produced by productively employing those endowments in international cooperation: they would be benefiting from a cooperative scheme by contributing resources to which they were not entitled to begin with.

Hence, there is good reason to think that both James and Miller would accept what we call the entitlement principle. Rawls' commitment to the principle

[15] See James, 'A Theory of Fairness' (n 11) 181, fn 9: the endowment adjustment is a means to identify the gains from trade, such that, once the gains of trade are identified, the gains must be shared equally (and no further adjustments are necessary).

[16] Miller, 'National Responsibility and Global Justice' (n 10) 395.

is beyond dispute. It is, in fact, at the very core of his theory of international justice. He holds (ignoring, for the moment, certain exceptional circumstances) that states are exclusively entitled to the wealth, goods, and resources they control and create. His justification for this view draws in part on an analogy with the institution of individual property. Property incentivizes agents to maintain and cultivate assets that would otherwise deteriorate or be wasted. Similarly, granting states an exclusive entitlement to the wealth in their territory incentivizes them to cultivate their land and resources.[17] Additionally, he denies that national prosperity depends on access to resources, instead crediting 'the political culture, the political virtues and civic society of the country, its members' probity and industriousness, [and] their capacity for innovation'.[18]

On this understanding of the causes of prosperity, Rawls considers it inappropriate to require the redistribution of wealth between states, for instance to correct inter-state wealth inequalities. He asks us to consider an example of states with effective political and social institutions at the same level of wealth. The first decides to industrialize while the other, 'preferring a more pastoral and leisurely society,' does not. Since the resulting wealth inequality is the result of the states' autonomous choices, it is inappropriate to require the former to redistribute its newly acquired wealth to the latter.[19] In this way, the entitlement of states to their national endowment is consistent with his emphasis on the importance of political autonomy and non-interference: the entitlement principle protects the political autonomy of states to shape economic, social, and political institutions according to the views of their citizens and to be responsible for the effects of those choices.

That Rawls is committed to the entitlement principle is perhaps easy to overlook as he does not include it (or a version of it) in the list of principles of international justice he defends.[20] This may explain why Charles Beitz, an otherwise insightful critic of Rawls, presents a somewhat misleading picture when he writes of the Rawlsian view that it lacks 'any principle of international distributive justice' and 'each state is assumed to have a right to the wealth of its territory, and [that] there are no moral rules regarding the structure and conduct of economic relations between states.'[21] It is true that Rawls's theory lacks a principle of distributive justice in the sense that Rawls denies that justice requires the regulation of distributive inequalities between states. Yet, the principle that

[17] Rawls, *Law of Peoples* (n 1) 8, 39.
[18] Rawls, *Law of Peoples* (n 1) 108.
[19] Rawls, *Law of Peoples* (n 1) 118.
[20] See Rawls, *Law of Peoples* (n 1) 37.
[21] Charles Beitz, *Political Theory and International Relations* (Princeton University Press 1999) 66.

states have a right to the wealth of their territory is *itself* a principle of distributive justice. It concerns the rights and duties of states in their relations concerning the distribution of wealth between them.

Implicit Acceptance in Practice

Rawls's commitment to what we call the entitlement principle has appeared to many of his readers to be ultimately untenable.[22] An early critic submits that Rawls's theory of international justice is obsolete, written for a 'vanished Westphalian world'.[23] Deep global political and economic integration has undermined the plausibility of his conception of states as politically autonomous, entitled to the wealth of their territory, and engaged in isolated practices of international cooperation.

Our aim is not to defend the society-of-states model of international justice against its critics. Rather, in this book we wish to show what justice requires in international tax policy, assuming the model is correct. We do so because we believe that the basic commitments of the theory, and its apparently conservative implications, are shared by many in the international tax community today.

The entitlement principle, in particular, is overt in the language of rights used by policymakers and researchers seeking to explain taxation as a phenomenon and as an impetus for international cooperation. The influence of the equal benefit principle is more visible in its historical violation than its acceptance, but its normative weight has become evident with the opening of the international tax policymaking realm to more states of different wealth and development levels. As such, recent iterations in international tax cooperation have exposed past unfairness and generated pressure to establish fair terms of cooperation going forward.

For instance, in the face of political pressure to address problems of tax avoidance by large multinational companies, the OECD calls for 'a realignment of taxation and relevant substance'[24] to restore the capacity of states to exercise their 'legitimate right to tax the profits of a taxpayer based upon income and

[22] The voluminous literature includes Beitz, *Political Theory* (n 21); Gillian Brock, *Global Justice: A Cosmopolitan Account* (Oxford University Press 2009); Darrel Moellendorf, 'Constructing the Law of Peoples' (1996) 77(2) Pac Phil Q 132–54; Martha Nussbaum, *Frontiers of Justice* (Harvard University Press 2006).

[23] Buchanan, 'Vanished Westphalian World' (n 2).

[24] OECD, *Action Plan on Base Erosion and Profit Shifting* (OECD Publishing 2013) 13.

expenses that can reasonably be considered to arise within their territory.'[25] The implicit concern is that if states cannot exercise their legitimate rights to tax, then not all returns, fairly attributable to domestic factors, will be retained in the domestic economy. The same sentiment is expressed in the OECD's aim of ensuring 'that profits are taxed where economic activities take place and value is created.'[26]

This idea has also been widely endorsed by governments, companies, and non-governmental organizations. It has recently been included in the Multilateral Convention to Implement Tax Treaty Related Measures to Prevent Base Erosion and Profit Shifting, signed in 2016 by over 100 countries and entered into force in 2018. A 2016 review of statements on tax strategies published by FTSE 100 companies revealed that about 25 per cent are committed to 'paying the right amount of tax where value is created.'[27] Non-governmental organizations and advocacy groups, including Oxfam, ActionAid, Christian Aid, Tax Justice Network, and the Fair Tax Mark, have accepted it as essential prerequisite for fair corporate taxation.[28] Indeed, the Fair Tax Mark, a 'fair trade'-style branding and marketing strategy established by tax justice advocates in 2014, accredits businesses that are 'good taxpayers.'[29] The basic premise of the Fair Tax Mark is that a business seeks 'to pay the right amount of tax (but no more) in the right place at the right time, where 'right' means that the economic substance of the transactions undertaken coincides with the place and form in which they are reported for taxation purposes.'[30]

These statements signal widespread agreement on the plausibility, at least in outline, of the society-of-states model of international justice: they imply that states are entitled to the wealth of their territory and must fairly share the

[25] OECD, *OECD Transfer Pricing Guidelines for Multinational Enterprises and Tax Administrations* (OECD Publishing 2017) 15, also 55.

[26] OECD, *Aligning Transfer Pricing Outcomes with Value Creation, Actions 8-10-2015 Final Reports* (OECD Publishing 2015) 3.

[27] Maya Forstater, 'Publishing Corporate Tax Strategies' Tax J (4 August 2016), <https://www.taxjournal.com/articles/publishing-corporate-tax-strategies-04082016>.

[28] Christian Aid, 'Tax and Sustainability: A Framework for Businesses and Socially Responsible Investors' (October 2011) 4 <https://www.christianaid.org.uk/sites/default/files/2017-08/accounting-for-change-tax-sustainability-october-2011.pdf>; Oxfam and others, 'Getting to Good: Towards Responsible Corporate Tax Behavior' (November 2015) 15 <https://www.oxfam.org/sites/www.oxfam.org/files/file_attachments/dp-getting-to-good-corporate-tax-171115-en.pdf>; Sol Picciotto, 'Taking the Tax Justice Debate Forward: Including Learning to Digest the "Double-Irish Dutch Sandwich"' (2016) TJN 8.

[29] Fair Tax Mark, 'Who We Are' <https://fairtaxmark.net/who-we-are>. For an analysis of the Fair Tax Mark and its role in influencing tax strategies of multinational businesses, see Allison Christians, 'Tax Justice as Social License: the Fair Tax Mark' in Richard Eccleston and Ainsley Elbra (eds), *Business, Civil Society and the New Politics of Corporate Tax Justice: Paying a Fair Share* (Edward Elgar 2018).

[30] Fair Tax Mark, 'Criteria and Standards' <https://fairtaxmark.net/getting-the-mark/criteria-and-standards/>.

benefits created by their cooperation. In expressing that the states in which 'value' is created have a right to tax, the OECD articulates something close to the entitlement and equal benefits principles; in drawing up rules to explain which states can lay a claim to multinational income and which (by exclusion) cannot, the OECD implicitly articulates the requirement of fair cooperation. This book is motivated by the desire to show the implications of the normative commitments implicit in much of the contemporary academic and policy debate in international taxation today.

1.2. Cooperation and Capital Mobility

On the society-of-states model of international justice, we can think of states as initially fully autarkic with fully closed economies, autonomously developing their own economies while practicing duties of non-interference in relation to other states. They may, however, consider it beneficial to engage in various forms of international cooperation. In particular, they may consider it beneficial to pursue policies of international economic integration. States would do so voluntarily and in pursuit of increasing national wealth. If they wish to cooperate in this way, for instance by establishing trading relationships, they must devise just terms to distribute the benefits of that cooperation between them. The benefits of such a cooperative effort compared to the baseline of autarky, we have suggested above, must be allocated in accordance with the equal benefit principle.

One of the main points in this chapter is that justice in international tax policy concerns the question of how to appropriately allocate the benefits of a certain type of cooperation: the facilitation of international capital mobility and investment expected to generate cooperative surpluses in the form of worldwide welfare enhancements. By facilitating international capital mobility through tax coordination, states pursue the mutual augmentation of national wealth giving rise to a cooperative surplus (compared to a situation where states do not permit international capital flows). More precisely, this cooperative surplus consists of the total gains in productivity (measured in terms of gains in gross national income, the total market value of all income) resulting specifically from facilitating capital mobility. There may, of course, be difficulties with the measurement of the gains of this specific form of cooperation. However, it is plausible that econometric methods can be employed to estimate them with some accuracy.[31]

[31] On the difficulties and practical possibilities specifically related to measuring the gains of international trade in goods and services, see James, *Fairness in Practice* (n 11) 179–83.

This raises a question of fairness, namely how to fairly distribute the cooperative surplus among the cooperating states. We will argue that on the society-of-states model of international justice, a theory of international tax justice is a theory that explains what fairness requires in the design of the institutions that regulate this cooperative effort.

We start by observing that it may be beneficial from a worldwide welfare perspective to facilitate the free flow of capital. From a theoretical point of view, the case can be based on the comparative advantage argument, traditionally used to explicate the benefits of free trade. The basic case for international trade suggests that by specializing in what they do best, their comparative advantage, and by relying on trade for the rest, all states (even those that lack an absolute advantage in anything) can productively contribute to a cooperative surplus. This requires the abolition of trade barriers, such as tariffs and subsidies, and the coordination of an international division of labour.

The comparative advantage argument applies in much the same way for international investment—conceived as trade of capital for labour—as it does for trade in goods and services.[32] When capital-rich states export their capital to labour-rich states, both capital and labour can be more productively employed and both states are expected to benefit. Note that investment abroad can be in the form of either foreign direct investment or foreign portfolio investment. Foreign direct investment establishes ownership of, or controlling share in a business abroad and gives rise to active income. Foreign portfolio investment generally gives rise to 'passive' income—that is, income that arises for the investor by virtue of their ownership of an asset rather than any of their own particular activity.

The core idea motivating the facilitation of international mobility of capital is that additional economic returns can be generated (over and above a situation where states do not permit international investment) in the form of income to private investors, wages for labour, knowledge spillovers into the local economy, or, ideally, a combination of these things. These additional or surplus gains are made possible only by states actively creating the conditions for cross-border investment and production, such that it is practically possible for the private sector to combine economic factors belonging to multiple states. By practically possible, we refer to the legal structures that protect private rights and interests as well as the range of necessary institutions that

[32] Eg Maurice Obstfeld, 'International Capital Mobility in the 1990s' (1993) National Bureau of Economic Research, Working Paper No. 4534; James, *Fairness in Practice* (n 11) 150, 265; Thomas Rixen, *The Political Economy of International Tax Governance* (Palgrave Macmillan 2008) 31.

facilitate cross-border transactions and activities. These include banking and financial services, transportation routes and carriers, and all manner of tangible and intangible inputs and intermediaries. States have a mutual interest in creating these conditions to facilitate international investment that is potentially welfare-enhancing, because capital can sometimes be more productively employed abroad than in the domestic economy.[33]

States have over the past century pursued fiscal coordination with this aim consciously in mind. The famous 1923 *Report on Double Taxation* prepared for the League of Nations was occasioned by the fear that the lack of fiscal coordination would interfere with 'economic intercourse and with the free flow of capital.'[34] It was the central concern of the international community in the late 1990s, as expressed in the OECD's warning that double non-taxation gives rise to 'potential distortions in the patterns of trade and investment' impeding sustainable economic growth and leading to reductions in global welfare, and it continues to motivate reform within the language of base erosion and profit shifting, most recently in particular with respect to highly digitalized firms.[35]

If states wish to create conditions in which international capital mobility gives rise to increases in worldwide welfare, they must ensure that their respective income tax systems do not excessively distort the investment decisions

[33] These productivity gains may include greater returns to capital but also gains due to increased domestic investment and employee compensation. Mihir Desai, C Fritz Foley, James R Hines Jr, 'Foreign Direct Investment and Domestic Economic Activity' (2005) National Bureau of Economic Research, Working Paper Nr. 11717. Note that international trade and investment are conceptually interchangeable, such that given frictionless international trade there is no need for international investment. Hence, '[f]or direct investment to thrive there must be some imperfection in markets for goods or factors, including among the latter technology, or some interference in competition by government or by firms, which separates markets' (CP Kindleberger, *American Business Abroad* (Yale University Press 1969) 13).

[34] GWJ Bruins and others, *Report on Double Taxation: Submitted to the Financial Committee* (League of Nations 1923) 3. Additionally, the promotion of international investment has been pursued with the aim of increasing global peace and security. See, eg, League of Nations (1922), Brussels Financial Conference 1920: The Recommendations and Their Application, Vol. 1 at p 228 (declaring that double taxation was a serious impediment to placing international investment abroad, and therefore a threat to global peace); *see also* Sunita Jogarajan, *Double Taxation and the League of Nations* (Cambridge University Press 2018) 16 (describing the League of Nations' interest in taxation as one element of their overall mission to 'promote international co-operation and to achieve international peace and security').

[35] OECD, *Harmful Tax Competition: An Emerging Global Issue* (OECD Publishing 1998) 14; OECD, *Base Erosion and Profit Shifting (BEPS) Action Plan Report on Addressing the Tax Challenges of the Digital Economy* (OECD Publishing 2015) 9. The prevention of distortions in investment patterns is one of the OECD's main concerns in international tax reform. In cases where double taxation came to be addressed by exclusively assigning the right to tax to one jurisdiction and denying it to the others, the opportunity to achieve double non-taxation by relocating income to non-taxing states arose. This outcome was tolerated over many decades until it eventually became too politically costly, thus eventually prompting the reconsideration of those provisions via the BEPS initiative. See Allison Christians, 'Tax Activism and the Global Movement for Development through Transparency' in Miranda Stewart and Yariv Brauner (eds), *Tax, Law and Development* (Edward Elgar 2013) 288–315; Allison Christians and Stephen Shay, *Assessing BEPS: Origins, Standards and Responses* (Int'l Fisc Assoc Cahier 102A, 2017).

of individuals and companies. This facilitates capital movement by removing tax obstacles to productive foreign investment.[36] An obstacle is here understood in terms of preventing a more productive worldwide allocation of capital, such that additional national income gains could have been achieved in its absence.[37]

The possibility of such tax obstacles follows from conventional views regarding the jurisdiction of states.[38] In broad strokes, 'source states'—that is, states that are the hosts of inbound capital investment—are thought to legitimately claim the income by virtue of the fact that they have jurisdiction over the territory where the income arises (the territory that forms the 'source' of the investor's income).[39] At the same time, residence states—the states where the investors are resident (sometimes referred to as the home states)—are said to be entitled to tax the income because they have jurisdiction over the person receiving the income, including when it arises abroad.[40]

If both source and residence states would exercise their jurisdiction to tax, the investor would be taxed twice.[41] Double taxation will discourage

[36] The prevention of distortions to investment patterns is, as noted, another of the OECD's main concerns in international tax reform. In cases where double taxation came to be addressed by exclusively assigning the right to tax to one jurisdiction and denying it to the others, the opportunity to achieve double non-taxation by relocating income to non-taxing states arose. This outcome was tolerated over many decades until it eventually became too politically costly, thus eventually prompting the reconsideration of those provisions via the BEPS initiative. See Allison Christians, 'Tax Activism and the Global Movement for Development through Transparency' in Miranda Stewart and Yariv Brauner (eds), *Tax, Law and Development* (Edward Elgar 2013) 288–315; Christians and Shay, *Assessing BEPS* (n 35).

[37] See Rixen, *The Political Economy of International Tax* (n 32) 31.

[38] Eg, Rutsel Martha, *The Jurisdiction to Tax in International Law* (Kluwer 1989), Chapter 2.

[39] The claim that the income finds its 'source' in the source state is ambiguous and can be understood in at least two ways. First, it can mean that the income of the investor arises in that state for accounting purposes. Second, it can mean that the income is attributable to economic factors of that state. The former does not entail the latter. Indeed, the point of the preceding discussion has been to note that in the context of capital mobility, income is attributable to the factors of multiple countries which therefore must be fairly shared between them. There is broad agreement across jurisdictions concerning the former conception—ie, when to allocate income to a specific state for accounting purposes—even though the specific practices of states in defining it in legal terms are often difficult to reconcile with any principle. For a discussion, see, eg, Lawrence Lokken, 'What Is This Thing Called Source?' (2011) 37(3) Int'l Tax J 25–31 (arguing that a general theory of source can be constructed by combining the benefit principle (taxes borne by a taxpayer should be related to the value of government services and protections received) and the ability to pay principle (the aggregate tax burden should be allocated among taxpayers in ways that reflect their relative abilities to pay taxes) by creating a source principle that 'apportions a taxpayer's ability to pay among jurisdictions in a way that reflects the governmental service and protections available to the taxpayer in profit-seeking activities', and examining the ways in which various US source rules seem to fit this articulation of the principle).

[40] As in the expression of the source principle, the residence principle is considered both ubiquitous and notoriously difficult to implement in practice. For discussion, see Allison Christians, 'Drawing the Boundaries of Tax Justice' in Kim Brooks (ed), *The Quest for Tax Reform Continues: The Royal Commission on Taxation Fifty Years Later* (Carswell 2013).

[41] The overlap of source and residence is one form of double taxation; other forms include overlapping source claims, in which two states both claim to be the state of source, and overlapping residence claims, in which two states both claim to be the state of residence. Tax treaties include various 'tie-breaker' rules to prevent these overlaps.

individuals to invest abroad if the anticipated returns after tax are expected to be lower than they would be on available domestic investments.[42] This would deter otherwise productive foreign investment. An analogous argument holds for double non-taxation. If returns to international investment remain untaxed, investors are incentivized to engage in otherwise unproductive or less productive foreign investment. In order to prevent such inefficiencies or distortions in the global allocation of capital, states may choose to coordinate their domestic tax regimes so as to create the appropriate incentives for their residents to invest abroad, in particular by preventing double taxation and its corollary, double non-taxation.

The risk of double (non-)taxation is a key reason for states to coordinate their fiscal policies and was the central issue when international tax policy first became an area of international attention. There is wide agreement that both double taxation and double non-taxation must be avoided in order to facilitate national income gains through international investment.[43]

Fiscal coordination alone is, of course, insufficient to establish this cooperative practice: states must also relax capital controls, including lifting prohibitions on, and reducing or abolishing taxes on, foreign investment transactions. However, absent fiscal coordination, the likelihood of double (non-) taxation, and more generally investor uncertainty about the tax consequences of investing internationally would risk eliminating the potential benefits resulting from facilitating international capital flows.

We treat the facilitation of international capital mobility as an isolated cooperative practice, to which principles of justice apply. It is true that states today cooperate on a range of economic as well as socio-political issues. International investment is only one aspect of global economic integration and market reliance in a number of different areas, including international trade and services. There are nevertheless two main reasons to conceive of international investment as a cooperative scheme in isolation.

[42] The actual impact in any given situation varies and a high enough pre-tax return might compensate for even double taxation in some scenarios. See, eg, Michael Keen and Peter Mullins, 'International Corporate Taxation and the Extractive Industries: Principles, Practice, Problems' in Philip Daniel and others (eds), *International Taxation and the Extractive Industries* (Routledge 2016) (noting that 'while the rhetoric commonly abhors "double taxation", what investors presumably care about (compliance costs aside) is not how many times they are taxed but how much').

[43] Rixen, *Political Economy of International Tax* (n 32) 31, speaks of the 'ideal of *single taxation*' ensuring that 'all factors are put to the most productive use from a worldwide perspective'. This is perhaps an overstatement since an efficient allocation of capital requires not only that income is taxed only once but also that the effective tax rate is the same wherever the investor decides to invest. Nonetheless, significant increases in allocational efficiency can be expected by preventing double taxation. See also Reuven Avi-Yonah, *International Tax as International Law: An Analysis of the International Tax Regime* (Cambridge University Press 2007) on the 'single tax principle'.

First, issues of fairness in international tax policy are intimately related to international investment. In a hypothetical world where economies would facilitate international trade while rigorously prohibiting international investment, many of the problems and puzzles of international tax policy would simply disappear. (We bracket here issues relating to the movement of people.) Much less often, if ever, would there be a risk of double (non-) taxation, nor would states likely face the ills of international tax avoidance and tax competition, issues we come back to later in the book.

Second, as will become clear below, international tax policy significantly affects how the benefits of the cooperative practice of facilitating international capital mobility and investment are allocated between states. This should be unsurprising as the international tax system forms part of the regulatory framework that facilitates cross border investment. We therefore treat the pursuit of welfare benefits through the facilitation of international capital mobility as a cooperative practice, independent of, and possibly existing side by side with, other cooperative practices such as the facilitation of international trade of goods and services.[44] We focus on international taxation while accepting, for the sake of the argument, that other forms of cooperation are also appropriately and effectively regulated by principles of justice.

Think of it as follows: imagine that states are facilitating international trade in goods and services while maintaining rigorous capital controls, rendering any international capital flows impossible. They then establish free flow of capital between them, the costs and benefits of which are to be assessed in relation to the counterfactual situation where no capital flows are permitted. A theory of international tax justice is a theory of the equitable distribution of the gains of a cooperative practice facilitating potentially welfare-enhancing international investment. The question is how this practice should be structured and what constitutes a fair division of the cooperative surplus.

At this point, one might object that the cooperative benefits of financial liberalization are uncertain at best.[45] For instance, studies show little to no correlation between capital market liberalization and economic growth in

[44] Conversely, note that in discussions of fairness in trade, the regulation of international capital mobility is often bracketed or neglected. See Mathias Risse and Gabriel Wollner, *On Trade Justice: A Philosophical Plea for a New Global Deal* (Oxford University Press 2019); Andrew Walton, 'Justice and Trade Policy' in Annabelle Lever and Andrei Poama (eds), *The Routledge Handbook of Ethics and Public Policy* (Routledge 2018); David Miller, 'Fair Trade: What Does it Mean and Why Does it Matter?' (2017) 14(3) J Moral Phil 249–69; James, 'A Theory of Fairness in Trade' (n 11).

[45] Eg, James, *Fairness in Practice* (n 11) 265–66.

low-income states.[46] When low-income states have reduced capital controls their economies have in many cases been harmed by (licit and illicit) capital flight.[47] Additionally, any advantages arising from capital mobility are likely to accrue to capital rather than labour as reflected in the fact that 'the average citizen has tended to see only modest benefits from financial globalization.'[48] Finally, capital market liberalization has tended to increase the prevalence and severity of financial crises which can ravage economies, especially those of less affluent states.[49]

We have three responses to these concerns. First, we accept the possibility that financial liberalization in the aggregate harms rather than helps states. In that case, there is no reason for states to cooperate to facilitate it and the advice would be to stop doing so. That would, however, also largely resolve the question that motivates this book, since in that case there would be little reason to be concerned about the taxation of international capital flows from the perspective of international justice. Second, our main point regarding the distribution of the costs and benefits of cooperation in accordance with the equal benefit principle would still stand: the (net) costs must be shared equally. Finally, many of the apparent harmful effects of financial liberalization noted here are caused by the structure of the existing international tax regime. It is precisely because the costs and benefits of financial liberalization are today not fairly shared that the international tax regime should be reformed, or so we will argue.

The question of how to equally share the gains of international capital mobility is increasingly relevant. Foreign investment is, together with international trade, among the most consequential phenomena in the globalization of the world economy today. Touted as a significant driver of economic growth and development, foreign investment has increased tremendously over the previous decades and in 2018 it formed, with flows of about $5 trillion, almost 6 per cent of global GDP.[50] Developing economies are increasingly deeply integrated in the global economy and received one third of total investments in the same year.[51]

[46] Dani Rodrik, 'Who Needs Capital-Account Convertability' in P Kenen (ed), *Should the IMF Pursue Capital-Account Convertability?* (International Finance Section, Department of Economics, Princeton University 1998).

[47] Paul Collier and Jan Willem Gunning 'Explaining African Economic Performance' (1999) 37(1) J Econ Lit 64–111; Paul Collier, Anke Hoeffler, and Catherine Pattillo, 'Flight Capital as a Portfolio Choice' (2001) 15(1) Wld Bank Econ Rev 55–80.

[48] James, *Fairness in Practice* (n 11) 266.

[49] Carmen Reinhart and Kenneth Rogoff, *This Time Is Different: Eight Centuries of Financial Folly* (Princeton University Press 2012).

[50] UNCTAD, *World Investment Report 2019* (United Nations Conference on Trade and Development 2019) 11 (laying out FDI, portfolio flows and other investment (bank loans)).

[51] UNCTAD, *World Investment Report* (n 50) 12.

The increasing importance of international capital for lower-income states is particularly visible in the case of foreign direct investment (FDI). Unlike FDI to high-income states, which has slumped in the last few years (caused primarily by the repatriations of foreign earnings by United States companies following tax reforms in the United States), foreign direct investment to developing economies has remained stable.[52] Foreign direct investment flows to developing economies now account for 54 per cent of global FDI ($706 billion).[53] This makes FDI the largest source of external finance for lower-income states.[54] Even the poorest states in the world are recipients of capital inflows. In 2018, the least developed economies (with a combined population of 1 billion) received 3 per cent of total cross-border capital flows, of which $24 billion consisted of FDI.[55] This is undoubtedly a small sum in light of global cross-border investment flows but it is substantial when measured against the size of the economies of these states.[56]

International investment is accordingly an important site for potentially mutually beneficial economic cooperation between richer and poorer states alike. The question is how to allocate the benefits.

Income Taxation and Capital Mobility

Fiscal cooperation today generally consists in one of (typically) two states yielding its entitlement to tax through a network of bilateral and multilateral tax treaties and instruments, which we will explore in more detail where relevant throughout the chapters that follow. Implicit is a continued commitment to income taxation. This is striking if one compares it to the attitude generally taken in the context of trade liberalization. Over the past decades, trade liberalization has been pursued (with various degrees of success) by progressively

[52] UNCTAD, *World Investment Report* (n 50) 12; U.S. Congress, H.R.1—An Act to provide for reconciliation pursuant to titles II and V of the concurrent resolution on the budget for fiscal year 2018 (commonly referred to as the U.S. Tax Cuts and Jobs Act of 2017) (hereafter TCJA).

[53] UNCTAD, *World Investment Report* (n 50) 2, 3. In 2018, FDI inflow to Africa increased by 11 per cent to $46 billion, inflow to Asia by 4 per cent to $512 billion, while contracting by 6 per cent in Latin America and the Caribbean to $147 billion.

[54] UNCTAD, *World Investment Report* (n 50) 12: Official development assistance was $149 billion, and remittances were $529 billion.

[55] UNCTAD, *World Investment Report* (n 50) 12.

[56] See Andrew Sumner, 'Is Foreign Direct Investment Good for The Poor?' (2015) 15 Dev Pr 269–85, at 269 ('when accounted for as a proportion of annual investment or as a proportion of productive assets, the flows are of significance in many, if not the majority of, developing countries'). See also OECD, *Development Co-Operation Report 2016: The Sustainable Development Goals As Business Opportunities* (OECD Publishing 2015) 56; Karl Sauvant, 'Attracting Foreign Direct Investment and Benefiting from It: Challenges for the Least Developed Countries' (2015) 7(2) Transnatl Corp Rev 125–27.

eliminating barriers to trade, including especially in the form of tariffs. In that context, it is generally agreed that the abolishment of border taxes should, at least in theory, be the policy aim of states committed to facilitating international trade to advance global welfare.[57] Analogously, one might wonder why financial liberalization could not be pursued through the progressive elimination of taxes on cross-border income flows.

The short answer is that doing so would undermine if not effectively eliminate income taxation not only on cross-border income but also on much domestic income as well, as investors in each state would be expected to respond to domestic investment opportunities facing a cost not imposed on readily available cross-border alternatives. Reduction of cross-border income taxation is only attractive from a worldwide welfare perspective if domestic income taxes are reduced too. That is clearly not something states are prepared to accept.

The commitment to continued taxation of income is consistent with the society-of-states model. Recall that on this model the principles of international justice regulating the relations between states are meant to protect and advance the autonomy of states in shaping their domestic political and socio-economic institutions. That is why states, among other things, have a duty of non-interference, why they must respect the territorial integrity of other states, and why they are entitled to the wealth of their territory.

The political autonomy of states would be significantly diminished if they were to give up their capacity to tax individual and corporate income, because doing so would remove what has become one of the primary sources of public revenue available to them. Personal and corporate income taxes on average make up 30 per cent of total government revenue of high-income OECD members.[58] If states can no longer tax (either foreign or domestic) income they would be significantly restricted in raising revenue necessary to fund public goods, social welfare programmes, and other desirable policy goals.[59] It would plausibly undermine their capacity to remain internally just.

[57] For an overview, William Miner, 'Modern History of Trade Policy' in William Kerr and James Gaisford (eds), *Handbook on International Trade Policy* (Edward Elgar Publishing 2007) 29–34.

[58] Mick Moore, 'Obstacles to Increasing Tax Revenues in Low Income Countries' (2013) International Centre for Tax and Development Working Paper 13/15, 7.

[59] In the context of trade liberalization, such public revenue considerations are less salient, as international trade taxes now make up just 2 per cent of the total government revenue of high-income OECD countries. In most middle- and high-income countries, the ultimate abolition of all tariffs is therefore generally seen as economically desirable even if in practice impossible. Some low-income countries, where trade taxes generally make up larger shares of government revenue, may be less enthusiastic about trade liberalization precisely because it hampers their ability to collect revenue.

Hence, in pursuing financial liberalization through the abolition of income taxation, states would voluntarily undermine the very conditions that the principles of international justice are meant to secure. Not only is this unwise, it may in fact be prohibited as a matter of justice. It is likely that domestic distributive justice requires income taxation. If one agrees with Rawls that justice is the first virtue of social institutions, then the pursuit of national wealth through international cooperation must be pursued, as any other desirable social end, in a manner consistent with what domestic distributive justice requires.[60]

Cooperation on international tax today is a balancing act: it is an attempt to facilitate potentially welfare enhancing international capital flows while simultaneously protecting the political autonomy of states. An institutional scheme that avoids double (non-)taxation resolves the jurisdictional conflicts that form obstacles to potentially welfare enhancing international capital flows, but makes no further attempts to harmonize domestic tax systems and in that sense is in some sense 'sovereignty preserving.'[61] States remain largely free to specify who is a taxpayer, what constitutes income, when income gives rise to tax, and perhaps, at what rate above a certain imagined threshold. We will turn to the implications of tax competition, but first, we need to address the appropriate allocation of tax rights while bracketing the dynamics of tax competition.

1.3. Allocating the Benefits of Cooperation

In the previous section, we argued that the aim of avoiding double (non-) taxation is acceptable in light of a commitment to the autonomy of states as they design a cooperative practice for the mutual augmentation of national wealth. States wish to facilitate international capital mobility while simultaneously protecting their capacity to impose income taxes. In this section, we show how the entitlement principle and the equal benefit principle must be applied to this cooperative practice.

Income and Other Benefits of Cooperation

We start by briefly considering how the principles apply to cases of purely domestic income taxation. Take the following example: a resident

[60] John Rawls, *Theory of Justice* (The Belknap Press of Harvard University Press 1971) 3.
[61] Rixen, *Political Economy of International* Tax (n 32) 64.

taxpayer receives income from a domestic investment (say, a local company that only produces and sells locally). In this case, the returns do not result from a cooperative practice and hence do not (in part or in whole) consist of a cooperative surplus that must be shared among multiple states. The returns on investment are fully attributable to national endowments to which the state is fully entitled on the basis of the entitlement principle. The state therefore may count the income as part of its national wealth and (at least insofar as international justice is concerned) may tax it as it sees fit.[62]

To this conclusion one might object that what appears to be a fully domestic case may in fact form part of a cooperative scheme in the following way: take the example of a state that is facilitating international trade, which gives rise to surpluses including in the form of higher returns to our investor. One could imagine a situation in which the investor benefits from the fact that international trade increases the size of the market in which it operates (even though it produces only for the local market). In this case, some of the returns of the investment that appear purely domestic are in fact part of a cooperative surplus to which the state is not fully entitled.[63]

In response, we observe that this objection only succeeds if the benefits of international trade are not yet fairly allocated, in accordance with the relevant principles of international justice. In that case, part of the income that appears fully domestic may indeed as a matter of justice be owed to another state. However, for purposes of our current discussion we assume that the benefits of international trade, as well as the benefits of other cooperative schemes states participate in are already fairly allocated: this is how we can isolate the question of how to fairly allocate the potential benefits of the mutual facilitation of international capital mobility. In the example discussed here, the income does not result from the facilitation of financial liberalization, which is the cooperative practice that concerns us here. We can therefore assume that the state is fully entitled to the income that accrues to residents from fully domestic investments.

[62] The proviso within brackets is meant to express the reservation that whether and how a state may tax its residents and citizens may be in various ways constrained by requirements of domestic distributive justice. We are here concerned with the right to tax only in relation to other states. The entitlement principle implies that in a just world, states lack obligations to transfer any of their own wealth to other states (or to individuals in other states) and that other states lack the right to seize extraterritorial wealth to increase their own national endowments.

[63] For an argument along these lines, see Adam Kern, 'Illusions of Justice in International Taxation' (2020) 48(2) Phil & Pub Aff 151–84, at 169ff.

Let us now consider the taxation of cross-border income flows. In that case there are potentially multiple conflicting tax jurisdictional claims that must be adjudicated.

As we outlined above, the entitlement principle holds that states are entitled to the returns they would have had had their inputs been employed in solely domestic production. Assuming these counterfactual returns could be estimated with some level of accuracy, the returns are conceivable as their own wealth since they form the opportunity cost of engaging in international production. In turn, the equal benefit principle holds that the economic gains of cooperation must be shared equally between the cooperating states. Applied to the international tax regime, the two principles require that states' coordination efforts be structured so as to ensure that the net gains of international capital mobility and investment are distributed equally among the states participating and upholding that regime. In other words, fairness requires the consideration of the overall distribution of the gains of financial liberalization *and* the way the allocation of tax rights between the source and residence state contributes to that distribution.

The equal benefit principle applies to the distribution of the *net* gains of cooperation—the benefits and burdens the cooperative practice creates. It does not apply to the wealth of the territory that is not created through cooperation, including the wealth it foregoes by participating in the cooperative scheme. Hence, states must first be compensated for the opportunity costs of participating in the cooperative scheme. That compensation is due by virtue of the entitlement principle.[64]

When considering how to allocate taxation rights or tax revenues among states, the two principles accordingly hold that any such allocation must ensure that the net gains of international capital mobility and investment be distributed equally among the states participating and upholding that regime.

In other words, the society-of-states model of international justice, applied to international taxation, suggests that questions regarding the fairness of the allocation of taxing rights or tax revenues must be answered with reference to the overall allocation of the benefits and burdens of international capital mobility. A difficulty in translating these observations into concrete policy advice is that the returns to a particular investor in the form of income do not constitute the only benefit of the cooperative scheme: other benefits may include

[64] Note that Kern, 'Illusions of Justice' (n 63) 175 implicitly accepts this use of the entitlement principle when he suggests that when income is generated in a cooperative scheme, the resident state is 'exclusively entitled to tax only . . . the "autarkic residual" '—the portion of the income that would have been earned under conditions of autarky.

additional salary for labour, technical know-how, and other positive spillovers elsewhere in the economy. It is therefore wrong to think that when applying the entitlement and equal benefit principles to the design of international tax policy we can focus solely on the division of revenues resulting from taxing international income flows.

This point was advanced by the economist Peggy Musgrave, particularly in the article 'Inter-nation equity,' co-authored with Richard Musgrave in 1972. They maintain that inter-nation equity concerns 'the allocation of national gain and loss'[65] where 'national gain' is understood not merely to include fiscal revenue or 'treasury gain,' but all benefits, including private income and intangible benefits that accrue to a state as we outlined them above. To consider only the allocation of treasury gains is to ignore the gains of international investment that accrue to private actors, for instance in the form of greater income than might have been possible in a counterfactual domestic investment. The possibility of realizing other gains, including positive spillovers, explains why states may be willing to forego the taxation of foreign investment gains: doing so potentially increases the inflow of capital leading to the augmentation of national wealth (even after the profits of that capital investment and possibly also the investment itself have been repatriated). This is why it would be myopic to focus exclusively on the distribution of the available tax revenues among states. What matters is not only which state gets to tax and how much, but the overall distribution of gains arising from the facilitation of international capital mobility and investment.

We seek to add three dimensions to these considerations. First, we suggest that the equity question the Musgraves are concerned with arises because states engage in a cooperative practice—the facilitation of international capital mobility with the associated potential welfare gains—that gives rise to benefits that must be shared fairly among the participating states. Second, we consider that the cooperative surplus should be allocated in accordance with the equal benefit principle, so as to ensure that, as much as is possible and feasible, the cooperating states receive an equal share of the benefits to which they all contribute. Finally, we propose that the division of taxation rights (that is, the norms agreed to with the aim of preventing both double taxation and double non-taxation) should be understood as instrumental to a fair allocation. In other words, rules coordinating international tax policy are fair when they

[65] Richard Musgrave and Peggy Musgrave, 'Inter-nation Equity' in Richard M Bird and John G Head (eds), *Modern Fiscal Issues: Essays in Honour of Carl S Shoup* (University of Toronto Press 1972) 68.

secure an overall equal allocation of the benefits of international capital mobility between the cooperating states.

Determinative for that distribution is whether, under the negotiated coordination regime, the source state retains the right to impose tax (and exercises that right). The reason is that it does not matter for the allocation of the benefits of international capital mobility whether the residence state taxes the income derived from international investment. Whether the resident state taxes profits realized by its resident taxpayers is irrelevant from the perspective of the allocation of wealth between states. It only determines whether those profits accrue as private income or as treasury gain: either way, the profits enhance the national wealth of the residence state. However, when a source state taxes the income, it reduces in equal measure the wealth that flows to the residence state. Unlike a residence state, if a source state wishes to augment its national wealth, it does not have the same policy choice to leave the returns to cross-border investment in private hands as it would in purely domestic cases.

On the society-of-states model of international justice, then, the basic policy issue of international taxation focuses on the question whether the source state should retain the right to tax in order to further an approximately equal distribution of the net gains of international capital mobility and investment.

The Case for Source Taxation

It is difficult to predict the (net) direction of capital flows in a just world, between states that are politically autonomous and universally observe the norms that regulate the society of states. Perhaps the international wealth inequalities would be limited and states would, on average, export as much capital as they import. In that case it would not matter much whether source states would be allocated the right to tax cross-border income. Whatever tax base is given up when in the role of source is recouped when in the role of residence. For example, while a state may give up source tax revenue by reducing its tax on dividends paid out to foreign persons, it will recoup the revenue thus lost by being able to collect more tax on dividends received by its residents from the other state than it would in the absence of the treaty.

However, in a world where some states are capital rich and others are capital poor, and some states will tend to be net capital importers while others net capital exporters, the introduction of a source tax does have distributive consequences. In order for foreign direct investment to contribute to domestic capital accumulation and economic growth, it is necessary that profit repatriation be lower than investment inflows.[66] In the absence of a source tax, the capital importer is almost always in the role of the source state, habitually losing its tax base and rarely if ever recouping it by sending capital abroad.[67] Conversely states that are habitual exporters of capital will often enjoy the reduction of tax at source as an increase of their own endowment, even if they do not choose to tax at residence. To ensure that less affluent source states capture a fair share of the benefits of foreign investment, it may therefore be especially important that they have the capacity to tax the returns to capital that are invested in their territories.[68] Tax competition is a key impediment to achieving this goal, as we will see in the next chapter.

To assess the distribution of the total (net) benefits of the cooperative practice of facilitating international investment then requires an economic analysis that may be difficult to carry out. However, as Musgrave and Musgrave have suggested, there is reason to think that in the absence of a source tax the residence state receives a disproportionate (ie, larger than proportionally equal) share of the cooperative surplus generated by international investment.[69] To be sure, when foreign capital is invested in a state, it is likely that some of the returns will accrue to the economy of that state, for instance, as noted above, in the form of local wages or technology spillovers, even if that state does not otherwise tax the income arising from the investment. But in the absence of a tax at (geographic) source, it is likely that most of the additional wealth

[66] Amitava Dutt, 'Direct Foreign Investment, Transnational Corporations and Growth: Some Empirical Evidence and a North–South Model' in Richard Kozul-Wright and Robert Rowthorn (eds), *Transnational Corporations and the Global Economy* (MacMillan Press 1998) 165–66, notes the possibility that due to 'high levels of profit repatriation (especially if one takes into account practices such as transfer pricing) new direct foreign inflows is in most periods less than capital outflows due to profit repatriation.'

[67] Richard Chisik and Ronald Davies, 'Asymmetric FDI and Tax-Treaty Bargaining: Theory and Evidence' (2004) 88(6) J Pub Econ 1119; Allison Christians, 'Tax Treaties for Investment and Aid to Sub-Saharan Africa: A Case Study' (2006) 71(2) Brook L Rev 639; Tsilly Dagan, 'The Tax Treaties Myth' (2000) 32 NYUJ Int'l L & Pol 939 reprinted in Tsilly Dagan, *International Tax Policy: Between Cooperation and Competition* (Cambridge University Press 2018).

[68] In what follows, we will use this vocabulary of 'source states' and 'residence states' and in particular we will draw on the common use of 'source states' to describe states that are relatively less affluent. We do this because as a rule, these states capture their share of the cooperative surplus arising from international income flows by taxing 'at source,' that is, by imposing tax on returns to foreign investments made within their territories (as opposed to 'at residence,' that is, capturing income earned by resident taxpayers that invest abroad). Relatively less affluent states are almost always in this role because they are almost always net capital importers rather than net capital exporters. (For an overview of average capital flows for countries at different levels of affluence over the last fifty years, see Andreas Steiner, *Global Imbalances, Financial Crises, and Central Bank Policies* (Academic Press 2016) 13–19.) We note that the simplifying language is imprecise in that every state that interacts in the global economy stands in the role of source state and most also stand in the role of residence state to some degree, but it is a useful shorthand for understanding how states generally frame their positions with respect to international tax norms and standards.

[69] This is particularly so, Musgrave and Musgrave, 'Inter-nation Equity' (n 65) 73, hypothesize, if the source state is capital poor but resource rich.

generated by international capital mobility will leave the state as earnings to the foreign investor.

Indeed, authors considering the positive effects of foreign investment traditionally count 'higher tax revenue from foreign profits' among the most significant direct gains for source states.[70] Yet, source states can only benefit in this way if they are both allocated the right to tax foreign income (either as a matter of commonly accepted source and residence definitions or when taxing rights are being divided among states, such as in the context of a tax treaty) and capable of exercising that right. A tax on income at source allows the state to enjoy the returns to which it is entitled, by receiving an approximately equal share in the surplus of productive gains created by international cooperation, that is, as we have defined it, the cooperative surplus.[71]

This argument for source state taxation is especially compelling in the context we will be exploring in the next chapters when we include in our analysis the existence of less affluent states with populations facing subsistence rights deficits. For such states, the benefits of foreign investment are often less certain. A large literature on the effects of foreign investment on economic growth and poverty reduction shows that a number of background conditions may have to be in place, such as a certain level of economic, human capital, and financial market development, before such investment benefits these states.[72]

One study on the role of technology spillovers and economic growth in lower income states, for instance, shows that the effective use of more advanced technologies introduced by foreign companies requires a sufficient level of human capital in the local economy (measured in that study by secondary school attainment), and suggests that, for states with very low levels of human capital, the effect of foreign direct investment on growth is close to nil.[73] By one measure, in order for foreign investment to contribute to domestic capital accumulation and economic growth, profit repatriation to other states (such as

[70] GDA MacDougall, 'The Benefits and Costs of Private Investment from Abroad: A Theoretical Approach' (1960) 36 Econ Rec 13–35, at 34.

[71] Musgrave and Musgrave, 'Inter-nation Equity' (n 65) 73.

[72] The literature is surveyed in Sumner, 'Is Foreign Direct Investment Good?' (n 56) 276–77, with reference to VN Balasubramanyam, M Salisu, and David Sapsford, 'Foreign Direct Investment as an Engine of Growth' (1999) 8(1) J Int'l Trade & Econ Dev 27–40; Eduardo R Borenzstein, Jose De Gregorio, and Jong-Wha Lee, 'How Does Foreign Direct Investment Affect Growth?' (1998) 45(1) J Int'l Econ 115–35; Magnus Blomstrom and Ari Kokko, 'Multinational Corporations and Spillovers' (1994) 12(3) J Econ Surv 247–77; Laura Alfaro and others, 'FDI and Economic Growth: The Role of Financial Markets' (2000) Harvard Business School Working Paper 01-083, Boston, MA: Harvard Business School. A more recent review is in Ann Harrison and Andrés Rodrîguez-Clare, 'Trade, Foreign Investment, and Industrial Policy for Developing Countries' in Dani Rodrick and Mark R Rosenzweig (eds), *Handbook of Development Economics*, vol 5 (Elsevier 2010).

[73] Borenzstein, Gregorio, and Lee, 'How Does Foreign Direct Investment Affect Growth?' (n 72) 134.

in the form of outbound payments of dividends, royalties, interest, and capital gains) must be lower than investment inflows.[74] This is especially important if foreign investments crowd out, rather than crowd in domestic investment, which could happen, for instance, if multinational companies make existing domestic producers less profitable or displace them altogether.[75] Possible additional factors include the level of export dependence and freedom of businesses from government intervention.[76]

Accordingly, an important policy tool to ensure that lower income source states benefit from foreign investment is the taxation of the returns to such investment, which can be effectuated through gross basis withholding taxes on outbound profit repatriations as well as net basis taxes on income associated with local business operations. We will review the different ways of taxing investment returns at source in later chapters, but for the present purposes it is sufficient to note that the need to tax such returns is broadly recognized by international organizations. The United Nations Conference on Trade and Development, for instance, submits that it is important for the least developed economies to have in place withholding taxes on dividends, royalties and interest payments, so as to permit them 'to obtain a fair share of tax revenues arising from [transnational corporate] activities.'[77] Taxes on the returns to foreign investment help ensure that some capital accumulation takes place in the source state and the benefits of foreign investment are thereby fairly shared between the source and residence state.

In the face of significant international wealth inequality, the application of the equal benefit principle likely requires that source states are allocated (and can exercise) a right to tax cross-border income.[78] In the following chapters we will further develop these observations, arguing that the case becomes

[74] Dutt, 'Direct Foreign Investment' (n 66) 165–66.

[75] Ana B Reis, 'On the Welfare Effects of Foreign Investment' (2001) 54(2) J Int'l Econ 411. For a more positive assessment of the effects of FDI on the productiveness of domestic capital, Manuel Agosin and Roberto Machado, 'Foreign Investment in Developing Countries: Does it Crowd in Domestic Investment?' (2005) 33(2) Oxford Dev Stud 149, 149, concluding that 'FDI has, at best, left domestic investment unchanged.'

[76] Dierk Herzer, 'How Does Foreign Direct Investment Really Affect Developing Countries' Growth?' (2012) 20(2) Rev Int'l Econ 396–414.

[77] UNCTAD, *Foreign Direct Investment in LDCs: Lessons Learned from the Decade 2001–2010 and the Way Forward* (United Nations Conference on Trade and Development 2011) 35.

[78] A qualifying remark is worth making: it is unlikely that an equal distribution of the net benefits of cooperation would in fact be secured by allocating the source state a right to tax. For one thing, the precise share of the cooperative surplus the source state receives is dependent (among other things) on the rate at which it decides to tax foreign owned income, something that is conventionally left to the determination of the state. However, the empirical observations cited here do give us good reason to think that a source tax at a reasonable rate is necessary to approximate such an equal distribution.

incontrovertible once the moral implications of extant subsistence rights deficits are considered.

1.4. Conclusion

In this chapter we have argued that the international tax regime structures a cooperative practice whereby states facilitate international capital mobility with the aim of increasing their respective national endowments. The international tax regime is a site where states cooperate in order to facilitate mutually beneficial foreign investment; moreover, it is relevant to determining how these gains are shared between the cooperating states. We suggested that the allocation of (exclusive) tax rights to source states is likely to further an approximately equal distribution of the costs and benefits of the cooperative practice. In turn, the equal benefit principle holds that when states cooperate for their mutual benefit, the net gains of that cooperation should be equally shared between them.

From the perspective of the conception of international justice presented in this chapter, the protection of the capacity of states to tax the income of individuals and companies can be justified with reference to the importance of the political autonomy of states. Political autonomy consists in the capacity of states to create and maintain minimally just domestic socio-economic institutions. It is plausible that the protection of the capacity of states to tax income and raising government revenue is a necessary requirement to secure minimally just institutions. The argument presented is that it is impossible for states to secure just domestic institutions if they pursue financial liberalization in a way that does not protect their capacity to tax income and with it, their political autonomy more generally.

The preceding analysis opens up two lines of inquiry, which we will examine in the chapters that follow. The first line of inquiry concerns the obstacles that prevent some source states today from taxing international income. We discuss these obstacles in the next chapter. In the rest of the book, we will show that, particularly given the extant subsistence rights deficits suffered by people around the world, these obstacles are unjust and must be removed.

The second line of inquiry is whether the parameters of the entitlement and equal benefit principles as we have explored them thus far can be said to be complete, even if they were fully reflected in the international tax regime. In particular, these parameters seem open to critique given that we live in a world in which a vast number of people contribute directly and indirectly to the economic returns to international investment but are deprived of their basic human right to subsistence. We ask whether the presence of subsistence rights deficits changes the nature of assessment of what international tax cooperation must be, in order for it to be just. In Chapters 3 and 4, we ask this question in the event that it is accepted that reasonably affluent states have a duty of justice to assist societies by making available financing to rectify subsistence rights deficits occurring within their borders. In Chapters 5 and 6, we ask the same question assuming that no such duty of assistance exists.

2

Obstacles to Fair Cooperation

In Chapter 1 we sought to demonstrate that, in a just world, states are entitled to the wealth of their territories and to share equally in any of the surplus returns that arise from their cooperation with each other. In exploring how taxation interacts with these principles, we saw that source states may have to tax away some of the investment returns earned within their territories in order to receive an equal share of the cooperative surplus, while residence states can choose to tax or not, according to internal policy considerations. The source state's action is key to the distribution of cooperative surplus: when gains arise from cross-border investment, the source state has the opportunity to tax some of them away before they ever get into the hands of the other state whether as private investment gain or tax revenue.

Knowing this, one might expect most source states to routinely impose taxes to the fullest extent on all returns to capital that they can plausibly link to their jurisdictions, at least within the bounds of accepted norms. In fact, the opposite is true: many states do not collect a share of the cooperative surplus of international capital mobility through source-based taxation, even—perhaps especially—when they keenly rely on inbound capital investment for economic development. In the previous chapter we suggested that this likely means that these states do not receive a fair share of the benefits of tax cooperation.

What explains the disconnect? We offer two explanations in this chapter, namely tax competition and peer pressure to conform to international tax norms, both through treaties and soft law. We examine why and how these factors impede the capacity of source states to tax cross-border income. We then review some of the reforms currently under consideration in multilateral fora, now that a confluence of factors has resulted in a willingness even among the most affluent states to consider modifications to traditional principles and norms of tax cooperation. This willingness has been a long time in the making as we show by briefly reviewing the global conversation that has been taking place in the last twenty years about the rise of what the OECD has called 'harmful' tax competition. Before developing our normative case for reform

Tax Cooperation in an Unjust World. Allison Christians and Laurens van Apeldoorn, Oxford University Press. © Allison Christians and Laurens van Apeldoorn 2021. DOI: 10.1093/oso/9780192848673.003.0003

and proposing a range of technical solutions in the following chapters, we conclude that this is an opportune moment to present our case.

2.1. Tax Competition

To the extent that source states must tax the returns to foreign capital investment in order to receive an approximately equal share of the cooperative surplus, tax competition stands as a clear obstacle to this aspect of fair cooperation. When states facilitate financial liberalization, they establish conditions for a competition between them for capital inflows. This competition tends to put downward pressure on their capacity and willingness to tax returns to capital. Left unchecked, tax competition leads states to refrain from imposing taxes even if all would agree that they may do so (as a normative matter or according to generally accepted tax standards or both). It undermines their capacity to exercise the tax rights allocated to them, harming their political autonomy and potentially undermining a fair distribution of the gains of the cooperative practice between them.

As such, it is important to understand how it is that tax competition impedes national political autonomy and with what effect for states of different levels of national affluence, as well as geo-political influence on tax policymaking. In opening this inquiry, it is necessary to contend with the inescapable fact that the tax system is instrumental to achieving all kinds of non-tax policy goals. As such, it is often called upon as a site for reform in the name of incentivizing or facilitating various social and economic outcomes, including capital accumulation. Taxation is not the only available policy tool to achieve these aims but it is frequently high on every state's list of possible strategies to employ. The desire for foreign capital in particular almost universally prompts lawmakers to consider taxation as a possible impediment to their economic policy goals rather than as a tool for achieving those goals. We introduced some of the reasons states seek foreign capital in the first chapter. We now expand this examination and consider in more depth how they use tax to do so.

Why States Compete for Capital

As we introduced in Chapter 1, the reason states compete to attract foreign capital is simple: the expectation is that increased capital investment will produce positive spillovers in the form of domestic capital accumulation, economic growth, and a rising standard of living for the society as whole. Whether the premise holds in fact depends on historical and contemporary social, economic, and political factors, but it is clear that the great promise of the post-World War II institutions was to achieve both peace and widespread prosperity through freer international trade and investment, and this remains a core mandate of the key intergovernmental organizations today.

States benefit differently from the flows of investment among them, and there is no guarantee that all states benefit from their participation in global capital markets to even some minimal extent.[1] In the previous chapter we noted that a states' capacity to benefit from capital inflows through various forms of positive spillovers is in part dependent on the characteristics of its economy. In some cases it may even hurt more than it helps, if states are unable to limit profit repatriation, for instance by imposing a source tax.[2] Despite these risks, the race to attract foreign capital persists.

In this race, each state has a different relative ability to compete, based on a combination of historical and contemporary social, economic, and cultural factors including the accident of geography. Virtually every state is therefore in a near constant re-evaluation of all of its available policy levers, with taxation an available tool alongside labour standards, environmental regulation, and other regulatory regimes.[3] The relative impact of tax policy at any given point in time depends in part on other regulatory influences on capital flows. For example, as global social standards respecting labour conditions and environmental regulation rise, the pressure to use taxation to attract capital intensifies.

Taxation is a tricky tool to deploy for this purpose, however. From one perspective, tax revenues are obviously needed to create the conditions for producing the spillovers described above.[4] This would require raising revenues to make the public investments needed to attract additional private investment. However, lawmakers must contend with the widespread perception that

[1] Andrew Sumner, 'Is Foreign Direct Investment Good for The Poor?' (2015) 15 Dev Pr 269–85.

[2] Amitava Dutt, 'Direct Foreign Investment, Transnational Corporations and Growth: Some Empirical Evidence and a North–South Model' in Richard Kozul-Wright and Robert Rowthorn (eds), *Transnational Corporations and the Global Economy* (MacMillan Press 1998) 165–66.

[3] Richard Caves, *Multinational Enterprises and Economic Analysis* (Cambridge University Press 1982); Helen I Safa, 'Runaway Shops and Female Employment: The Search for Cheap Labor' (1981) 7(2) Signs: J Women Cult & Soc 418–33.

[4] At a minimum, to create the fundamental building blocks of social order through the rule of law. See, eg, Stewart Macaulay, 'Law and the Behavioral Sciences: Is There Any There There?' (April 1984) L & Pol'y 149–87, abr 1984, p 152 (explaining that the rule of law is not free); Stephen Holmes and Cass R Sunstein, *The Cost of Rights: Why Liberty Depends on Taxes* (WW Norton & Company 1999) (explaining that property rights protections depend on taxation); Colin Farrelly, 'Taxation and Distributive Justice' (2004) 2 Pol Stud Rev 185–97, 190; Colin Farrelly, *Justice, Democracy and Reasonable Agreement* (Palgrave Macmillan 2007) (explaining that property rights are costly).

taxation reduces the net expected private return to investment. Whether this is empirically true or not is not always the material deciding factor when it comes to making tax policy choices. To the extent it is feasible within socially accepted norms, the best strategy of the private sector has always been to reap maximum private rewards while contributing minimally to public coffers—even extracting subsidies from public coffers if that is possible.

Even if reduced public spending on core infrastructure is the result of low tax levels, and even if reduced infrastructure also negatively impacts private gains, the persistent perception of tax as a cost feeds a generalized acceptance that firms are rationally averse to taxation. The sentiment is captured in the adage that the primary duty of the firm is to increase shareholder returns—an idea that is contested but still exerts a powerful intuitive force in tax policy discourse.[5] Since tax is a salient cost to investors while the private benefits to be had from public spending are often less so, some resistance to the payment of taxes is assumed to be a permanent fixture in any lawmaker's political assessment involving the use of tax policy to attract investment.

How States Use Tax to Attract Capital

Since reducing taxation is a primary objective for the private sector, a state that seeks to tax the returns to foreign-owned capital is wary that taxpayers will either fight the tax by adopting increasingly aggressive tax avoidance practices, or flee it in search of higher post-tax returns in other states. Tax considerations are significant, though perhaps not decisive, when they consider in which jurisdiction to invest. If firms are considering cross-border expansion, taxation levels will play a role in their determination of the relative costs and benefits of locating production abroad. From the perspective of the investor, taxes appear (at least in the short term) as pure costs, the reduction of which can increase profits or long-term firm value or both.

States wishing to tax returns to foreign-owned capital through corporate income taxes therefore run the risk of losing investment to other jurisdictions that impose lower tax burdens. Certainly, the tax treatment investors receive will not be the only consideration featuring in investment decisions.[6] After all,

[5] See eg Reuven S Avi-Yonah, 'Corporate Taxation and Corporate Social Responsibility' (2014) 11(1) NYU J L Bus 1.

[6] See, eg Philipp Genschel 'Globalization, Tax Competition and the Welfare State' (2002) 30(2) Pol & Soc 244–74; Steffen Ganghof, *The Politics of Income Taxation: A Comparative Analysis of Advanced Industrial Countries* (ECPR Press 2006).

other state specific factors—including public goods provision, the legal environment, and quality and costs of labour—may also influence the returns investors can expect, hence also playing a role in their investment decisions.[7] Nevertheless, multiple studies showing that there is an inverse relationship between capital inflows and raising taxes give states reasons for concern.[8] Conventional economic wisdom accordingly teaches that states seeking foreign investment should not tax at source.

However, this advice only makes sense if firms facing little or no tax at source will also face little or no tax at home, including when they repatriate their profits, such as when they pay out dividends or gains to a parent company in their home state. If a firm were to escape tax at source only to meet it at residence, the advice to forego tax at source would not make sense. It does make sense, however, when we see that the global trend has been to gradually eliminate residence-based taxes on repatriated profit as well. This trend makes source-based taxation increasingly difficult for states seeking to attract investment capital with all available tools in play.

An example in some detail is helpful in explaining why. We can imagine a traditional cross-border investment model as one that involves a multinational firm that gathers capital in the residence state and uses it to make an investment in the source state—namely, by buying assets or inventory, or hiring workers to perform various functions. This is a traditional investment and things look different in highly digitalized firms (such as Facebook or Google) but it is a good place to start the analysis.

In making its cross-border investment, our imagined multinational firm subjects itself to regulation by both jurisdictions, thus creating the opportunity for both to tax it. The source state might tax profits earned by the firm within its territory (separate and apart from any sales or consumption taxes that might also apply to local buyers), while the residence state might tax the firm as its resident, whether on income or some other tax base.[9] Both states act

[7] Taxes will not be the only or even the most important consideration in many cases, but all other factors being equal, sensitivity to taxation levels may influence investment location decisions. See, eg, OECD, *Corporate Tax Statistics* (2nd edn, OECD Publishing 2020) 16 ('It is well understood that cross-jurisdiction competitiveness is not solely driven by the tax costs associated with an investment; many other factors, such as the quality of the workforce, infrastructure and the legal environment, affect profitability and are likely to have significant impacts on investment decisions'); see also Michael P Devereux and Rachel Griffith 'Evaluating Tax Policy for Location Decisions' (2003) 10 Int'l Tax & Pub Fin 107–26.

[8] Ruud de Mooij and Sjef Ederveen, 'Corporate Tax Elasticities: A Reader's Guide to Empirical Findings' (2008) 24(4) Oxford Rev Econ Pol'y 680–97.

[9] Lawrence Lokken, 'What Is This Thing Called Source?' (2011) 37(3) Int'l Tax J 53; Stephen E Shay, J Clifton Fleming, Jr and Robert J Peroni, '"What's Source Got to Do with It?"—Source Rules and International Taxation' (2002) 56 Tax L Rev 81; Svetislav Kostic, 'In Search of the Digital Nomad: Rethinking the Taxation of Employment Income Under Tax Treaties' (2019) 11(2) World Tax J.

appropriately, according to generally accepted views of tax jurisdiction as we saw them in Chapter 1: the source state is entitled to tax any base that derives from economic sources within it, while the residence state is entitled to tax any of its residents on any base it chooses. But the combination has the potential to create a substantially higher tax on foreign income relative to what the multinational would face had it confined its operations to its home state.

The risk that this could occur motivates the firm to lobby for a different result. It might lobby foreign states for tax breaks and subsidies, or it might lobby its home state to negotiate a mutually agreeable way to share the tax base to prevent this result—an idea we will explore in more detail below. Cooperation is not a foregone conclusion: either or both states could simply decide to accept the possibility that the firm will face double taxation, and either or both could act unilaterally to prevent double taxation without coordinating with the other.

Assuming away cooperation for the moment, the two states face different prospects in making their deliberations. From the residence state perspective, lawmakers must consider whether to help the firm investing outside of the state by ceding the residence-based tax, or, conversely, to discourage the export of capital by allowing the possibility of double taxation to stand. Lawmakers in the source state will make the inverse calculation, deciding whether to help the firm considering foreign investment opportunities by ceding the tax at source or providing subsidies, or, conversely, to do nothing and accept the risk that less capital might be imported if it faces a higher tax burden. As such, neither state strictly requires the cooperation of the other in order to ensure the free flow of investment capital.[10] All that is needed is for at least one of the two states to choose not to tax despite its widely accepted jurisdictional right to do so.

Three Possible Outcomes

As tax jurisdictions overlap, there are accordingly three possible outcomes: one or the other state will cede its right to tax; neither will cede, thus potentially making cross-border investment less profitable than domestic investment; or both will cede, thus making cross-border investment potentially more profitable than domestic investment. Each state seeks to make its own choice in light of how it expects or observes other states to act.

[10] Tsilly Dagan, 'The Tax Treaties Myth' (2000) 32 NYUJ Int'l L & Pol 939 reprinted in Tsilly Dagan, *International Tax Policy: Between Cooperation and Competition* (Cambridge University Press 2018).

As it turns out, the third outcome has been the dominant strategy for most of the history of modern income taxation, but there have been moments of recalibration toward ensuring that capital faces a tax either at source or at residence at some point. The recent development of consensus around global minimum tax rates, albeit limited to a modest number of very large multinationals, is the latest and most impactful recalibration to date, as we discuss further below.

The course of action chosen by lawmakers in residence states, to the extent their political strategies respond to dominant economic theory, will depend on whether they believe there are national gains to be achieved by overseas investment relative to domestic investment. If so, the residence state can cede its right to tax by either providing a credit for taxes paid in the source state or simply by exempting all foreign income from tax all together, whether or not it faces tax in the source state.

States that choose a credit system are typically referred to as 'worldwide' tax states in the sense that they nominally tax all income of their residents wherever derived throughout the world, with offset for foreign taxes paid. In contrast, states that choose to exempt foreign income from taxation all together are typically referred to as 'territorial' tax states, because they effectively tax only the income arising in their own territories. No state is purely one or the other; worldwide and territorial are two extremes that represent the opposite ends of a spectrum. Whether the choice is made to be predominantly worldwide or territorial, lawmakers will likely design safeguards to ensure that foreign investment is not overly attractive relative to domestic investment, including by capping the amount of foreign taxes that can be credited, or limiting exemption to a specified type or amount of income.

Yet the choice between credit and exemption, that is, between worldwide and territorial, is not a neutral one when assessed from a global perspective. A given state's choice potentially impacts the range of choices thereafter available to other states that are prospective importers of capital. If the major capital-exporting or residence states were to choose credit systems and tax any residual profits earned abroad, then firms' location decisions would be less sensitive to tax at source, at least so long as the source tax does not exceed the creditable amount. Conversely if residence states choose exemption systems, the possibility of residual taxes falls away and firms' location decisions will become much more sensitive to tax at source. In the latter case, firms will typically use all available means to reduce taxes at source, whether by engaging in direct negotiation with potential host governments to achieve individualized tax reductions, lobbying for more general tax reductions, or through tax avoidance.

When residence states adopt territorial tax systems by exempting (or permitting indefinite deferral of taxation on) foreign income, they therefore create pressure on source states to compete for investment by also reducing taxes on income earned by foreign residents.[11] Conversely, if residence states mostly had worldwide tax systems with tax credits for source-based taxes, the pressure on source states would be alleviated. Of course, not all residence states have the same impact on global capital flows; what matters is the behaviour of the strategically important capital exporters. The degree of influence varies for different source states and over time but China and the member states of the OECD, especially the United States, are currently dominant in this respect.

Accordingly, whether source states choose to tax depends in large part on the overall trend toward territoriality versus toward worldwide taxation within influential capital-exporting states.[12] All tax systems in the world have elements of both systems, but over the past several decades the clear trend among states that export significant volumes of capital is toward territoriality.[13]

Predictably, the move to territoriality has been accompanied by a proliferation of tax incentive schemes to attract foreign capital. Strategies include a range of creative approaches including unilaterally reducing withholding taxes on income flows (dividends, interest, royalties, and capital gains), reducing corporate tax rates on local profits when earned within specified industries or geographic zones, or when earned in connection with specified intellectual property rights (such as so-called 'patent box' regimes), and even providing direct subsidies in cash and in kind. These measures are in use by states the world over even when it is not clear whether they are effective as a lure or

[11] If a multinational firm is based in a territorial state, its baseline tax rate on foreign income is effectively zero. This includes situations in which the 'territorial' state is a worldwide state that exempts active foreign income (for example, Canada); imposes excessive restrictions on creditability (the United States); allows deferral (the United States prior to the 2017 reform), or has flexible rules for the qualification for tax purposes of foreign subsidiaries (the United States with check-the-box rules).

[12] OECD, *Action Plan on BEPS* (n 7); Rosanne Altshuler and Harry Grubert, 'The Three Parties in the Race to the Bottom: Host Governments, Home Governments and Multinational Companies' (2005) 7 Fla Tax Rev 137.

[13] Michael Keen and Peter Mullins, 'International Corporate Taxation and the Extractive Industries: Principles, Practice, Problems' in Philip Daniel and others (eds), *International Taxation and the Extractive Industries* (Routledge 2016) 15–16 (naming the United States, Ireland and South Korea as mainly worldwide states, and Australia, Austria, Belgium, Canada, France, Germany, Luxembourg, the Netherlands, Norway, Switzerland, and the United Kingdom as mainly territorial states).

whether the investment thus attracted actually ends up creating net local benefits relative to autarky.[14]

It should be noted that the trend toward territoriality also creates more pressure on residence states themselves, as firms seek to strategically relocate their headquarters to the most favourable jurisdiction. Some residence states adopt various safeguards, including so-called anti-inversion rules, to protect themselves against this kind of competition, even though the opportunities for tax avoidance can be traced back to some of their own policy choices.[15] A multilateral trend back to worldwide taxation might reverse some of these pressures for residence states as well, thus making such a move a mutually beneficial policy choice. As we will explore more below, the likelihood that major capital-exporting states might go in this direction has recently increased, partially in response to the major revenue needs arising from the Covid-19 pandemic.

Thus, embedded in cross-border tax relations, tax competition looms large for those seeking to understand which states can tax effectively and which cannot. Yet tax competition is not the only source of explanation; it is accompanied, and arguably furthered, by the hard and soft law sources that make up the international tax regime.

2.2. Peer Pressure

Proposing terms of cooperation that facilitate international capital flows has always been a major goal of the great powers but protecting source-based taxation has not. The need to find a mutually agreeable way to compel states to yield their entitlement to tax in specified circumstances initially led geopolitically powerful states to agree to a set of tax-base sharing norms in the early twentieth century—the rules of tax jurisdiction discussed above being a major component of this grand compromise. These early norms have remained remarkably constant since then, presumably because they served the geopolitical powers well overall, even if lawmakers, policy observers, and scholars have constantly observed the system to be flawed—even predatory[16]—in multiple technical, economic, and normative respects. It is only recently that

[14] Afton Titus and Tracy Gutuza, 'The Relationship between Tax Incentives and Human Rights Obligations in the Drive to Attract Foreign Direct Investment: Are African Developing Countries Getting it Right?' (2018) 1 Acta Jur 149–82.

[15] Adam Rosenzweig, 'Defining a Country's "Fair Share" of Taxes' (2015) 42 Fla St L Rev 373; Senate Finance Committee release, 'Grassley Announces Bill to Rein in Corporate Expatriation' *Congressional News Releases* (Washington 2002) TNT 71–29.

[16] See Steven Dean, *Predatory Cooperation*, Intertax Debate (Kluwer Law 2021).

technological innovation and the erosion of the applicability of traditional conceptions of tax jurisdiction have led the geo-political powers of the day to consider potentially significant overhaul, but fidelity to the concepts of source and residence, no matter how flawed, is likely to survive any norm reconstruction.

These concepts are at work in national tax laws and international treaties, as they are in a range of model international agreements, guidelines, standards, and other influential documents drafted in intergovernmental forums over the years.[17] The collection of pluralistic legal agreements and processes are commonly referred to as a regime, a system, or an order, not always with detailed explanation.[18] Their function is to enable states to achieve mutually beneficial cross-border investment to generate the surplus gains described above, some share of which each then seeks to protect as part of its national endowment.

The main form of law in this system consists of a network of several thousand bilateral tax treaties, all based on a common model and related guidance primarily developed by the OECD.[19] Two other influential model conventions with different terms are promulgated by the United States and the United Nations, but all three models share core characteristics, and the OECD's version is typically referred to as the key source of international tax norms.[20] The influence of the OECD Model Tax Convention is further entrenched by a set of interpretative guidelines it produces as 'commentaries' to the model. The commentaries elaborate, clarify and provide examples intended to express the OECD's view of the consensus of its member states as to the meaning of the various provisions and terms used in the Model Tax Convention. By implication, as regulations are to domestic statutes, the commentaries serve as interpretive guidance for tax treaties actually in force. Because they reflect the consensus of the OECD member states, the commentaries are seen as persuasive in many states, including beyond the OECD membership, even if they are not formal or 'hard' law.

17 For a description of the relevant actors, institutions, elements and processes, see, eg, Yariv Brauner, 'An International Tax Regime in Crystallization' (2003) 56 Tax L Rev 263; Arthur Cockfield, 'The Rise of the OECD as Informal 'World Tax Organization' Through National Responses to E-Commerce Tax Challenges' (2006) 9 Yale J L & Tech 59; Allison Christians, 'Hard Law and Soft Law in International Taxation' (2007) 25 Wisc J Int'l L 325; Allison Christians, 'Networks, Norms, and National Tax Policy' (2010) 9 Wash U Glob Studies L Rev 1.

18 By using these popular terms interchangeably we intend to be loosely descriptive and do not take a position regarding the range of legal implications that might flow from using one or the other.

19 OECD, *OECD Model Tax Convention on Income and on Capital* (2017). For discussion of the reasons that led states to adopt tax treaties, see Sunita Jogarajan, 'The Conclusion and Termination of the 'First' Double Taxation Treaty' (2012) 3 Brit Tax Rev.

20 United States Treasury, *United States Model Income Tax Convention* (2016); United Nations, *Model Double Tax Convention between Developed and Developing Countries* (United Nations 2017) 318.

Soft Law

As such, the OECD model and commentaries are often referred to as soft law instruments. This characterization potentially elevates their stature, allowing the OECD to accept and even advertise its role as the world leader in tax policy, compelling adherence to its norms through modelling and peer pressure.[21] Through these mechanisms, the tax policy preferences of the OECD member states have widespread influence well beyond the organizational membership, and the organization has continuously reinforced and expanded this reach over the course of several decades. When the OECD defines tax policy norms, it impacts states the world over.

This influence is seen clearly in the OECD Model Tax Convention's tax-base sharing structure, which seeks to implement the first outcome of the three described above in the discussion on tax competition, namely by having one or the other state cede its right to tax in order to prevent double taxation. It does so by significantly limiting source state taxation. This is accomplished by capping source state withholding rates on portfolio investment returns and by restricting source state taxation of active income via thresholds to taxation and a prescribed method of allocating business profit across states.[22]

Rate caps are found in a series of provisions delineating the various types of income to be paid out, while the threshold rules are embodied in the concept of the 'permanent establishment,' a threshold concept that allows full source state taxes of business operations only once they have met agreed conditions, and then only in respect of income associated with that above-threshold activity.[23] These rules involve the source state generally agreeing to refrain from taxing income earned by nonresident firms unless it is attributable to business activities that meet physical presence requirements, and even then, in some cases, only if the activities are conducted for a given duration or rise to a specified level of involvement.[24]

[21] See Frank Engelen, 'Some Observations on the Legal Status of the Commentaries on the OECD Model' (2006) 60(3) IBFD Bull 105 (arguing that states can by implicit conduct bind themselves to OECD guidance as a matter of international law); David R, Tillinghast, 'Commentaries to the OECD Model Convention: Ubiquitous, Often Controversial; But Could They Possibly Be Legally Binding?' (2006) 35 Tax Mgmt Int'l J 580.

[22] See, eg, OECD, *Model Tax Convention* (n 19) Arts. 10–13 (reducing source based withholding taxes on specified income items); Art. 5 (restricting the tax base with threshold rules).

[23] See OECD, *Model Tax Convention* (n 19 Art. 5; UN, *Model Tax Convention* (n 20) Art. 5; US, *Model Tax Convention* (n 20) Art. 5. A limited force of attraction is accepted in the UN Model, but not in the OECD Model. See S Sagar 'How "Limited" Is Limited Force of Attraction? An Analysis of the Relevant Case Law and the Potential Implications of the OECD/G20 BEPS Initiative' (2017) 71 Bull Int'l Taxn March/April 180–213, at 182.

[24] Peripheral and ancillary activities include exploratory or preparatory functions such as research and development, as well as activities considered incidental to the economic source of the income,

The profit allocation norm at play involves two intersecting concepts, namely separate entity and arm's length pricing. The separate entity concept is that for tax treaty purposes, a group of related or affiliated companies (that is, those joined through common control or as the OECD refers to them, 'associated enterprises') should not be treated as a single entity but rather each of the companies should be treated as a distinct person with the attendant obligation to compute and pay its tax liabilities based on its own income. Arm's length pricing then holds that in computing each separate entity's income for tax purposes, any prices set for transactions occurring among these separate associated enterprises ought to reflect the prices that unrelated enterprises would be expected to pay in the same transactions. The separate entity and arm's length pricing standards are implied if not explicitly required by the OECD, UN, and US Model Tax Treaties. Each also contains a corollary for unincorporated enterprises, that is, the concept of business profits attributable to permanent establishments.[25]

As an example of rate capping, a state might have a domestic tax rate of 25 per cent on all dividends paid out to foreign shareholders, but the OECD Model Tax Convention limits source states to a maximum 5 per cent rate for inter-company dividends and 15 per cent for all other dividends.[26] As a result, most of the world's tax treaties cap source taxation at these rates, with most exceptions running in the direction of lower rates at source, despite the UN Model Tax Convention providing some support for a higher cap.[27]

As an example of base restricting, a state might tax all income earned from any business operating within its territory with no exception, but the OECD Model Tax Convention prevents states from taxing business profits earned by foreign residents unless the business exceeds certain physical presence factors (and in some cases time factors).[28] In particular, the permanent establishment definition in the OECD Model Tax Convention requires a business to

such as storage, display, or delivery of goods. See OECD, *Model Tax Convention* (n 19) Art. 5; UN, *Model Tax Convention* (n 20) Art. 5; US, *Model Tax Convention* (n 20) Art. 5. For a comparison of the thresholds among the Models and their implications, see Michael Lennard, 'The UN Model Tax Convention as Compared with the OECD Model Tax Convention—Current Points of Difference and Recent Developments' (2009) 49 Asia/Pac Tax Bull 8.

[25] OECD, *Model Tax Convention* (n 19) Article 9, Associated Enterprises, and Article 7, Business Profits; UN, *Model Tax Convention* (n 20). The norms are laid out in guidelines published with periodic updates by each institution to reflect the evolving consensus of their respective memberships. OECD, *OECD Transfer Pricing Guidelines for Multinational Enterprises and Tax Administrations* (OECD Publishing 2017); United Nations, *Practical Manual on Transfer Pricing* (United Nations 2017).

[26] OECD, *Model Tax Convention* (n 19) Article 10, paragraph 1 (in all versions).

[27] UN, *Model Tax Convention* (n 20) Articles 10–13.

[28] OECD, *Model Tax Convention* (n 19) Article 5, Permanent Establishment.

have established material physical operations in the territory, defined to include things like having an office with employees or operating a factory, but excluding things like selling inventory out of a local warehouse and other so-called 'preparatory or auxiliary' functions even if there are local contractors dedicated full time to the business.[29] The UN Model Tax Convention follows suit but with a lower threshold for taxation.[30] Bilateral tax treaties typically contain these core principles with minor variations.

Finally, the profit allocation standards for incorporated entities and attribution of profits to permanent establishments are found not in treaties themselves but in separate 'guidelines' developed and updated periodically by the OECD and the United Nations states either adhere to or view as persuasive.[31] The adverse effects of these norms for some source states is a complex topic we will return to in some detail.

Formal Neutrality

The treaty-based restriction of tax at source is not targeted to one set of states or another; it is neutral in the sense that it is generally reciprocal. Each party to a tax treaty might be the residence state in one situation and the source state in another, so a reciprocal reduction of tax at source ultimately harms neither so long as capital investments flow between them in roughly equal amounts. In theory, whatever tax base is given up when in the role of source is recouped when in the role of residence. For example, while a state may give up source tax revenue by reducing its tax on dividends paid out to foreign persons, it will recoup the revenue thus lost by being able to collect more tax on dividends received by its residents from the other state than it would in the absence of the treaty (because in the absence of the treaty, it would feel obliged to credit the higher source tax rate or exempt the income all together to prevent double taxation). Accordingly, tax treaties among economically similarly states are commonly described as having little revenue effect to either state.

When states are likely to exchange capital investments in roughly equal measure, treaties covering these exchanges are typically characterized as mere coordinating systems for the benefit of the taxpayers, with little overall revenue effect on either state.[32] The referenced benefit to the taxpayer is avoiding the

[29] OECD, *Model Tax Convention* (n 19) Article 5, paragraphs 1–4 (in all versions).

[30] UN, *Model Tax Convention* (n 20) Article 5.

[31] OECD, *Transfer Pricing Guidelines* (n 25); to a lesser extent, UN, *Model Tax Convention* (n 20).

[32] See, eg, Staff of the Senate Foreign Rel Comm, 105th Cong, Report on the Tax Convention with Ireland 17 (Comm Print 1997) ('the proposed treaty is estimated to cause a negligible change

complication of having to reconcile the overlapping taxation of the two states through duplicative filing, cross-crediting, and the like. The characterization of neutrality due to reciprocity holds even in the case of complete elimination of source state taxation.

For example, the US Joint Committee on Taxation typically issues explanatory material in conjunction with the enactment of US tax treaties, often including a statement of the expected economic impacts of the treaty for the United States. One such explanation accompanied a proposed 'protocol' (effectively, an addendum to the existing treaty) to the Australia-US tax treaty that reduced the previous rate for source-based tax on specified inter-company dividends paid to beneficial owners in the other state from five percent to zero. The explanatory material stated that even though the proposed protocol would eliminate all US taxes of the income paid out to Australian investors in these cases, the treaty would bring 'immediate and direct benefits to the United States as both an importer and an exporter of capital'. The explanation went on to say that '[t]he overall revenue impact of this provision is unclear, as the direct revenue loss to the United States as a source country would be offset in whole or in part by a revenue gain as a residence country from reduced foreign tax credit claims with respect to Australian taxes.'[33]

Reciprocity has long been a key commitment underlying the OECD Model Tax Convention since it is directed at and works most effectively between states that exchange capital and services with each other in roughly reciprocal amounts—which generally describes the founding member states of the OECD. But the story of reciprocity quickly falls apart when the states are not likely to exchange capital investments in roughly equal measure. This is the case for most of the states outside the OECD membership in relation to member states.

Substantive Non-Neutrality

Restricted tax base and reduced withholding tax rates equally for both parties does not make sense if one party is habitually the capital exporter and the other the capital importer. In that case, the capital importer is almost always

in . . . Federal budget receipts'); Staff of the Senate Foreign Rel Comm, 108th Cong, Report on the Tax Convention with the United Kingdom 16, 17 (Comm Print 2003) (same).

[33] See, eg, Staff of the Joint Comm on Taxation, 108th Cong, Explanation of Proposed Protocol to the Income Tax Treaty Between the United States and Australia (Comm Print 2003).

in the role of the source state, habitually losing its tax base and rarely if ever recouping it by sending capital abroad.[34] Conversely states that are habitual exporters of capital will enjoy the source rate reduction as an increase of their endowment, even if they do not choose to tax at residence, as we saw in Chapter 1.

In fact, there is no uniformly neutral way to treat cross-border investment flows for tax purposes. In the 1960s, Peggy Musgrave was among the first economists to develop this insight in the language of capital export neutrality and capital import neutrality and the point became a mainstay in international tax policy when developed in co-authorship with Richard Musgrave.[35] The Musgraves noted that in a multi-state world, worldwide taxation with foreign tax creditability is neutral as to capital exports, while territoriality is neutral as to capital imports, but the types of neutrality created by exemption versus credit are mutually exclusive policies to the extent that the tax base and effective tax rate diverges among states, which is the current reality. As the policies cannot be reconciled, governments commonly revisit their positions, often in response to choices made by their major investment partner states.

Responding to the perhaps unforeseen aspects of relationships between more and less affluent states that result from the substantive non-neutrality of tax policy choices, the United Nations formed a Group of Experts on International Cooperation in Tax Matters with the intent of studying how best to preserve source state taxation.[36] It did so by providing for lower business tax thresholds and higher withholding rate caps for investment income in its own Model Tax Convention, first released in 1980.[37] However, relatively more

[34] Richard Chisik and Ronald Davies, 'Asymmetric FDI and Tax-Treaty Bargaining: Theory and Evidence' (2004) 88(6) J Pub Econ 1119; Allison Christians, 'Tax Treaties for Investment and Aid to Sub-Saharan Africa: A Case Study' (2006) 71(2) Brook L Rev 639.

[35] Peggy Richman [Musgrave], *Taxation of Foreign Investment Income: An Economic Analysis* (Johns Hopkins Press 1963); Peggy Richman [Musgrave], *United States Taxation of Foreign Investment Income: Issues and Arguments* (Law School of Harvard University 1969); Richard Musgrave and Peggy Musgrave, 'Inter-nation Equity' in Richard M Bird and John G Head (eds), *Modern Fiscal Issues: Essays in Honour of Carl S Shoup* (University of Toronto Press 1972); Richard Musgrave and Peggy Musgrave, *Public Finance in Theory and Practice* (5th edn, McGraw-Hill 1989) 15.

[36] The group, formally entitled the 'Ad Hoc Group of Experts on International Cooperation in Tax,' was established by the UN Secretary-General in 1968. It was transformed into a permanent committee, the Committee of Experts on International Cooperation in Tax Matters, by resolution of the UN Economic and Social Council (ECOSOC) in 2004. In 2015, the United Nations announced its plan to enhance the resources of the Committee in order to strengthen its effectiveness, namely by increasing the frequency of its meetings to two sessions of four days each per year, increasing its engagement with the Economic and Social Council, and seeking voluntary funding to support the increased participation of developing country experts at subcommittee meetings. United Nations, Resolution adopted by the General Assembly on 27 July 2015.

[37] United Nations, *United Nations Model Double Taxation Convention between Developed and Developing Countries* (United Nations Publications 1980). For discussion, see Honey Lynn Goldberg, 'Conventions for the Elimination of International Double Taxation: Toward a Developing Country Model' (1983) 15 L & Pol'y Int'l Bus 833.

affluent states have generally not embraced these terms in their tax treaty negotiations. On the contrary, some have aggressively pursued reduced source state taxation through tax treaties even when it is clear that the effects of such reductions will not be reciprocal.[38] Martin Hearson confirms in particular that power asymmetries between tax treaty signatories 'lead to more unequal distributions of taxing rights away from developing countries.'[39]

2.3. 'Fair' Versus 'Harmful' Tax Competition

The discussion above makes clear that between tax competition and international peer pressure, it is currently very difficult for states seeking to attract international investment to tax at source. Even so, a global conversation has been taking place over the last two decades or so about whether and in what forms it should be considered acceptable for states to engage in tax competition, and what role, if any, tax treaties should have in stopping it. In the rest of this chapter we survey the trajectory of the debate of the international community and indicate some of the hopeful signs indicating a willingness of states to consider more significant reforms of the terms of tax cooperation today.

The origins of this discourse developed in mid 1996 when the OECD released an OECD Ministerial Communiqué announcing the initiation of multilateral talks to define and eliminate harmful tax competition.[40] Following a meeting of the G-7 countries later in the same year, the G-7 Finance Ministers and Central Bank Governors declared that '[t]ax schemes aimed at attracting financial and other geographically mobile activities can create harmful tax competition between States, carrying risks of distorting trade and investment and could lead to the erosion of national tax bases,' and they 'strongly urge[d] the OECD to vigorously pursue its work in this field.'[41] The OECD's work was

[38] Kim Brooks, 'Canada's Evolving Tax Treaty Policy Toward Low-Income Countries' in Arthur Cockfield (ed), *Globalization and its Tax Discontents: Tax Policy and International Investments* (University of Toronto Press 2010) 189–211; Festud Aukonobera, 'Uganda' in M Lang, Pasquale Pistone, and Josef Schuch (eds), *The Impact of the OECD and UN Model Conventions on Bilateral Tax Treaties* (Cambridge University Press 2012).

[39] Martin Hearson, 'When do Developing Countries Negotiate Away Their Corporate Tax Base?' (2018) 30(2) J Int'l Devel.

[40] See Council of the OECD, *Ministerial Communiqué*, 21–22 May 1996, par xv <http://www.g8.utoronto.ca/oecd/oecd96.htm> (instructing the OECD to 'analyse and develop measures to counter the distorting effects of harmful tax competition on investment and financing decisions, and the consequences for national tax bases').

[41] Statement of G7 Finance Ministers and Central Bank Governors (Sept 20, 1997) <www.g7.utoronto.ca/finance/fm970920.htm>; *Lyon Summit Communiqué: Making a Success of Globalization for the Benefit of All*, 7 U.S. Dep't of State Dispatch Supplement 1, 5 (June 1996).

further spurred on by rising attention to international tax in the popular media and later the rise to prominence of the tax justice movement, which framed tax incentive regimes and corporate tax avoidance practices as fundamentally unjust. The narrative of harmful tax competition alongside the evolving language of tax justice implied that some uses of a tax system to compete for capital are justified, while others are not.

But lawmakers and justice advocates are not always clear about how they drew the line between these categories. In particular, the OECD's work on the subject drew the reasonable criticism that the member states of the OECD were quick to decry the tax incentive strategies of non-member states, while reluctant to recognize their own policies as harmful to other states. In particular, the harm at stake, according to the OECD, was created by states that had little or no tax base—popularly referred to as tax havens. The OECD said that in reducing their effective income tax rates, these states 'encourage[d] the location of activities for tax rather than business purposes,' which made it 'harder for the home country to take defensive measures.'[42] By home country, the OECD tacitly meant its member states whose exported capital was routed through states offering themselves out as offshore financial centres before finally being invested in real economic activities elsewhere.

The OECD accordingly targeted 'tax havens and harmful preferential tax regimes' in the abstract, and stated its intention to reduce 'the distortionary influence of taxation' on location decisions involving financial and service activities.[43] Without ever expressly confronting the lines it was drawing in this exercise, the OECD identified some of the main practices it viewed as facilitating corporate and individual tax avoidance and evasion. On the list were narrow 'money box' schemes, as well as the broadly systemic choice of territorial taxation, which the OECD simply defined as the practice of exempting all foreign-source income from tax.[44] These practices were stated in OECD documents using abstract language and without specifically naming any offending states,

[42] OECD, *Harmful Tax Competition: An Emerging Global Issue* (OECD Publishing 1998) 27, 29, 32. See also Bev Dahlby, 'Globalization and the Future of the Corporate Income Tax' (2002) ATAX Discussion Paper #9, <http://ideas.repec.org/p/nsw/discus/09.html> accessed 31 August 2020 (explaining that globalization puts downward pressure on corporate income taxation and may lead to abandonment of foreign tax credit systems in favour of exemption systems as capital is increasingly invested abroad).

[43] OECD, *Harmful Tax Competition* (n 42) 7, 9 (in addition seeking 'to safeguard and promote an open, multilateral trading system and to encourage adjustments to that system to take into account the changing nature of international trade, including the interface between trade, investment and taxation'). Diane Ring, 'Democracy, Sovereignty and Tax Competition: The Role of Tax Sovereignty in Shaping Tax Cooperation' (2008) 9 Fla Tax Rev 555; Luis Calderon Gomez, 'Transcending "Tax" Sovereignty and Tax Standardization: Three Questions' (2020) 45 Yale J Int'l L 191.

[44] OECD, *Harmful Tax Competition* (n 42) 32.

but it was widely assumed that the OECD had a number of small jurisdictions in scope and would exempt its own membership from both scrutiny and sanction. This made it virtually impossible for the OECD to speak with moral authority even as it increasingly used the language of fairness and equity, a situation that only worsened as the discussions unfolded further.

'Tax Sovereignty'

Upon further deliberation among the member states, the issue of national autonomy over tax matters—often referred to in tax-law scholarship as 'tax sovereignty'—arose, and with it, disagreements about the merits of any OECD action considering the widespread view that states had the (unfettered) right to choose a tax system according to internal domestic policies. The OECD never defined or questioned the concept of tax sovereignty, and the term soon came to dominate all discussion.[45]

Lacking consensus on any position that would speak to the overall design of the tax system and therefore dictate the circumstances under which states could be prevented from choosing *not* to tax—by international sanction if necessary—the OECD ultimately moved away from broad, systemic policy choices in order to focus its efforts on issues that might be less susceptible to tax sovereignty as a defence. The language of national tax rates and systemic tax policy choices receded and the number and scope of targeted tax practices narrowed to those that facilitated tax evasion, namely through a combination of tax exemption and bank secrecy.

This turn made the narrative more palatable, but it erased the key sources of contention. These would later re-remerge in the aftermath of the harmful tax practices initiative, but by 2004, the OECD had settled on information exchange as the primary means to meet the goal of ending harmful tax practices, now redefined as promoting a 'level playing field' upon which 'to achieve high standards of transparency and information exchange in a way that is fair, equitable, and permits fair competition between all countries.'[46] Thus, judging its initiative as normatively appropriate, the OECD wrapped up its work by forming an expanded forum of participating states whose practices would be subject to peer review going forward.

[45] See Laurens van Apeldoorn, 'BEPS, Tax Sovereignty and Global Justice' (2018) 21(4) Crit Rev Int'l Soc & Pol Phil 478.

[46] OECD, 'A Process for Achieving a Global Level Playing Field' (OECD Global Forum on Taxation 2004) 2.

Base Erosion and Profit Shifting

Since the OECD's definition of fairness and equity remained implicit and the normative implications were never addressed, it should not have been a surprise when the same concerns that motivated the harmful tax practices work soon resurfaced in another form. As noted, a new cycle of tax cooperation began after the fiscal crisis of 2008 brought widespread austerity measures across OECD member states, even as stories about the low taxes paid by some of the world's largest firms splashed across popular media headlines.

With public scrutiny focused on the corporate taxation of multinationals, the OECD launched an initiative to counter what it coined 'base erosion and profit shifting', or BEPS.[47] The language of profit shifting, aimed at multinationals, combined with the nature-based metaphor of base erosion, cast the problem as one that involved firms with great power and states as hapless victims rather than the architects of tax policy, driven by natural forces rather than institutional choices. The metaphor of erosion hearkens to similarly vivid descriptions in the literature on harmful tax practices, which spoke of 'fiscal termites'[48] and the 'corrosive' nature of tax havens.[49] With the BEPS initiative, OECD member states revisited the unfinished consensus they had built in the harmful tax practices project.

This time, however, with broader public scrutiny, the OECD had little choice but to focus on the practices of its own membership, and in particular the series of rather arcane rules including those aimed at allocating profits among the geographically dispersed branches and affiliates of multinationals, discussed above as part of the soft law of international tax. The OECD defined the problem of BEPS as an unfair allocation of the tax bases of states that distorts trade and investment patterns and may 'hamper the application of progressive tax rates and the achievement of redistributive goals.'[50]

In recalibrating the rules, the language of fairness and the metaphor of a 'level playing field,' first raised in the harmful tax practices work, reemerged as a central unifying theme. These terms indicate the OECD's view that the present level of tax competition is normatively objectionable, and the targets of

[47] OECD, *Addressing Base Erosion and Profit Shifting* (OECD Publishing 2015).

[48] Vito Tanzi, 'Globalization, Technological Developments, and the Work of Fiscal Termites' (2001) 26 Brook J Int'l Law (characterizing eight trends in taxation, including the proliferation of low tax jurisdictions and regimes, as 'gnawing at the foundations of the tax systems' of industrialized OECD member states).

[49] See, eg, Peter Dietsch, *Catching Capital: The Ethics of Tax Competition* (Oxford University Press 2015) 121–22.

[50] OECD, *Harmful Tax Competition* (n 42) 14.

reform pinpoint some of the locations for the perceived injustices. The BEPS initiative ultimately targeted four areas of reform to be implemented through hard law (treaties and domestic rule sets) and multiple adjacent areas to be implemented through soft law, including peer review, monitoring, and the development of guidance.

Opinions differ on whether the BEPS initiative as a whole introduced major reforms or only cosmetic ones, but perhaps the most notable aspect of the BEPS initiative is the one issue area that first defied agreement, was put aside, and ultimately reemerged as arguably the OECD's most significant effort on cooperation to date. That issue area is the taxation of highly digitalized firms and the digitalized economy, initially introduced as the first action item in the BEPS project.[51] The parameters of this area are contested and still in flux, yet they are distinguished from all of the other OECD work to date. For the first time since the original tax norms were forged by committee over a century ago, states are considering a fundamental change to the scope and limits of tax jurisdiction, including with some level of global minimum taxation for a select group of multinational companies. We will return to these developments in later chapters.

Though not always acknowledged as such, the global conversation on tax competition and tax cooperation is fundamentally an ongoing referendum on the normative implications of both tax competition and the peer pressure of prevailing cooperation norms. This can be seen in the OECD's language of harmful versus fair tax cooperation, its implied acceptance of tax sovereignty as a matter of political autonomy, and the persistently unexamined metaphors of 'equal footing' and a 'level playing field,' which have featured prominently in the BEPS initiative.

The discussion is charged because the choice of some states regarding the taxation of international income flows, and their relative position vis à vis each other as primarily importers or exporters of capital, clearly produce distributional implications. Many states, especially lower-income ones, are consistently disadvantaged by both tax competition and the tax-base sharing norms that states developed in the name of tax cooperation. An IMF study concludes that capital outflows related to tax competition for lower income states are significant, possibly more so than for more affluent states, putting the revenue

[51] OECD, BEPS Action 1; OECD Programme of Work on Digitalisation; OECD, 'Brief on the Tax Challenges Arising from Digitalisation: Interim Report' (OECD Publishing 2018), <www.oecd.org/tax/beps/brief-on-the-tax-challenges-arising-from-digitalisation-interim-report-2018.pdf> accessed 12 April 2021.

losses currently at around 1.3 per cent of GDP on average.[52] The cost to states of peer pressure to adopt OECD consensus norms is difficult to measure but there are signs of great disparity among differently situated states.

Disparate Effects on Tax Capacity

Disparate impacts can be seen especially in the global decline of corporate taxation, a phenomenon that coincided with the liberalization of capital controls over the previous decades in many states worldwide.[53] Statutory rates have decreased in states at all levels of affluence, but with different effects for states of different means.[54] In relatively affluent states, the economic impact of corporate tax rate reductions has been limited, with corporate tax revenue as a share of gross domestic product (an admittedly rough measure) remaining relatively low but stable over time owing to a mix of base broadening and shifting of the tax mix to other factors, especially labour and consumption.[55]

Many lower income states were not similarly able to offset reductions in corporate tax rates with base broadening and shifting, and have seen reductions in corporate tax revenue as a share of their economy.[56] Since lower-income states rely more heavily on corporate income tax than high-income states, due to the

[52] Ernesto Crivelli, Ruud De Mooij, and Michael Keen, 'Base Erosion, Profit Shifting and Developing Countries' (2015) IMF Working Paper WP/15/118.

[53] Michael Keen and Alejandro Simone, 'Is Tax Competition Harming Developing Countries More Than Developed?' (2004) 1317 Tax Notes Int'l 1320–21; Michael Keen and Alejandro Simone, 'Tax Policy in Developing Countries: Some Lessons from the 1990s, and Some Challenges Ahead' in Sanjeev Gupta, Benedict Clements, and Gabriela Inchauste (eds), *Helping Countries Develop: The Role of Fiscal Policy* (International Monetary Fund 2004) 302; Titus and Gutuza, 'Tax Incentives and Human Rights Obligations' (n 14).

[54] OECD, *Corporate Tax Statistics* (n 7) 9 ('Statutory CIT [corporate income tax] tax rates have been decreasing on average over the last two decades, although considerable variation among jurisdictions remains. The average combined (central and sub-central government) statutory tax rate for all covered jurisdictions was 20.6 per cent in 2020, compared to 20.7 per cent in 2019 and 28.0 per cent in 2000').

[55] OECD, *Corporate Tax Statistics* (n 7) 4 (revealing 'a slight increase in both the average of CIT [corporate income tax] revenues as a share of total tax revenues and as a share of GDP between 2000 and 2017' across 93 jurisdictions studied for which data was available).

[56] Vito Tanzi, *Taxation in an Integrating World* (The Brookings Institution 1994) 130–31; Odd-Helge Fjeldstad and Lise Rakner, *Taxation and Tax Reforms in Developing Countries: Illustrations from Sub-Saharan Africa* (CMI Report 2003) 6 (Value added taxes were adopted to facilitate a shift away from other forms of tax but they did not bring new groups into the tax net or demonstrably improved revenue generation); IMF, *Rwanda: Letter of Intent, Memorandum of Economic and Financial Policies, and Technical Memorandum of Understanding* (25 March 2005) (despite Rwanda's adoption of VAT, revenue losses occurred due to a reduced reliance on income taxes and tariffs, and excise taxes were expected to make up the difference); M Shahe Emran and Joseph E Stiglitz, 'On Selective Indirect Tax Reform in Developing Countries' (2005) 89(4) J Pub Econ 599 (finding that adopting VAT produced few or no gains in revenue coupled by losses in distributional equity); Choifor I Saahdong, 'Indirect Tax Reforms and Revenue Mobilization in Cameroon' (Master's thesis, University of Oslo 2008) (in Cameroon, 'VAT remains rigid to revenue mobilization after the 1999 tax reform').

relative ease of administration and collection, such a decrease in corporate tax revenue 'jeopardizes a convenient and much-needed tax handle.'[57] The decline in rates is only aggravated by the proliferation of tax incentives many lower income states have implemented to attract foreign investment.

As seen above, the disappearance of tax at source limits domestic capital accumulation, potentially inhibits the prospects for positive spillovers, and may even result in net capital outflows. As Andrew Sumner puts it, 'liberalisation, conceptually at least, removes many of the policy instruments that might assist extraction of economic benefits to the local economy.'[58] When that is the prevailing outcome, source states do not stand to benefit from international cooperation in comparison to autarky.

We think that is the prevailing outcome and would therefore consider curtailment of tax at source normatively unjustifiable whether it is the product of tax competition or substantively non-neutral international tax norms.[59]

2.4. Prospects for Reform

The combination of competitive and legal impediments to source taxation discussed above demonstrates that residence states both enable and act as a ceiling on source states' ability to tax. Whether or not it is normatively or politically acceptable, the actions of residence states have these effects on source states. No matter how embedded in thought and assumption the notion of tax sovereignty, there actually is no neutral position in which all states can make any choices they want when it comes to taxation. If capital-exporting states choose to tax the foreign income of their residents, this choice will have one effect on states that mostly import capital. If capital-exporting states choose not to tax the foreign income of their residents, this choice will have a different effect. There is no escaping the international impact of domestic regulatory choices in the context of the thoroughly interconnected global economy in which we find

[57] Keen and Simone, 'Is Tax Competition Harming Developing Countries' (n 53) 1324. See also Kim Brooks, 'Canada's Evolving Tax Treaty Policy toward Low-Income Countries' in Arthur J Cockfield (ed) *Globalization and the Impact of Tax on International Investments* (University of Toronto Press 2010) 189–211 ('The revenue that low-income countries are able to raise from the income earned in their countries on cross border trade and investment flows is often significant and is critical for the development of their economy and for raising the standard of living of their impoverished residents.')

[58] Sumner, 'Is Foreign Direct Investment Good for the Poor?' (n 1) 282.

[59] We recognize, however, that others may disagree. For example, Tsilly Dagan has emphasized the importance of foreign investment in stimulating growth in developing economies, which she identifies as an important requisite of global justice. In Dagan, *International Tax Policy* (n 10) she goes as far as rejecting multilateral cooperation as unjust, insofar as it limits low-income states in their ability to attract investment through tax competition.

ourselves today. As such the question is not whether states should cooperate when it comes to tax: they already have cooperated and they continue to cooperate to create and maintain the conditions in which taxation has these inescapably global effects.

If there is no residence state tax and there are viable alternative destinations for investment capital, states vying for such capital will find it more difficult to tax the income arising within their borders that is fairly attributable to their domestic factors. Source states would no longer face this hurdle if and to the extent that this income would face an inescapable residual tax in an equal or higher amount in the residence state of the investor. Given that thousands of tax treaties in place have been structured to prevent taxation at source, greater taxation at residence would create more room to tax at source only if these terms were reformed to reverse those past decisions.

In order to change direction, the world's major residence states would have to move back on the spectrum toward worldwide taxation and away from territorial taxation.[60] There is some momentum materializing in this direction in the wake of the adoption of what amounts to a global minimum tax rate by the United States in the form of its 'global low taxed intangible income' regime, followed by a similar proposal in the OECD programme of work on the taxation of the digital economy.[61] The US regime potentially pushes back in the direction of worldwide taxation with respect to some forms of capital investment, even though it is within a larger structural move toward territoriality that leaves the US system in an overall position of impeding source taxation by other states.[62]

Other developments that could support a move back in the direction of worldwide taxation can be seen within the OECD's work on transforming the tax system to allocate more multinational profits away from low- and nil-tax jurisdictions through the BEPS initiative, and more particularly in its efforts to address the difficulties posed by the digitalization of the economy. The latter project explicitly includes a proposed global minimum corporate tax rate and

[60] Martin Hearson, 'Transnational Expertise and the Expansion of the International Tax Regime: Imposing "Acceptable" Standards' (2018) 25(5) Rev Int'l Pol Econ 647–71.

[61] U.S. Tax Cuts and Jobs Act of 2017.

[62] Athiphat Muthitacharoen and Krislert Samphantharak, 'Tax-Motivated Profit Shifting and Anti-Avoidance Stringency: Firm-Level Evidence from Developing Countries' (2019) Puey Ungphakorn Institute for Economic Research Pier Discussion Papers No. 111, <https://ideas.repec.org/p/pui/dpaper/111.html> accessed 31 August 2020 (modelling the negative effect of the U.S. Tax Cuts and Jobs Act on the ability of ASEAN states to impose source taxation); Dorine Boumans and others, 'Expected Effects of the US Tax Reform on Other Countries: Global and Local Survey Evidence' (2019) CESifo Working Paper No. 7491 (showing a 'negative impact on tax revenues and investment in countries with close economic ties' to the United States following the adoption of the Tax Cuts and Jobs Act).

harmonization of the global tax base through models, norms, standards, and guidance.[63] A related result of the BEPS initiative is the European Union's implementation of the Anti-Tax Avoidance Directive, which requires member states to adopt stricter rules for the taxation of passive income earned through controlled foreign affiliates. The Directive would generally impose residence-based taxation of foreign income streams where the source state's effective tax rate on such income falls below 50 per cent of the tax rate in the residence jurisdiction.[64]

These reforms might be seen by some as an objectionable curtailment of tax sovereignty in the sense that they effectively allow residence states to override the policy choices of source states. But overriding the policy choices of source states is also the outcome of the movement toward territoriality that residence states have been undertaking over the past few decades. Raising the overall expected level of tax for multinationals relative to the levels that were customary before the BEPS initiative began, even in the form of a global minimum tax that is effectuated by the actions of residence states, would arguably increase the overall level of tax sovereignty in that it would provide states that wish to expand source-based taxation a greater ability to do so.

2.5. Conclusion

This returns us to the starting point, that is, to try to understand what justice requires when it comes to tax cooperation among states. We began the discussion by outlining the normative guidance to be found within the entitlement and equal benefit principles, and we concluded Chapter 1 by observing that, leaving aside for the moment some of the problematic claims of states' entitlement to territorial wealth that accrue in an unjust world, it is clear that when states cooperate for their mutual benefit, the net gains of that cooperation should be equally shared between them. We have indicated in the present chapter that several obstacles today prevent source states from taxing cross-border income. The current terms of tax cooperation are marked by competition and peer pressure that works to the disadvantage of capital-importing states, especially those that are relatively less affluent than the capital-exporting

[63] OECD Programme of Work on Digitalisation (2019) (Pillar Two, describing the plan of work on a global minimum tax rate broadly following the US 2017 tax reform).

[64] Reuven S Avi-Yonah, 'The Great Recession and the International Tax Regime' (*Kluwer International Tax Blog*, 23 April 2019), <http://kluwertaxblog.com/2019/04/23/the-great-recession-and-the-international-tax-regime/> accessed 12 April 2021.

states whose domestic and international policy choices have forged and maintained all of these terms to date.

Given the requirement that relatively affluent states facilitate rather than thwart source taxation under a coherent application of the entitlement principle and under baseline circumstances of fair cooperation, lower income states are entitled to an institutional tax order that immediately prioritizes the kinds of reforms that would make it feasible for source states to impose tax on foreign investors and that would return taxing rights to source states in tax treaties that to date have removed these rights. Doing so is made legally difficult by the sheer volume of existing bilateral tax treaties that establish a firm commitment to reduction of tax at source.[65] As a starting point, the dominant Model Tax Convention promulgated and supported by the OECD requires major revision. Its current allocation of taxing rights promotes injustice, not only by curtailing the rates and the bases of tax at source, but also because the successful harmonization of tax policy through the OECD creates enormous international pressure to conform to its models and norms even when doing so perpetuates unjustifiable outcomes.[66] This is inconsistent with the entitlement principle which is otherwise well represented throughout policy documents promulgated in defence of various international coordination efforts.

Even on a rudimentary reading of the entitlement and equal benefit principles, fundamental reforms of the international tax system are not only justified but they are required. As the next chapters demonstrate, a more comprehensive examination of the entitlement principle in light of existing injustice in the world establishes that these fundamental reforms are only a starting point: much more will be needed to ensure that states are equally positioned to protect their entitlements to the wealth in their territories.

[65] Martin Hearson and Jalia Kangave, 'A Review of Uganda's Tax Treaties and Recommendations for Action' (2016) Institute of Development Studies International Centre for Tax and Development Working Paper No. 50.

[66] Reuven Avi-Yonah, *International Tax as International Law: An Analysis of the International Tax Regime* (Cambridge University Press 2007) 4 (observing that the freedom of most countries to adopt international tax rules is severely constrained, even before entering into any tax treaties, by the need to adapt to generally accepted principles of international taxation). Avi Yonah notes in particular that 'Mexico was required to abandon its long tradition of applying formulas in transfer pricing and adopt rules modeled after the OECD guidelines' in order to be able to join the OECD; Brazil is currently in accession talks with the same requirement in place despite signals that the OECD itself is now willing to consider moving toward methods commonly attributed to Brazil's international tax system. Avi-Yonah also notes that South Korea changed its broad interpretation of what constitutes a permanent establishment to conform to OECD norms, while Bolivia abandoned an attempt to adopt a cash flow corporate tax because it was ruled not creditable in the United States. He notes that 'Even the United States is not immune to this type of pressure to conform, as can be seen if one compares the 1993 proposed regulations under 482, which led to an international uproar, with the final regulations, which reflect the OECD guidelines.'

3
Subsistence Rights and the Duty of Assistance

The previous two chapters introduced two principles for tax cooperation and indicated their implications for international tax policy in a world that is just. In this chapter and the next, we examine the implications of the entitlement and equal benefit principles if one accepts that states have a duty of assistance given the degree of subsistence rights deficits we see in the world today. The duty of assistance, in brief, holds that when states are unable or unwilling to secure the subsistence rights of their populations, other states that are relatively affluent and well-ordered have a duty to assist in securing such subsistence rights. We think the duty to assist imposes a substantial condition on the entitlement and equal benefit principles, and we aim to show why that is so and to what effect for tax rules around the world.

We begin by discussing the breadth and severity of subsistence rights deficits and analysing the normative case that the universal protection and fulfilment of subsistence rights is required within the society-of-states model of international justice. We explain why subsistence rights deficits create obligations not only for the state where the deficits occur, but also for third-party states, which have a duty to act as backup rights protectors in specified circumstances. We then establish how the duty to assist impacts the two principles, showing that their application to cooperative schemes is conditional on subsistence rights being fulfilled in the cooperating states. When international capital mobility and investment involves states with populations facing subsistence rights deficits, any cooperative surplus generated must be viewed as the national endowment of the states in which subsistence rights are yet to be fulfilled, until such time as they are fulfilled.

We conclude that claims of relatively wealthy, well-ordered states to the (full) wealth of their territory are invalid until subsistence rights are realized in all states. This conclusion carries significant implications for the design of tax rules, which we will examine in detail in the chapter that follows.

Tax Cooperation in an Unjust World. Allison Christians and Laurens van Apeldoorn, Oxford University Press. © Allison Christians and Laurens van Apeldoorn 2021. DOI: 10.1093/oso/9780192848673.003.0004

3.1. The Breadth and Severity of Subsistence Rights Deficits

In order to explain how and why the entitlement principle is conditioned by national duties related to subsistence rights deficits around the world, it is necessary to introduce a relatively modest requirement of international justice. This consists of a noncomparative standard of what counts as a minimally decent life, expressed in terms of a threshold set by the human right to subsistence. The universal fulfilment of this right, we submit, is a necessary (if not sufficient) requirement for international justice.

The human right to subsistence, as we understand it, is a moral claim-right held by every person to assistance, if necessary, in securing clean air, food, water, clothing, shelter, basic healthcare, physical security, and the opportunity to provide for oneself the means to subsistence through work in favourable conditions.[1]

This right is also articulated in various legal instruments, including the Universal Declaration of Human Rights (UDHR) which in article 3 protects individuals' right to life and security and in article 25 defines the right to an adequate standard of living.[2] Of particular relevance to the analysis we will develop in this and following chapters, the right to subsistence includes *inter alia* the right to a living wage, that is, a wage that is adequate to meet basic needs and to attain and maintain a minimally decent life. UDHR article 23(3) states for example that workers have 'the right to just and favorable remuneration' allowing them to ensure for themselves and their family 'an existence worthy of human dignity, and supplemented, if necessary, by other means of social protection.'[3] The right to a living wage protects the subsistence interests of

[1] James Nickel, 'Poverty and Rights' (2005) 55(220) Phil Q 385 288. See also Henry Shue, *Basic Rights* (2nd edn, Princeton University Press 1996) 23. Note that we include physical security among the things protected by the right to subsistence, which in effect merges two of the 'basic rights' Shue identifies. Closely related is the conception of human rights advanced famously by then-US Secretary of State Cyrus Vance in his Law Day speech at the University of Georgia in 1977, which *inter alia* declared human rights to include 'the fulfillment of such vital needs as food, shelter, health care and education.' Cyrus Vance, 'Human Rights and Foreign Policy' (1977) 7 Ga J of Int'l & Comp L 223.

[2] Universal Declaration of Human Rights, Adopted and proclaimed by UN General Assembly resolution 217 A (III), 10 December 1948 (hereafter UDHR). UDHR Art. 25 (Setting out the 'right to a standard of living adequate for the health and well-being' of workers and their families, 'including food, clothing, housing and medical care and necessary social services, and the right to security in the event of unemployment, sickness, disability, widowhood, old age or other lack of livelihood in circumstances beyond [the worker's] control.') Economic and social rights are also included in other human rights legal instruments, such as the International Covenant on Economic, Social, and Cultural Rights (16 December 1966) 999 U.N.T.S. 3 (hereafter ICESER), the Convention on the Rights of the Child, the Convention on the Elimination of Discrimination Against Women, and the Conventions of the International Labor Organization.

[3] The ICSECR further elaborates in article 7 that workers ought to be provided, at a minimum, 'fair wages,' as well as safe and healthy working conditions and rest, leisure and reasonable limitation of working hours. For an overview of the widespread international support for a living wage, see

individuals and their families, especially where social insurance schemes provided by states are insufficient or non-existent. A living wage is one requisite, perhaps the most important requisite, allowing individuals to secure for themselves and their families a minimally decent life.[4]

Beyond the UDHR framework, the right to subsistence is seen in nearly universal legal bans on certain economic exchanges such as selling oneself or one's children into slavery or selling one's body parts. We note that the existence of such exchanges, besides being intrinsically repugnant, can only be the result of systemic market distortions in that those who 'would sign a contract for indentured service' or 'take out a loan to cover basic consumption' demonstrate 'vast differences in the bargaining power of [market] participants.'[5] As we will show later in the discussion, this structural market imbalance is not only relevant to identifying subsistence rights deficits but also to understanding how we recognize, define, and geographically distribute income from multinational activity for tax purposes.

The legal instantiation of subsistence rights in international conventions and national legal frameworks supports the judgement that the right to subsistence is widely accepted as protecting urgent and vital interests of individuals worldwide and is therefore helpful to explain our reasoning as we examine the implications of the entitlement and equal benefits principles in an unjust world.[6] However, we primarily treat the right to subsistence as a moral, not a legal right, and part of a philosophical theory of international justice. For our purposes, the normative force of the right to subsistence does not depend on its legal embodiment, acceptance, or justiciability in fact. On the contrary, to the extent the law fails to live up to the moral theory, there is a strong case for legal reform.

Richard Anker, 'Estimating a Living Wage: A Methodological Review' (2011) Conditions of Work and Employment Series No. 29 <https://ideas.repec.org/p/ilo/ilowps/994663133402676.html accessed 31 August 2020>.

[4] UDHR Art. 25(1) (listing as requisite 'food, clothing, housing, and medical care and necessary social services'); ICSECR Art. 11 (declaring the 'right of everyone to an adequate standard of living for himself and his family, including adequate food, clothing and housing' and stating that everyone has the right 'to be free from hunger'); see also ICESCR 6,7,10 (declaring 'the right to work, [and] to free choice of employment'); UDHR Article 3 (declaring the 'right to life, liberty and security of person').

[5] Arthur M Okun, 'Equality and Efficiency: The Big Tradeoff' (Brookings 1974, 2015 ed), 16–19. Contra, see eg Jason Brennan and Peter Martin Jaworski, 'Markets without Symbolic Limits' (2015) 125(4) Ethics 1053.

[6] This is the case even though there have been long-standing debates about the legal status of some social and economic rights, especially as outlined in the ICSECR. See eg David Beetham, 'What Future for Economic and Social Rights?' (1995) 43(1) Pol Stud 41–60, 43.

Scope of Subsistence Rights Deficits

The scope of need relating to subsistence rights is vast. Currently, at least a fifth of the world's population face deficits of this right, even under conservative definitions. Plausible as a proximate measure of subsistence rights deficits is the Global Multidimensional Poverty Index, developed by the Oxford Poverty and Human Development Initiative, which includes a number of different indicators covering health, education, and standard of living.[7] According to the Initiative's most recent report, 1.3 billion people globally are multidimensionally poor, 84.3 per cent of whom are based in low- and lower-middle-income states.[8] The finding that so much of the world's population faces subsistence rights deficits is broadly consistent with a World Bank report finding that approximately 1.8 billion people live on less than USD $3.20 purchasing power parity per day.[9] This is the poverty line the World Bank uses to reflect poverty assessments in lower-middle-income states.

Approximately half of those living below this poverty line are workers: the International Labour Organization estimates that in 2019 there were a total of 630 million workers in developing and emerging economies who lived in working poverty (that is, below the World Bank poverty line of less than USD $3.20 purchasing power parity per day).[10] This included 30 per cent of all workers in Southern Asia and 54 per cent of all workers in Africa (of which more than half lived in extreme poverty, on less than USD $1.90 purchasing power parity per day).

These figures likely underestimate the number of people experiencing subsistence rights deficits. A 2020 report of the UN Special Rapporteur on extreme poverty and human rights characterized the World Bank's definition of poverty as 'flawed' because it 'mistakenly gauges progress in eliminating poverty by reference to a standard of miserable subsistence rather than an even minimally adequate standard of living' which 'downplays

[7] *Global Multidimensional Poverty Index 2020* (Oxford Poverty & Human Development Initiative) <http://hdr.undp.org/sites/default/files/2020_mpi_report_en.pdf>; see also Sabina Alkire and James Foster, 'Counting and Multidimensional Poverty Measurement' (2011) 95(7–8) J of Pub Econ 476. Multidimensional poverty refers to the recognition that poverty has many forms and dimensions, which can be measured in various ways.

[8] *Global Multidimensional Poverty Index* (n 7).

[9] World Bank, *Reversals of Fortune: Poverty and Shared Prosperity 2020* (World Bank Group 2020) 39. Purchasing power parity is a broadly used metric to make meaningful comparisons of economic conditions across countries.

[10] ILO, *World Employment and Social Outlook: Trends 2020* (International Labour Organization 2020) 13, 40, 53.

the parlous state of impoverishment in which billions of people still subsist'.[11]

Subsistence Rights and the Sustainable Development Goals

The international community has responded to the circumstances we describe above by setting out the 2030 Agenda for Sustainable Development. Adopted in 2015 by the UN General Assembly (representing 193 countries), the 2030 Agenda for Sustainable Development, alternately referred to as the Sustainable Development Goals and the 2030 Agenda, forms an ambitious development agenda with broad support.[12] It aims to continue the work started with the Millennium Development Goals, which had previously aimed to reduce poverty worldwide by addressing human deprivation in its various forms while ensuring the sustainable use of resources and protecting the environment.[13] The 2030 Agenda contains objectives for all states, but it has particular significance for lower income ones, many of which have lacked the capacity and resources to adequately address the problems it targets. In this chapter we treat the Sustainable Development Goals as geared towards securing subsistence rights, some of them directly, others by means of policies that are instrumental to their fulfilment.[14]

Many of the seventeen Sustainable Development Goals, and the detailed targets contained within them, directly support the universal and robust fulfilment of the right to subsistence. Goal 1 aims to end poverty and includes the targets of eradicating extreme poverty and reducing by half the poverty in all its dimensions according to national definitions and implementing social protection measures. Goal 2 aims to end hunger and achieve food security, and includes targets to ensuring universal access to food and improving sustainable and resilient agricultural production. Goal 3 aims to secure universal basic healthcare with targets including reducing maternal mortality, ending

[11] Philip Alston, 'The Parlous State of Poverty Eradication' Report of the UN Special Rapporteur on extreme poverty and human rights, A/HRC/44/40 (United Nations, 2 July 2020).

[12] UN, *Sustainable Development Goals* (United Nations 2015). To the extent the goals of the Sustainable Development Goals remain unfulfilled in 2030, the minimum conception of global justice central to its scope would be expected to continue into any future such agenda-setting.

[13] UN, *Transforming Our World: The 2030 Agenda for Sustainable Development* (United Nations 2015) par 2. The Millennium Development Goals, adopted by the United Nations in 2000, sought to meet eight development targets by 2015, including eradicating extreme poverty, promoting gender equality, reducing child mortality, providing universal primary education, and ensuring environmental sustainability. United Nations Millennium Declaration, UN Resolution 55/2, 18 September 2000.

[14] The 2030 Agenda is explicitly 'grounded in the UN Charter, the Universal Declaration of Human Rights, [and] international human rights treaties.' UN, *2030 Agenda* (n 13) par 10.

preventable child deaths and providing universal health coverage. Goal 5 includes the targets of ending all forms of discrimination and violence against women and girls, and ensuring women have equal rights to economic resources and access to property. Goal 6 aims to achieving universal access to sanitation and safe and affordable drinking water, Goal 7 aims to ensure universal access to affordable, and sustainable energy services, and Goal 11 aims to improve cities and settlements, including by ensuring access to adequate housing, and by reducing the adverse socio-economic impact of natural disasters.

A subset of the Sustainable Development Goals indirectly supports the universal fulfilment of the right to subsistence. These Goals include targets that reveal a commitment, on the one hand, to poverty alleviation through public investment and economic growth, and on the other hand, to do so in a way that reduces the environmental impact and material footprint of economic production and consumption.[15]

For instance, Goal 8 includes the target of sustaining economic growth, increasing economic productivity, and achieving full and productive employment and decent work for all, supported by Goal 9, which includes the target of developing reliable and sustainable infrastructure. Preventing climate change and ensuring the sustainable use of natural resources is revealed as a necessary condition to protect the poorest and most vulnerable populations world-wide from the hazards related to resource depletion and climate change. Accordingly, Goals 12, 13, 14, and 15 promote the achievement of sustainable management of natural resources, taking climate change measures, increasing the adaptive capacity to climate-related hazards and natural disasters, sustainably managing and protecting marine and coastal ecosystems, and more generally conserving and sustainably using biodiversity and ecosystems.

Some of the Sustainable Development Goals may seem to go beyond the baseline conception of a minimally decent life captured by the right to subsistence. For example, Goal 10 aims to reduce socio-economic inequality within and among states by targeting the achieving and sustaining of a higher than national average income growth rate for the bottom 40 per cent of the population and adopting fiscal and social protection policies. One might argue that the justification of this goal requires drawing on a more robust conception of global egalitarian justice. However, even the concern to reduce wealth and income inequality can be defended as a means to ensure the universal satisfaction of a

[15] The material footprint of an economy is an indicator providing 'a consumption perspective of resource use'. Thomas O Wiedmann and others, 'The Material Footprint of Nations' (2013) 112(20) Proc Nat'l Acad Sci U S A 6271.

baseline of a minimally decent life for all, which no doubt requires increasing the share of the world's poorest people in the benefits of economic growth.

Similarly, Goal 4 includes targets to provide universal primary and secondary education, substantially increase literacy and numeracy, and to eliminate gender disparities in education. Again, these targets might be characterized as going beyond securing subsistence rights. But here too a persuasive case can be made for the instrumental importance of basic education for poverty alleviation since secure access to basic education and healthcare increases a person's capacity to secure for themselves the means to subsistence through work while also making it possible for them to understand the domestic laws that are in place to protect their rights, such as those banning child labour.

3.2. The Duty of Assistance

Having established that the attainment of the Sustainable Development Goals is—practically—a necessary and sufficient condition to secure a minimally decent life for all, the question of responsibility remains. We seek to make the case that, first, reasonably affluent, well-ordered states have what Rawls calls a 'duty to assist' societies to tackle subsistence rights deficits within their borders and, second, that these duties must in part be discharged by making available additional resources to the societies in question.

The duty of assistance is a backup duty.[16] Backup duties, as we define them, are duties that may come into existence if those who are seen as primarily responsible are either unable to discharge their duties due to lack of capacity, or unwilling to do so due to negligence. In many cases, subsistence rights deficits are likely the result of a combination of both a lack of capacity and negligence. A more precise assessment heavily depends on contestable judgements about what is economically and politically feasible in particular circumstances, and what can therefore be reasonably required of the governments in question. For the moment we treat each of the arguments independently and argue that in both cases it is reasonable to assign backup duties of justice to foreign states.

Although states are generally held responsible for guaranteeing subsistence rights within their territory and to attain the Sustainable Development Goals more generally, some may in fact be unable to do this without help from abroad. Following Rawls, we refer to these as 'burdened' states.[17] Rawls

[16] The term 'backup duty' is from Shue, *Basic Rights* (n 1) 171.

[17] John Rawls, *The Law of Peoples, with The Idea of Public Reason Revisited* (Harvard University Press 1999) 5, 65.

characterizes states as burdened if they face unfavourable conditions that prevent them from being capable of independently achieving reasonably just institutions, where any reasonably just regime must at least secure a set of human rights that include the rights 'to the means of subsistence and security'.[18] Even if the governments of these states do whatever can be reasonably demanded of them, they will be unable to fulfil the subsistence rights of their citizens due to a combination of unfavourable environmental, political, and socio-economic conditions. Negligent states are conversely those that possess the economic capacity to address subsistence rights deficits within their territories, yet consistently fail to do so.

Perhaps few states are fairly characterized as purely lacking in capacity or purely negligent; instead, it is probably true that virtually all states with subsistence rights deficits suffer from both ailments to various degrees. We must acknowledge further that there are probably very few states in the world in which the entire population can be said to have their subsistence rights fully realized. Even in the most advanced economies, there are those who experience deprivation, sometimes as the legacy of historical strife and conquest. Yet states that do not suffer from systemic lack of development generally do not tolerate or trade on these conditions. Instead they typically invest (or at least, continuously commit to invest) in the physical and social infrastructure necessary to eliminate them.

As such, we understand the duty to assist to exist alongside the duty to guarantee subsistence rights within the territory, and we will argue that advanced economies cannot use their own subsistence rights deficits as a reason for failing to undertake the duty to assist states with fewer resources. We acknowledge that this position would make for complex decision making in practice, but we liken the analysis to that which drives the expectation of common but differentiated responsibilities in the trade law context and similar areas of law.

Assistance to Burdened States

The duty of assistance is, in the starkest of terms, a claim that third-party states that cannot be said to be directly or legally responsible for subsistence rights deficits in a given place can nevertheless have relatively demanding obligations to intervene. The judgement that a duty of assistance exists in the case of burdened societies is shared by a large number of philosophers across a spectrum

[18] Rawls, *Law of Peoples* (n 17) 65.

of positions. David Miller, for instance, argues that if states 'make reasonable attempts to provide subsistence' but fail to do so, then 'outsiders will have remedial responsibilities to come to the aid of the citizens in question'.[19] Miller explains that 'if people are unable to lead decent lives as a result of events outside of their society for which they cannot be held responsible, this imposes a general responsibility to assist 'outsiders as a duty of justice.'[20]

James Nickel similarly concludes that if some states 'are genuinely unable to implement' the right to subsistence, it is up to 'secondary and back-up addressees to come forward and provide meaningful assistance'.[21] Regarding the International Covenant on Economic and Social Rights, Nickel observes that 'duties of richer countries to assist low-income countries in realizing basic economic and social rights should have been specified abstractly but explicitly.'[22]

Others have defended similar, although in some cases more tentative, views. For example, James Griffin suggests that if lower-income states cannot manage their obligations, rich nations may be obliged to act, with the caveat that defining such nations and allocating the obligations among them is difficult: it would require deciding which states should be seen as rich, how much can be expected of them as a group, and how they should share the burden amongst themselves.[23] Similarly, Mathias Risse acknowledges that '[t]he most plausible way of thinking about such obligations [based on human rights] is in terms of a duty of assistance in ensuring that (in this case other) states effectively can, and are organized such that relevant forces are motivated to, provide such [human rights] protection.'[24] Charles Beitz agrees that these are cases involving 'strong beneficence' where 'the threatened interest is maximally urgent,' 'there is a set of "eligible" agents with the resources, position, and capacity to act so as to alleviate the threat or mitigate its consequences . . . [and] the costs of action, if shared among these agents and regarded from their perspectives, would be only slight or moderate'.[25]

Rawls, too, accepts that burdened states are owed assistance by reasonably affluent and well-ordered states. Rawls is categorical in claiming that relatively affluent and well-ordered states owe assistance not to individuals facing

[19] David Miller, 'National Responsibility and Global Justice' (2008) 11(4) Crit Rev Int'l Soc & Pol Phil 396–97; also D Miller, *National Responsibility and Global Justice* (Oxford University Press 2007) 166–67.
[20] Miller, *National Responsibility* (n 19) 254.
[21] Nickel, 'Poverty and Rights' (n 1) 400–01.
[22] Nickel, 'Poverty and Rights' (n 1) 400–01.
[23] James Griffin, *On Human Rights* (Oxford University Press 2008) 104.
[24] Mathias Risse, *On Global Justice* (Princeton University Press 2012) 80.
[25] Charles Beitz, *The Idea of Human Rights* (Oxford University Press 2009) 167.

subsistence deficits but to the states to which those individuals belong. He explains that states owe each other a duty of assistance in order to help each to develop the capacity to be politically autonomous and 'able to manage their own affairs reasonably and rationally.'[26] The consensus among these positions is that states with the means to do so are obliged to assist in meeting the subsistence rights of individuals in foreign states.

Assistance to Negligent States

There is less agreement about backup duties in the philosophical literature when it comes to negligent states—states that are able but nevertheless fail to guarantee the subsistence rights of their populations. Miller, for instance, accepts the existence of backup duties of justice on the part of outsiders in case aid is necessary owing to causes beyond the control of domestic governments. He would presumably also accept that outsiders have a duty of justice not to violate subsistence rights directly, regardless of the level of negligence of local governments. Yet he holds that if domestic governments negligently fail to create or preserve institutions that effectively protect individuals against violations of their subsistence rights, then outsiders lack stringent duties of justice to assist the deprived.[27] Miller concedes there may be remedial duties even in such cases, but he views these remedial duties as less stringent, implying they are voluntary or charitable in nature rather than a strict requirement.[28]

There are, however, good reasons to think that even in the case of negligence, the duty to assist is a stringent duty of justice. Henry Shue has shown that the right to subsistence is correlated with a complex set of duties, at least some of which concern the protection of individuals from the effects of potential non-compliance of others.[29] His central claim is that subsistence rights are rights to the robust enjoyment of the means to subsistence. In his view individuals must be protected against 'standard threats,' which requires social and economic institutions that prevent some from violating the rights of others and aid those who are deprived of their rights even when such rules and institutions are in place.[30] Shue therefore concludes that all states have a duty

[26] Rawls, *Law of Peoples* (n 17) 111.

[27] This concerns only violations by domestic actors, since otherwise Miller would likely accept the existence of a remedial duty on the outsiders responsible for violations.

[28] Miller, *National Responsibility* (n 19) 257–58.

[29] Shue, *Basic Rights* (n 1).

[30] Shue, *Basic Rights* (n 1) 62.

to create and maintain effective institutions to protect all the rights that individuals are entitled to enjoy.[31] The purpose of these institutions is to prevent individuals from violating the right—that is, by preventing rights-holders from enjoying the means to subsistence—and to aid them if they are nevertheless deprived of their right. Under this duty fall not just the prevention of immediate deprivations but also more complex institution-building related to sustainable and resilient social and economic planning and development.

In light of Shue's argument, Miller's position looks less plausible. Why should we conclude that outsiders lack a backup duty of justice to ensure institutions protect against threats to subsistence if the harms are caused by negligent governments? Even if the duty to protect individuals from deprivation could normally be discharged by domestic governments, the cases under consideration suggest that the institutional enforcement of subsistence rights should not be left entirely to them.[32] Instead, the argument seems to be that there should be institutions—perhaps global in scope—that protect individuals from standard threats to their right to subsistence, including specifically in the form of failings of their own governments. Where governments negligently fail to effectively guarantee the subsistence rights of their populations even though that can reasonably be demanded of them, effective assistance must be provided with the aim of robustly protecting individuals from subsistence rights deficits in the future.

We conclude that relatively affluent, well-ordered states have a duty to assist states with populations facing subsistence rights deficits, regardless of whether these deficits are due to a lack of capacity or a lack of political will. The populations of both burdened and negligent states have a right to their ability to live a minimally decent life being robustly protected, if necessary by third-party states that have no causal responsibility for their suffering.

Wealth and the Duty of Assistance

We now argue that the duty of assistance must in part be observed by making available additional resources to the burdened or negligent state in question. Some argue that the duty of assistance cannot effectively be fulfilled through wealth transfers but must be addressed largely or even solely through reform of

[31] Shue, *Basic Rights* (n 1) 17 (stating that states have a 'duty to create, if they do not exist, or, if they do, to preserve, effective institutions for the enjoyment of what people have rights to enjoy').

[32] Shue, *Basic Rights* (n 1) 56 agrees with this conclusion.

domestic institutions. Absent the right institutions in place, the argument goes, wealth transfers are likely to do little to alleviate the conditions of the poor and may even be counter-productive because they put resources into the hands of those perpetuating harms.

Rawls has influentially defended this position. He holds that the causes of national wealth and poverty lie in a societies' culture and traditions and 'industriousness and cooperative talents of its members, all supported by their political virtues'.[33] Hence, he concludes that that 'merely dispensing funds will not suffice to rectify basic political and social injustices'.[34] That is why it may be impossible to fulfil the duty of assistance by means of transfers of wealth. Risse agrees, in that he questions the availability of global institutional reforms that would improve the position of the global poor, if growth and prosperity depend on the quality of domestic institutions including the rule of law, administrative capacity, and the prevention of fraud and government corruption. In that case, he says, 'money in isolation, detached from an institutional environment in which it can do good, may well be ineffective or cause harm when seized by the wrong people.'[35]

This 'institutional thesis' carries through to reports about and policy prescriptions for development, including in the realm of taxation. It is, for example, expressly reflected in the Sustainable Development Goal 16, which among other things targets the promotion of the rule of law, the reduction of corruption and bribery, and the development of effective and accountable institutions as well as responsive and representative decision-making.[36] It is also reflected in development policy prescriptions that focus on tax capacity, such as a 2014 OECD report on tax and development which opined that strong tax institutions are key to achieve progress (defined in terms of GDP growth). The OECD report described such strength by reference to 'sustained political commitment at the highest levels, administrative reforms that are aligned closely with policy changes and strong leadership by the revenue administration.'[37] Noting that 32 African states collected less than USD $1 of tax per person per

[33] Rawls, *Law of Peoples* (n 17) 108.

[34] Rawls, *Law of Peoples* (n 17) 108.

[35] Mathias Risse, 'How Does the Global Order Harm the Poor?' (2005) 33(4) Phil & Pub Aff 349, 373; also Mathias Risse, 'What Do We Owe the Global Poor?' (2005) 9(1/2) J Ethics 81–117. For this position, Risse cites *inter alia*, Douglass North, *Institutions, Institutional Change, and Economic Performance* (Cambridge University Press 1990); David Landes, *The Wealth and Poverty of Nations: Why Some are So Rich and Some So Poor* (W.W. Norton & Company 1998); Robert Hall and Chad Jones, 'Why Do Some Countries Produce So Much More Output Per Worker Than Others?' (1999) 114(1) Q J Econ 83.

[36] UN, *2030 Agenda* (n 13), Goal 16.

[37] OECD, *Development Co-operation Report 2014: Mobilising Resources for Sustainable Development* (OECD Publishing 2014).

day and that those with the lowest tax-to-GDP ratios also tended to be those with the lowest tax collection per person, the report lamented that reforms aimed at building the necessary institutions often meet with concerted political opposition.[38]

Defined as such, low tax capacity is often characterized as the result of domestic failures such as weak revenue administrations burdened by rent-seeking and corruption, poor tax-payer morale, and related governance failures.[39] Given this framework, it is no surprise that proposed solutions to lack of funding for development primarily focus on local institutional reforms to root out mismanagement and fraud.[40]

Yet low tax capacity is not solely or even primarily a problem of local corruption.[41] The capacity of a government to raise funds for public spending by extracting capital from the private sector is powerfully shaped by the availability of resources and the structural constraints that come with attempting to tax a poor population. As the 2030 Agenda establishes, many of the world's poorest states have very significant investment needs that well exceed available local resources. In order to attain the Sustainable Development Goals, these states must significantly increase public investment, including in physical infrastructure, food security, health, and education.[42] Public spending is essential since it is one of the primary ways in which states can improve the position of the poor, either directly through social spending, or indirectly by investing in areas that

38 OECD, *Development Co-operation Report 2014* (n 37) 93.

39 Mick Moore, 'Obstacles to Increasing Tax Revenues in Low Income Countries' (2013) International Centre For Tax and Development Working Paper 13/15, 18–19; Augustine Nwabuzor, 'Corruption and Development: New Initiatives in Economic Openness and Strengthened Rule of Law' (2005) 59(1–2) J Bus Ethics 121, 123; European Parliament Directorate General for External Policies, 'Cost of Corruption in Developing Countries—How Effectively is Aid Being Spent?' (European Union, April 2015) 9 (outlining 'the main ways in which corruption, illicit financial flows and mismanagement of public financial resources hamper development, and presents available estimates of the size and scope of flows, as well as financial and non-financial losses'); Transparency International, 'How Corruption Weakens Democracy' (Transparency International, 29 January 2019) <www.transparency.org/news/feature/cpi_2018_global_analysis>; Maria De Beneto, 'Corruption and Controls' (2015) 17(4) Eur J L Reform 479, 479 ('Administrative corruption seems to be developing into an epidemic, characterized by exponential growth all over the world, especially during recent years').

40 Jonathan Finer, 'World Bank Focused on Fighting Corruption: Graft and Bribery, Once Tolerated, Punished by Blacklisting' Washington Post (4 July 2003). <https://archive.globalpolicy.org/pmscs/30085.html>; World Bank, 'Combating Corruption' (4 October 2018) <www.worldbank.org/en/topic/governance/brief/anti-corruption> (outlining a number of institutional reforms required to curb vulnerabilities to corruption and noting that '[f]ighting corruption requires political will to create strong fiscal institutions that promote integrity and accountability throughout the public sector').

41 Michael Johnston, 'Why Do So Many Anti-Corruption Efforts Fail?' (2012) 67(3) NYU Ann Surv Am L 467, 477. ('Lack of nuance plagues our broader visions of what reform might look like: we frequently justify proposed changes, estimate the damage done by corruption, and gauge the success of reform by comparison to an efficient, rational, corruption-free state that does not actually exist anywhere.')

42 UNCTAD, *World Investment Report 2019* (United Nations Conference on Trade and Development 2019) xi.

significantly impact economic growth (such as infrastructure, education, and health),[43] with growth being strongly correlated with the rise of incomes of the poor.[44]

In many of the Sustainable Development Goals the provision of public services and public investment is called for, either explicitly or indirectly. Regarding the goal of ending poverty in all its forms everywhere (SDG 1), the UN General Assembly notes the need to '[e]nsure significant mobilization of resources from a variety of sources, including through enhanced development cooperation, in order to provide adequate and predictable means for developing countries, in particular least developed countries, to implement programmes and policies to end poverty in all its dimensions.'[45] Ending hunger (SDG 2) requires increased investment 'in rural infrastructure [and] agricultural research . . . in order to enhance agricultural productive capacity in developing countries.'[46] Achieving universal health coverage and access to essential health-care services (SDG 3) calls for a substantial 'increase [in] health financing and the recruitment, development, training and retention of the health workforce in developing countries, especially in least developed countries.'[47] Significant public investment is also envisioned for the goals of ensuring universal access to inclusive and equitable education (SDG 4), affordable, reliable and sustainable energy (SDG 7), and the building of sustainable and resilient infrastructure capable of supporting economic development and human well-being (SDG 9).[48] Attaining these Sustainable Development Goals requires significant public investments, particularly by the least affluent states.

Public investment is also indirectly, via growth promotion, an important means to the attainment of goals included among the Sustainable Development Goals. The reduction of inequality within and among states (SDG 10) is unlikely to be achieved without targeted government spending to address poverty and ensure fair equal opportunity in labour markets for the

[43] For infrastructure spending see C Briceño-Garmendia, A Estache, and N Shafik 'Infrastructure Services in Developing Countries: Access, Quality, Costs and Policy Reform' (2004) World Bank Policy Research Working Paper 3468, 5; C Calderón and L Servén, 'The Effects of Infrastructure Development on Growth and Income Distribution' (2004) Policy Research Working Paper Series no. 3400, 26. For social spending see E Baldacci and others, 'Social Spending, Human Capital, and Growth in Developing Countries: Implications for Achieving the MDGs' (2004) IMF Working Paper WP/04/217; D Bloom and D Canning 'Population Health and Economic Growth' World Bank Working Paper 47588.

[44] D Dollar and A Kraay, 'Growth Is Good for the Poor' (2002), 7 J Econ Growth 195, 219. See also D Dollar, T Kleineberg, and A Kraay, 'Growth, Inequality, and Social Welfare: Cross-Country Evidence' (2016) World Bank Policy Research Working Paper No. 6842.

[45] UN, *2030 Agenda* (n 13) 15.

[46] UN, *2030 Agenda* (n 13) 16.

[47] UN, *2030 Agenda* (n 13) 17.

[48] UN, *2030 Agenda* (n 13) 17–20.

least well-off. Similarly, to promote 'sustained, inclusive and sustainable economic growth, full and productive employment and decent work for all' (SDG 8),[49] the provision of public services and infrastructure must factor in the solution. Sustainable economic growth may, moreover, contribute to attaining the Sustainable Development Goals by reducing poverty and alleviating human deprivation more generally.

In 2014, a UN report projected that the spending needs for all developing economies combined to attain the Sustainable Development Goals would range from USD $3.3 trillion to USD $4.5 trillion annually and that they would face an annual financing gap of approximately US $2.5 trillion, given existing spending levels.[50] Another study found a combined financing gap of USD $1.4 trillion per year for low-income and lower-middle-income states.[51] The Addis Ababa Action Agenda speaks of an annual financing gap of US $1 trillion to $1.5 trillion for infrastructure in developing countries.[52]

In the face of the financing needs of lower-income states, the primary policy advice has been to 'mobilize domestic resources'. The Addis Ababa Action Agenda [2015], endorsed by the UN General Assembly, presents a program for the implementation of the Sustainable Development Goals and emphasizes 'the mobilization and effective use of domestic resources' as 'central to our common pursuit of sustainable development.'[53] These claims are echoed in IMF, OECD, European Commission, and World Bank publications.[54]

However, it is clear that domestic resource mobilization will be insufficient in isolation. The financing gaps for many lower-income states are simply insurmountable in light of their tax capacity. A recent IMF study calculated that the additional spending in forty-nine low-income developing

[49] UN, *2030 Agenda* (n 13) 19.

[50] UNCTAD, *World Investment Report* (n 42), xi.

[51] Guido Schmidt-Traub, 'Investment Needs to Achieve the Sustainable Development Goals—Understanding the Billions and Trillions' (2015) UN SDSN Working Paper Version 2.

[52] UN, 'Addis Ababa Action Agenda: Monitoring Commitments and Actions' (2016) 14. A financing gap of $US 1.5 trillion annually for developing countries is also mentioned in OHCHR, *The Other Infrastructure Gap: Sustainability, Human Rights and Environmental Perspectives* (Office of the United Nations High Commissioner for Human Rights 2018) 13.

[53] UN, 'Addis Ababa Action Agenda' (n 52) 20.

[54] See, eg, 'Domestic Resource Mobilization' (*The World Bank*, 2018) <www.worldbank.org/en/topic/governance/brief/domestic-resource-mobilization> accessed 31 August 2020; European Commission, International Cooperation and Development: Domestic Resource Mobilization, <https://ec.europa.eu/europeaid/policies/financing-development/domestic-resource-mobilisation_en>; OECD, 'Strengthening Tax Systems to Mobilise Domestic Resources in the Post-2015 Development Agenda Element 11 Paper 2' (OECD no date) <www.oecd.org/dac/Post%202015%20Domestic%20Resource%20Mobilisation.pdf> accessed 31 August 2020; OECD, 'Platform for Collaboration on Tax to Discuss Domestic Resource Mobilisation Challenges on 9 October' (OECD 2018) <https://www.oecd.org/tax/platform-for-collaboration-on-tax-to-discuss-domestic-resource-mobilisation-challenges-on-9-october.htm> accessed 31 August 2020.

countries required for a 'high performance' across the SDG areas of education, health, roads, electricity, water and sanitation, would require on average 15.4 per cent of GDP in 2030 (over and above existing government spending).[55] This requires on average more than doubling the tax take of low-income countries. For low-income countries the ratio of tax revenue to GDP is on average 13 per cent, compared to on average 35 per cent of GDP for high-income OECD.[56] Personal income tax revenues in low-income countries amount to an average of 1–2 per cent of GDP, compared with 9–11 per cent in high-income countries.[57] A 2017 IMF report noted that 'fragile' states—those with tax to GDP ratios below fifteen percent—struggle to expand their tax revenues, and that any gains they do realize are difficult to sustain over time.[58] These constraints on tax capacity are largely due to structural features in their economies. Low-income states generally have largely non-urbanized, agricultural economies with small firms and extensive informal sectors.[59] In some estimates, up to 60 per cent of the GDP of low-income states is located in the informal economy and is therefore hard or impossible to tax.[60] These realities quickly raise tax collection costs to a prohibitive level.[61]

The policy advice to mobilize domestic revenue should also come with a further disclaimer: it may harm the poor more than it helps them (certainly in the short term), even if the generated revenues are spent progressively. This is because, particularly for low-income states, it is difficult to also progressively allocate the tax burden. Progressive property and other wealth taxes are difficult

[55] Vitor Gaspar and others, 'Fiscal Policy and Development: Human, Social, and Physical Investment for the SDGs' (2019) IMF Staff Discussion Note, SDN/19/03, 9.

[56] Moore, 'Obstacles to Increasing Tax Revenues' (n 39) 7; OECD, *Revenue Statistics 2018: Tax Revenue Trends in the OECD* (OECD 2018)2 ('New OECD data in the annual Revenue Statistics 2018 publication show that tax revenues as a percentage of GDP (ie the tax-to-GDP ratio) have continued to increase since the low-point experienced in almost all countries in 2008 and 2009 as a result of the financial and economic crisis. The average tax-to-GDP ratio in OECD countries was 34.2 per cent in 2017 compared with 34.0 per cent in 2016 and 33.7 per cent in 2015'); but see Bernardin Akitoby and others, 'Tax Revenue Mobilization Episodes in Emerging Markets and Low-Income Countries: Lessons from a New Dataset' (2018) International Monetary Fund 7 ('Tax revenue has been rising in LICs and EMs over the last fifteen years. Between 2000 and 2015, two broadly similar points in the business cycle, the average tax revenue increased by 3.5 per cent of GDP, and measured 16.4 per cent in 2015 on (an unweighted) average).

[57] Michael Carnahan, 'Taxation Challenges in Developing Countries' (2015) 2(1) Asia Pacific Pol'y Stud 169 at 179, at 176.

[58] IMF, *Building Fiscal Capacity in Fragile States* (International Monetary Fund 2017) 12.

[59] Moore, 'Obstacles to Increasing Tax Revenues' (n 39) 14–15.

[60] IMF, *Revenue Mobilisation in Developing Countries* (International Monetary Fund 2011) 8.

[61] Timothy Besley and Torsten Person, 'Why Do Developing Countries Tax So Little?' (2014) 28(4) J of Econ Perspectives 112.

to implement for political reasons,[62] whereas progressive income and capital gains taxes are relatively easy to avoid or evade.[63]

Instead, low-income states must predominantly rely on indirect taxes such as value-added or sales taxes, which often have a regressive effect on income equality.[64] One study shows that, when using a USD $2.50 poverty line, in eight of twenty-five lower-income states there are more individuals made poorer as the result of government taxing and spending than there are individuals benefitting from these activities.[65] The conclusion is a caution for those who wish to pursue poverty alleviation by asking the governments of lower-income states to tax their individual populations more heavily: '[t]he big risk in setting an ambitious domestic resource-mobilization agenda is that governments will impoverish poor people even further.'[66]

Hence, many of the least affluent states simply lack the resources and capacity to mobilize the resources necessary to make genuine progress meeting the Sustainable Development Goals. It is recognized that, '[p]ublic finances, though central and fundamental to investment in Sustainable Development Goals, cannot alone meets SDG-implied demands for financing.'[67] And the 2030 Agenda accepts that '[i]nternational public finance plays an important role in complementing the efforts of countries to mobilize public resources domestically, especially in the poorest and most vulnerable countries with limited domestic resources,' which would be consistent with the backup duties described above.[68] Indeed, a recent *Sustainable Development Goals Report* notes ominously, although perhaps predictably, that 'the rate of global progress is not keeping pace with the ambitions of the Agenda, necessitating immediate and accelerated action.'[69]

[62] Moore, 'Obstacles to Increasing Tax Revenues' (n 39) 30; Ehtisham Ahmad and Nicholas Stern, 'Taxation for Developing Countries' in Hollis Chenery and TN Srinivasan (eds), *Handbook of Development Economics*, vol 2 (Elsevier 1989) 1017.

[63] RM Bird and EM Zolt, 'The Limited Role of the Personal Income Tax in Developing Countries' (2005) 16(6) J Asian Econ 928–46, 933.

[64] Ahmad and Stern, 'Taxation for Developing Countries' (n 62) 1021.

[65] Nora Lustig, 'The Sustainable Development Goals, Domestic Resource Mobilization and the Poor' in Jose Antonio Ocampo and Joseph Stiglitz (eds), *The Welfare State Revisited* (Columbia University Press 2018) 132.

[66] Lustig, 'Sustainable Development Goals' (n 65), 132.

[67] UNCTAD, *World Investment Report* (n 42) 137.

[68] UN, 'Addis Ababa Action Agenda' (n 52) 26. It additionally recognizes that 'international assistance as appropriate' will be 'critical to realizing sustainable development and achieving the sustainable development goals' (UN, 'Addis Ababa Action Agenda' [n 52] 11).

[69] UN, *The Sustainable Development Goals Report 2018* (United Nations 2018) 4. The IMF noted that in recent years the fiscal positions of low-income countries have worsened, which it explains as the result of 'rising expenditure requirements,' including 'rising debt service costs' and the observation that 'domestic revenue mobilization efforts have generally fallen short.' IMF, *World Economic Outlook, April 2018, Cyclical Upswing, Structural Change* (International Monetary Fund 2018) 29.

Contrary to the view of those who maintain that the duty of assistance cannot be discharged through the transfer of wealth, the widespread consensus is that lower-income states face significant obstacles raising the revenue needed to invest in the public goods and services that would help attain the Sustainable Development Goals and effectively protect and fulfil the subsistence rights of their populations. Certainly, institutions are important: government revenues badly spent or misappropriated will do little to improve the plight of the poor. Yet, given the enormous financing needs, good institutions in isolation will hardly be sufficient to set many low-income states on a path to becoming minimally just societies.

The implication is that there is a duty of assistance on the part of relatively affluent states to make additional funds available that allow lower-income states to make the necessary investments. The promise of international tax cooperation as a location for discharging the duty of assistance is that it does not just make available additional wealth to lower-income states but also that this wealth arrives in the budgets of the governments themselves and become directly available for public spending. It will have to become clear whether such redistributive effects can be accomplished through revising the terms of international tax cooperation. This task will be addressed in the next chapter.

3.3. The Entitlement Principle and the Duty to Assist

In the previous discussion we argued that reasonably affluent, well-ordered states have backup duties of justice to assist societies to tackle subsistence rights deficits within their borders and that these duties must be discharged by making available additional resources to the societies in question. We now consider the implications of this conclusion for international tax cooperation by revisiting the applicability of the entitlement and equal benefit principles as we introduced them in the first chapter.

Duty of Assistance as Duty of Justice

We start by arguing that the duty of assistance is a duty of justice, rather than a humanitarian duty.[70] Humanitarian duties are not only less stringent than

[70] Here we follow Rawls, who holds that that the claims of foreigners, correlative to the duty of assistance, are of equal standing to (if not, have priority over) the claims of fellow citizens to a fair share of the domestic cooperative product. Individuals are entitled only to a fair share of the societal wealth

duties of justice, they also relate differently to the entitlements of states. One way of expressing the distinction is to say that duties of justice are logically prior to the establishment of a just distribution of holdings, while humanitarian duties are logically consequent to it. If the duty of assistance is conceived as humanitarian duty, then states are obliged to use *their* holdings in performing the duty; if it is conceived as a duty of justice, then states are required, by performing the duty, to establish a just distribution of holdings, a distribution that allocates to states what is *theirs*.

In the latter case, as Brian Barry explains, even before any actual transfer has taken place, the required resource is 'as much that country's as it is now normally thought that what a country produces belongs to that country'.[71] The receiving state is entitled to those resources being transferred in precisely the same way as it is entitled to whatever wealth it already justly holds. The state performing the duty of assistance, conversely, lacks an entitlement to the wealth or resources it is required to transfer or employ. This means that, if the duty of assistance is indeed a duty of justice, it concerns precisely the same type of claim a state might have to its wealth as the entitlement principle introduced in the first chapter. To say that a duty of assistance requires a state to transfer some of its wealth, is (at least partly) equivalent to saying that the state lacks an entitlement to this wealth on the basis of the entitlement principle.

The plausibility of treating the duty of assistance as a duty of justice can be brought out by noting the implications of pressing the entitlement principle in the face of subsistence rights deficits abroad. To this effect, Henry Shue asks us to consider the analogy with individual property, and argues that only once individuals have secured a minimally decent life can others legitimately exclude them from the use and enjoyment of goods on the basis of an institution of property. As he explains, 'institutions governing the ownership and transfer of

that remains available after their state has performed the duty of assistance. See, eg, Samuel Freeman, 'Distributive Justice and The Law of Peoples' in Rex Martin and David A Reidy (eds), *Rawls's Law of Peoples: A Realistic Utopia?* (Blackwell 2006) 248, who writes that 'for Rawls, the duty of assistance to burdened peoples . . . is to be satisfied . . . before determining the distributive shares of the least advantaged in one's own society under the difference principle.' This assessment is not shared by all of Rawls' readers. Miller, *National Responsibility* (n 19) 255; Laura Valentini, *Justice in a Globalized World* (Oxford University Press 2011) 74, and Kok-Chor Tan, *Justice without Borders: Cosmopolitanism, Nationalism, and Patriotism* (Cambridge University Press 2004) 67–68, conceive of Rawls's duty of assistance as a humanitarian duty. See Caleb Yong, 'Rawls's Duty of Assistance: Transitional not Humanitarian or Sufficientarian' [2012] Nuffield College Working Papers Series in Politics <www.nuffield.ox.ac.uk/politics/papers/2012/Yong_working%20paper_2012_05.pdf> accessed 31 August 2020, for a more extensive discussion of these authors and an argument for our position.

[71] Brian Barry, 'Humanity and Justice in Global Perspective' in J Roland Pennock and John W Chapman (eds), *Ethics, Economics, and the Law* (New York University Press 1982) 248.

property can be fair only if possession of the commodities required for the satisfaction of subsistence needs is guaranteed to those from whom compliance with the institutions is demanded.'[72] This is a reformulation of Locke's view that the right to accumulate private property is limited by a universal right to subsistence, because the acquisition of property is possible only 'where there is enough, and as good left in common for others.'[73]

Analogously, the entitlement of states to the wealth in their territory is conditional on the absence of subsistence rights deficits abroad. It would be unfair to demand that individuals accept an institutional scheme if it prevents them from attaining and maintaining a minimally decent life. The institutional scheme in question is the society of states, the global institutional structure within which states exist and interact with each other. Given the presence of subsistence rights deficits, to institutionalize the entitlement principle as an unconditional regulating ideal of the society of states is analogous to a system of individual property with *not* 'enough and as good' left in common for others. Those facing subsistence rights deficits can legitimately reject an institutional structure that allocates states an unqualified right to the wealth in their territory in the face of their suffering.

The analogy between individual property and the entitlements of states can be extended to cover cases where domestic governments negligently fail to guarantee the subsistence rights of their citizens. In the case of individual property, those facing subsistence rights deficits are asked to accept a property regime that only adequately enforces and protects the property of the rich, while leaving them vulnerable to a life under a minimal baseline. From their perspective it does not much matter if the deficits are caused by full compliance with defective law, or by habitual non-compliance due to defective enforcement of otherwise non-defective law (in the sense that full compliance would fulfil subsistence rights). Any institution of individual property that enforces the rights of the rich but leaves the poor vulnerable to subsistence rights deficits is equally illegitimate. Analogously if the entitlement principle is treated as an unconditional norm governing the society of states, and this prevents individuals from living a minimally decent life given the negligence of their governments, individuals again have a reason to reject that norm as illegitimate.

One might object that it would be pointless to make available additional funds to states that lack a concern for the basic needs of their populations, as

[72] Shue, *Basic Rights* (n 1) 125.

[73] See John Locke, *Two Treatises of Government* (Cambridge University Press 1988) 288; Shue, *Basic Rights* (n 1) 153.

these funds would not likely be spent in ways that benefit the poor. We have three responses.

First, we are considering cases where effective assistance *can* be provided through wealth transfers. Negligence is not active obstruction, although it may render performing the duty of justice on the part of relatively affluent states more expensive. For instance, consider a situation in which subsistence rights deficits are due to widespread tax evasion by the state's rich, leaving the state's poor without the necessary assistance that could and would have been provided had citizens obeyed and the government enforced fiscal law. This kind of negligence does not prevent international wealth transfers from being effective in addressing subsistence rights deficits through public spending of the kind urged by the 2030 Agenda.

Second, we admit that in many cases merely transferring wealth is not enough, and that it is also necessary to assist in improving and strengthening domestic institutions, as recommended by those favouring the 'institutional thesis.' However, the empirical observations concerning the financing needs of low-income states as we laid out above show that institution building in isolation is simply insufficient. The 2030 Agenda cannot be successful if lower-income states are left financially to their own devices.

Finally, we note the perverse incentive implied by the alternative view: since reasonably affluent and well-ordered states would lack a duty to make additional funds available as long as the states in question remain negligent, they are incentivized to do nothing to tackle the causes of that negligence.

It is worth noting that Thomas Nagel, who in 'The Problem of Global Justice' presents his famously sceptical assessment of the demands of justice beyond the state, also appears committed to the view that the duty of assistance is a duty of justice (at least with reference to subsistence rights deficits in burdened states). He argues that only within states, between co-citizens subject to the same political and socio-economic institutions, does it make sense to ask whether the distribution of economic goods between them is just or unjust. Beyond the state this question has no answer since for Nagel it is an 'inappropriate site for claims of justice.'[74] Rather, beyond the state are only 'duties of humanity,' global in scope, owed to those 'threatened with starvation or severe malnutrition and early death from easily preventable diseases.'[75]

Given the distinction introduced above, one might suspect these humanitarian duties are less stringent than the duties of justice and that they operate

[74] Thomas Nagel, 'The Problem of Global Justice' (2005) 33(2) Phil & Pub Aff 113, 138.
[75] Nagel, 'Problem of Global Justice' (n 74) 118.

logically subsequent to the establishment of the entitlements of individuals or states. This appearance, however, is not borne out, because Nagel draws the distinction differently than we did: he takes humanitarian duties to hold 'in virtue of the absolute rather than the relative level of need' of individuals, while duties of justice are concerned with the comparative inequality between them.[76]

Accordingly, in an earlier article, aptly titled 'Poverty and Food: Why Charity is Not Enough,' Nagel presents an argument, akin to that of Shue, consistent with treating his humanitarian duties as duties of justice as we have understood them.[77] He notes that a system of property on the basis of which it is possible to have claims of right or entitlement can be criticized as morally illegitimate if it allows extreme poverty to arise and persist and that such a critique may 'cast doubt on the moral importance of the fact that something belongs to someone under that institution of property.'[78]

Nagel takes the world economy to have the characteristics of a system of property (even if it depends on the mutual recognition by states of their respective property regimes that shape their domestic markets), and he holds that there are feasible alternative arrangements that would reduce the number of subsistence rights deficits. As a result, he concludes that the world economy is 'illegitimate in this way.'[79] Again, this argument gives us reason to conclude that reforms are required as a matter of justice, which is to say that insofar as reforms result in the transfer of wealth, the receiving party is entitled to that wealth in a way that overrides the entitlement principle as it would otherwise be understood to apply. The reason for this, in Nagel's terms, is that the holdings prior to that transfer were based on a property regime that is morally illegitimate.

Nagel appears to have remained committed to this position in his more recent work on global justice. Although he describes humanitarian duties as involving 'charity',[80] he also writes that the 'urgent current issue is what can be done in the world economy to reduce extreme global poverty' and even suggests that, in the face of extreme poverty, securing domestic distributive justice may be 'a side issue.'[81]

[76] Nagel, 'Problem of Global Justice' (n 74) 119. See Miller, *National Responsibility* (n 19) 256, for a critique of drawing the distinction in this way.

[77] Thomas Nagel, 'Poverty and Food: Why Charity is Not Enough' in Henry Shue (ed) *Food Policy: The Responsibility of the United states in the Life and Death Choices* (1st edn, Free Press 1977) 54–62.

[78] Nagel, 'Poverty and Food' (n 77) 57.

[79] Nagel, 'Poverty and Food' (n 77) 58.

[80] Nagel, 'Problem of Global Justice' (n 74) 140.

[81] Nagel, 'Problem of Global Justice' (n 74) 118.

International Tax Policy and the Duty of Assistance

Even if it is true that the duty of assistance of affluent states to lower-income states with populations facing subsistence rights deficits can and must be performed through wealth transfers, an objection might arise that the international tax regime is an inappropriate location for such transfers. An argument against the use of international tax rules for this purpose would be that tax policy coordination is rightly focused on securing mutually beneficial cooperation in international investment. On this argument, if justice requires cross-border redistribution of wealth, this should be tackled directly such as by cash transfers rather than by changing the terms of cooperation in this, ultimately unrelated, policy area.[82] We disagree with this argument and argue to the contrary.

As we have argued above, if states have a duty of assistance and if this duty requires the cross-border transfer of wealth, these two factors invalidate the entitlement principle. This is to say that having failed to fulfil their duty of assistance, states lack an unqualified right to the wealth in their territory. This, in turn, impacts what counts as fair cooperation.

Recall our argument above that fair cooperation in international taxation requires that the burdens and benefits of facilitating international capital flows are shared equally between the cooperating states. The equal benefit principle presupposes that states have an entitlement to the wealth in their territory: that is to say that it can only be true that states have a right to share in the benefits produced from their mutual cooperation if they have an entitlement to the wealth of their territories in the first place.

We can now see that the persistence of an unmet duty of assistance invalidates this standard of fair cooperation. States may still have reason to engage in mutually beneficial cooperation—indeed, they may have a duty to do so, if it helps make available additional resources in those states that need it to tackle subsistence rights deficits. But having examined the nature and scope of subsistence rights deficits, it is now clear that what counts as fair cooperation is determined by the duty of assistance: the cooperative effort must be structured in such a way that it contributes, where feasible and to the extent possible, to

[82] Peter Dietsch and Thomas Rixen, 'Tax Competition and Global Background Justice' (2014) 22(2) J Pol Phil 150–77, 166, present a version of this objection when they argue that redistributive obligations by states 'should not be discharged in the form of a bias in the way the jurisdictional structure of international taxation is set up. It should, rather, be dealt with via explicit redistribution.' In more recent work, Dietsch accepts that redistribution is a legitimate function of cooperation in taxation. Peter Dietsch, 'The State and Tax Competition: A Normative Perspective' in Martin O'Neill and Shepley Orr (eds), *Taxation: Philosophical Perspectives* (Oxford University Press 2018) 203–23.

assisting vulnerable states in robustly protecting and fulfilling the subsistence rights of their populations.

The duty of assistance could, in theory, be discharged in any number of ways, including by direct wealth transfers among states. However, in the absence of such transfers, and given the persistence of subsistence rights deficits, the theoretical availability of alternatives cannot form an objection to changing the terms of tax cooperation. Tax cooperation is an appropriate site to perform the duty of assistance because that is what fair cooperation requires when cooperating parties have populations facing subsistence rights deficits: given the inapplicability of the principles that normally regulate cooperation, the terms of cooperation must be established that allocate wealth as the duty of assistance requires.

3.4. Conclusion

In the first chapter, we introduced two principles of tax cooperation: the equal benefit principle and the entitlement principle. On the society-of-states model of international justice, these two principles apply to the distribution of wealth between states that are cooperating in a global economy. When states cooperate for their mutual benefit, they are entitled to equally share in the (net) benefits produced by such cooperation. This equal benefit principle presupposes a commitment to the entitlement principle. It is only because states have an entitlement to their national endowments, that they may share in the benefits when those endowments are employed productively in a cooperative scheme.

We further argued that in the context of international taxation the relevant benefits concern the surplus benefits created by international capital mobility, and international tax reform should be focused on securing an approximately equal distribution of those benefits among the cooperating states. This chapter adds a crucial proviso to this argument: the argument only holds if states have honoured the duty of assistance. If states have failed to do so, the entitlement principle lacks application and fairness in international tax cooperation is not necessarily captured by the equal benefit principle. If states lack an unqualified entitlement to their wealth, they also lack an unqualified right to share in the benefits that are produced by means of it.

In light of the existence of widespread subsistence rights deficits suffered across the globe today, it is plausible that reasonably affluent states, considered as third-party states with a duty to act as backup rights protectors, have insufficiently honoured the duty of assistance. We have demonstrated that the duty to assist arises when subsistence rights go unfulfilled due to capacity constraints, but also when rights go unfulfilled due to negligence on the part of those with the primary duty to protect and fulfil those rights. The duty to assist implicates the entitlement principle because it demonstrates that contrary to popular intuition, it is not the case that each state is unconditionally entitled to the wealth of its territory. Instead, other states may have a greater moral claim to some of this wealth.

The entitlement principle (and by extension the equal benefit principle) must therefore be understood as conditional on the elimination of subsistence rights deficits. When applied to cross-border investment gains that involve states in which subsistence rights are significantly unmet, each state is entitled to the wealth created in its territory only so long as it fulfils its duty of assistance. This result connects directly to tax norms, rules and institutions because it demonstrates that an injustice is being perpetuated when states with populations facing subsistence rights deficits are constrained in their ability to tax, whether due to tax competition or the persuasive power of consensus-based tax policy making.

To make the moral claim that affluent states are entitled to their own wealth is therefore to deny that some less affluent states have a morally stronger claim. The argument in this chapter shows this is wrong. The morally stronger claim of less affluent states has important implications for the assessment of international tax policy that transcend the issues currently being tackled by the international community with respect to taxing rights and tax capacity.

The implications of the duty to assist and its constraint on the entitlement principle go directly to the design of policies that allocate taxing rights across states. Because they are built upon the entitlement principle as a normative foundation, tax norms and rules are both a necessary and appropriate location to address subsistence rights deficits. The conclusion is that we cannot unreflexively rely on the entitlement principle in the design of equitable tax rules, at least when it comes to relatively affluent states. Instead, the entitlement principle must be interpreted to mean that when cross-border investment involves states with subsistence rights deficits, the entitlement to tax belongs solely to such states until such time as subsistence rights are met. In the next chapter, we explore what kinds of reforms relatively affluent states would need to adopt in order to fulfil their obligations as we have laid them out.

Even though our position should be read as conservative given our minimal conception of subsistence rights, we acknowledge that our claim that the duty to assist conditions the entitlement principle will make some uneasy. If so, the arguments about the tax policy implications that follow will induce similar if not stronger opposition. We will ultimately revisit the philosophical theory for a second best option in light of the anticipated rejection, but our first task is to explore the stronger case. As we will show in the next chapter, that stronger case in effect calls for relatively affluent states to take immediate measures to cede tax to relatively poorer states in ways that will reduce rather than increase the pressures that stifle taxation at source.

4

Tax Cooperation with a Duty of Assistance

Chapter 3 made the case that the claims states can legitimately make on the basis of the entitlement principle are conditional on them having fulfilled their duty to assist states with populations suffering from subsistence rights deficits. Since tax rules effectuate entitlements by distributing the cooperative surplus created by cross-border investment, this suggests that affluent states are entitled to far less of the cooperative surplus than they are currently claiming under prevailing norms. The corresponding claim is therefore that states with populations suffering from subsistence rights deficits are entitled not only to more of the benefits arising from cooperation but also a reduction in the pressures that impede taxation as a means of capturing those benefits. We examined the framework of these impeding factors in Chapter 2 and noted that there are some national and international efforts underway to alter the status quo by reconfiguring which states may tax the income earned by multinationals and to what extent. We now need to revisit the prospects for structural change in light of the duty to assist as a condition of the entitlement principle.

This chapter accordingly examines how relatively more affluent states could help create a world in which states with populations suffering subsistence rights deficits would be able to capture more of the benefits of cooperative surplus through taxation. We will show that one way in which states can relinquish unjust claims of entitlement is to make room for source-based taxation with two main approaches to be pursued in tandem.

The first step is for states that export significant capital to other states to expand their existing pass-through regimes for corporate income taxation, while guarding against both double taxation and tax competition with carefully designed foreign tax credits. The effect of this step, which we explain in more detail below, is to create a backstop[1] or minimum level of corporate taxation, which will reduce some of the kinds of tax competition that effectively prevent some states from exercising their entitlement to a share of the benefits of cooperative surplus through taxation. The second step is for states with

[1] Or, as Ruth Mason describes it, a 'fiscal failsafe'. Ruth Mason, 'The Transformation of International Tax' (2020) 114(3) Am J Int'l L 353–402.

Tax Cooperation in an Unjust World. Allison Christians and Laurens van Apeldoorn, Oxford University Press. © Allison Christians and Laurens van Apeldoorn 2021. DOI: 10.1093/oso/9780192848673.003.0005

populations suffering subsistence rights to exercise their entitlement to co-operative surplus benefits.

These two steps for reform of the international tax system are not radical departures from the status quo. Rather, they can be characterized as, in the case of Step 1, a return to standards that were common across OECD states in the not-too-distant past and in the case of Step 2, a take-up of an alternative but still broadly neutral division of cooperative surplus in line with some of the earliest proposals for international tax cooperation and consistent with the ongoing work of the United Nations and other institutions. Moreover, both steps are broadly compatible with current developments in international tax policy discourse, both in terms of the OECD's work on the taxation of highly digitalized firms and in terms of recent national and regional tax policy developments across OECD members states and beyond.

Following our convention of using the common parlance of 'source states' to describe states with large populations that are suffering subsistence rights deficits as we described in the first chapter, we briefly need to revisit this shorthand. As noted, states with large populations suffering from subsistence rights deficits are almost always in the role of the source state, but every state that interacts in the global economy stands in the role of source state in some contexts while most relatively affluent states expect to regularly stand in the role of residence state as well, ideally in equal measure. Keeping this detail in mind helps explain how states generally frame their positions (and, if the context requires, change their views) with respect to the overall framework of international tax consensus building.

For example, we can see the different residence and source state interests at work by considering the recent move to revisit some of the foundational international tax principles owing to the tax challenges associated with the rise of the digitalized economy. Before the rise of the digital economy, it was commonly observed that OECD members were in roughly equivalent positions as both source and residence states vis à vis each other, each exporting and importing capital in relatively even amounts, such that tax treaties allocating taxing rights between them were long assumed to be more or less neutral in terms of their impact on national revenue collection. In relations between these states, restricting taxation at source to preserve taxation at residence or doing the opposite is theoretically a simple matter of deciding by consensus since either decision is acceptable so long as it is coordinated.

The assumption of rough neutrality rapidly changed for some OECD states with the emergence of highly digitalized multinationals, most of which are ultimately resident in the United States and China. With this rise of big tech, some states saw that being mainly on the receiving end of investment capital in this important sector with little or no established right to tax meant that they stood to gain very little of the cooperative surplus gains associated with these firms. An unfairness appeared to some states to result from the apparently neutral bargain they had heretofore supported. This realization prompted the current OECD-led initiative to rebuild consensus so as to geographically reallocate the income of such firms so that each state could again claim its 'fair share' of the cooperative surplus benefits produced in this specific context.

From this example, we can see that the terms residence and source are situational and contextual: no state is exclusively one or the other, but relatively affluent states have traditionally expected to be in both positions in roughly equivalent amounts. When that expectation changed, so did the apparent neutrality in the existing international tax consensus. Relatively less-affluent states have traditionally expected to be primarily in the role of source and have long sought change in the international consensus in different ways. For these states, the sudden interest of some relatively affluent states in revisiting the consensus presents a welcome opportunity for meaningful reform, but there are still important differences among states in the source category. The sequence of events described above demonstrates that when a state is alternately in the role of source and residence state, the general framework for distributing income and taxing rights under the current consensus tax rules seems relatively benign but when a state finds itself primarily or only in the source role, the fact that the consensus prevents tax at source appears more objectionable and even unfair.

We use the simplifying language of residence and source for ease of reading but also to reflect these terms and assumptions in common use among tax experts. Using this vocabulary makes it easier to explain how states with populations suffering subsistence rights deficits can use the prevailing norms and standards applicable to source and residence taxation to exercise claims of entitlement over cooperative surplus in a way that is readily recognized and understood across the international tax community. Yet we remain cognizant that the roles are fluid and the capacity of any given state to protect their interests depends on the particular facts and circumstances surrounding their involvement in international investment flows.

With these assumptions and cautions in mind, the discussion that follows considers how states could accomplish the two steps we propose to make room for tax at source, demonstrates that the first step is a necessary backstop to ensure that the second step results in greater taxation by states with subsistence rights deficits, and argues that where they apply, the terms and procedures in many existing tax treaties could be used to support the proposed adjustments rather than work against them. The chapter concludes by noting that even if there is scepticism that the duty to assist warrants the approaches we suggest, some of the tax reform proposals currently under multilateral negotiation would at least partially implement the principle that states' entitlement to the wealth in their territories is conditioned on the universal realization of subsistence rights.

4.1. Why Make Room for Taxes at Source

As we demonstrated in earlier chapters, taxation is a main means by which states distribute the cooperative surplus created by cross-border investment, but prevailing trends in international taxation, including tax competition, tend to skew the distribution of the cooperative surplus toward relatively more affluent states. If, as we have claimed, these relatively more affluent states are obligated to assist in the fulfilment of subsistence rights, and if doing so requires them to claim none of the cooperative surplus associated with such deficits until such time as all subsistence rights are fulfilled, there seem to be two paths forward: either such states will have to increase their taxes on the income that arises from cross-border investment and transfer all of the revenues associated with the cooperative surplus to states with populations suffering subsistence rights deficits, or in the alternative, relatively affluent states will have to effectively eliminate their claims on global tax revenues in such a way as to enable states with populations suffering from subsistence rights deficits to realize their own entitlement to tax.

Even if there is an argument for relatively more affluent states to raise most of the revenues and make transfers to states with populations suffering subsistence rights deficits, whether as a matter of relative administrative capacity or efficiency or other reasons, we reject this approach. To structure the international tax system in this way would be to assign the responsibility to collect and distribute tax revenues principally to the relatively affluent states that, according to our analysis, are not ultimately entitled to such revenues at all.

This would be problematic for a number of reasons. For example, the states assigned the task of collecting the revenues and making the appropriate transfers might simply fail to deliver on the latter, and it is difficult to imagine what sort of credible institutions could be created, and by whom, to police these actions.[2] Further, assigning the right to collect and the obligation to transfer

[2] For such feasibility concerns specifically in relation to tackling tax competition, see also Peter Dietsch and Thomas Rixen, 'Redistribution, Globalisation, and Multi-level Governance' (2014) 1(1) Moral Phil & Pol 61–81.

revenues primarily to relatively affluent states risks creating confusion about which states are actually entitled to the tax revenues thereby collected and distributed. This confusion could create additional political obstacles to fulfilment of the duty to transfer the revenues, for example by opening up conversations about whether the relatively more affluent states are also entitled to accountability from other states regarding the use of tax revenues that are to be transferred to them.

Instead, the better solution is to eliminate the claims of relatively affluent states to international income as far as possible to enable states with populations suffering from subsistence rights deficits to realize their own entitlements instead, until such time as subsistence rights deficits are universally eliminated. In practical terms, this means that the international tax system must be designed in such a way that states with populations suffering subsistence rights deficits are able—both in the sense of being assigned the primary right and in the sense of not being impeded by competitive pressure—to tax the income flows to which they contribute by being hosts of international investment flows. Since, as we noted above, states with large populations suffering from subsistence rights deficits are almost always in the role of the source state rather than the residence state, the most straightforward way to accomplish the task is to make it more possible for these states to tax at source than the current status quo permits.

Accordingly, we focus our attention on contracting taxes at residence to make room for tax at source. As we will show, however, such contraction paradoxically requires residence states to nominally impose *more* taxes at residence, rather than less. An explanation can be found within the structural interdependence of residence- and source-based taxation. We explore this interdependence by examining two steps for tax reforms that would facilitate a shift in income allocation to source states without necessarily increasing tax competition.

The first step is to expand existing pass-through taxation of corporate income at residence and the second is to reallocate the primary right to tax multinational income to source states when the claiming state is suffering subsistence rights deficits. Each step is discussed in turn.

4.2. Step One: Expand Pass-Through Taxation

The first and arguably most direct solution to (partially) fulfilling the duty to assist is for significant capital-exporting states to create a world in which all business profits are subject to tax at residence, while respecting the right of the source state to tax first. This task would be initiated by pass-through taxation at residence. As we will explain, pass-through taxation can create room for source-based taxation by effectively imposing a global minimum tax on corporate income earned through cross-border investment, but careful attention to the creditability of source-based taxes is key to preventing both double taxation and tax competition.

Pass-through taxation means treating shareholders (whether immediate or through chained ownership) as the direct earners or beneficiaries of the income otherwise legally earned by corporations. Doing so requires tracing income as it is earned through whatever forms and chains of ownership exist, in order to get at a beneficial owner who is a tax resident. The relevant shareholder could be a corporation itself, so long as domestic law effectively taxes the income of corporations at a rate that is not substantially lower than the personal tax rate. So long as at least one of the corporate entities in a chain is subject to current taxation on the underlying income of the entities below it, pass-through taxation will create a backstop to taxation at source.

Taxing at residence on a pass-through basis creates a backstop (or residual or minimum) tax in the sense that it only applies if and when the source state declines to tax the income first. A simple example is illustrative: imagine that Taxpayer A resident in State A owns all of the stock of Corporation B, which earns income from State C sources. As we have explored above, State C has a well-recognized claim of entitlement to the income and may decide to exercise its entitlement by taxing the income earned by Corporation B, or not. If State C declines to do so, Corporation B has earned income that faces no source tax. Assuming that Corporation B is not a resident of State A, a pass-through tax regime would allow State A to treat its resident Taxpayer A as having directly earned the income from State C and would accordingly impose tax. If instead State C decided to impose a tax on the income, State A should no longer impose its tax. As we will see below, a foreign tax credit rule in State A would serve as the technical means of accomplishing this overall outcome.

The broad precedent for passing corporate income through to the ultimate owners is the tax treatment of partnership income (and any corporate form effectively treated as a partnership or disregarded for tax purposes, such as limited liability companies), with the tax treatment of trusts an additional comparator. Steve Bank has characterized the choice to treat corporations differently from partnerships in this respect as 'one of the greatest puzzles in income taxation.'[3] Historical and contemporary arguments for and against the full pass-through taxation of corporate entities focus on a number of factors. First is the idea that the corporation should be fully respected an entity separate from its owners.[4] Second is complexity: existing flow-through regimes for partnerships and trusts feature a number of difficult compliance and administration challenges.[5] Finally, accurately tracking the relevant owners of a corporation at any given time can be quite onerous, especially given publicly traded securities which can change hands at high volume and frequency.[6] Further complexities arise across a number of dichotomies, including private versus public companies, local versus global companies, and high versus low tech companies. These distinctions among the various forms and structures of company ownership and operation make any one-size-fits-all rule for looking through the corporate form difficult to imagine.[7]

Even so, pass-through taxation for corporations already exists in piecemeal form, as readily seen throughout the world in the form of deeming rules that treat some forms of income as having been paid out to shareholders or other ultimate owners. So-called global minimum tax rules such as the US Global Low Taxed Intangible Income (GILTI) regime (and similar past and emerging proposals) and the OECD's corollary, the Global Anti-Base Erosion (GloBE) proposal are variations of this kind of approach.[8] A minimum tax rule is in

[3] Steven Bank, 'A Capital Lock-In Theory of the Corporate Income Tax' (2006) 94(4) Geo LJ 88.

[4] E Merrick Dodd, Jr, 'For Whom Are Corporate Managers Trustees?' (1932) 45 Harv L Rev 1160 ('The traditional view of our law is that a corporation is a distinct legal entity . . . its entity character has been thought of as something conferred upon it by the state which, by a mysterious rite called incorporation, magically produces *e pluribus unum*'); William Klein, 'Income Taxation and Legal Entities' (1972) 20 UCLA L Rev 13, 43 ('In both nontax and tax law the corporation is the epitome of entity theory in action. Indeed, the concept of the corporation as a separate entity has led one leading authority to suggest that the taxation of corporate profits can be justified on the ground that the corporation *is* an entity—not that is must be seen or treated as a separate entity for certain purposes, but that it *is* one'); David Millon, 'Theories of the Corporation' (1990) Duke LJ 201, at 202 ('From the early years of the 19th century, certain legal attributes of incorporation encouraged Americans to conceive of the corporation as an entity existing separately from its shareholders and other participants. . . . The idea of the corporation as an entity is also apparent in courts' routine statutory construction of the term "persons" ' to include corporate as well as natural persons.')

[5] Curtis Berger, 'W(h)ither Partnership Taxation?' (1991–1992) 47 Tax L Rev 105.

[6] Edward C Moore, Jr, 'Corporate Taxation' (1884) 18 Am L Rev 762 ('Assessing all corporate taxes to the corporation instead of to its shareholders, certainly appears to be the better method. It is simpler, both to understand and to apply; it does not give such opportunities for evasion of taxes, and it does not necessitate so many special exceptions and provisions.'); Thomas Cooley, *Treatise on the Law of Taxation* (Callaghan and Company 1886) 30: (taxes on dividends 'are more easily collected and do not usually involve inquisitorial proceedings. Dividends come from corporations whose proceedings are usually semi-public, and while the privacy of individuals is not invaded, neither are the demands of the government liable to serious evasions.').

[7] Treasury Dep't, Report on Integration of the Individual and Corporate Tax Systems (1992).

[8] Organisation for Economic Co-Operation and Development [OECD], 'Global Anti-Base Erosion Proposal ('GLoBE') Pillar Two' (8 November 2019) <http://www.oecd.org/tax/beps/public-consultation-document-global-anti-base-erosion-proposalpillar-two.pdf.pdf>; 26 USC § 951A, 'Global Intangible Low-Taxed Income Included in Gross Income of United States Shareholders'; OECD,

practice a pass-through rule that deems corporate income to have been earned by a different taxpayer, namely, the one that is considered tax resident under traditional residence rules.

The simplest version of pass-through treatment, whereby the corporate form is respected but certain forms of corporate income are deemed to be paid out to the owners, can be seen in rules defining and taxing personal holding companies.[9] In broad strokes, when an income tax system taxes individuals at a higher effective rate than companies, as many income tax regimes do, taxpayers have an incentive to set up companies to hold all of their income-producing assets so as to access the lower rate until such time as they distribute the earnings to themselves (such as in the form of dividends or capital gains). Virtually any personal income tax system requires a personal holding company regime of some kind as a safeguard to prevent individuals from using legal structures for this kind of tax avoidance, lest the progressive rates on individual income become meaningless. A personal holding company rule can prevent tax avoidance-motivated incorporation schemes either by treating all personal holding company income as having been earned by the individual owner (pass-through taxation, as in the example above) or taxing specified types of income earned by the personal holding company at the individual's (highest marginal) tax rate. Both strategies seek to eliminate the tax advantage that would otherwise accrue if the taxpayer could use a corporation to defer the higher rate of tax to the future or indefinitely. Thus, a personal holding company rule seeks to treat an individual that directly owns their investment portfolio in the same manner as one who incorporates a holding company to own all of their portfolio investments.

Pass-through taxation is not a radical idea. It is in fact in use throughout the international tax system, most commonly seen in the form of controlled foreign corporation and other passive foreign investment inclusion rules. These regimes are the logical extension of personal holding company rules. Instead of preventing tax arbitrage between the personal and the corporate rates within a single state, these rules prevent tax arbitrage between the domestic and the foreign tax rate.[10] Typically limited to highly mobile investment income, these

Programme of Work, Pillar II. For a clear explanation of how GILTI works to create space for source country taxation by acting as a backstop, see Susan C Morse, 'International Cooperation and the 2017 Tax Act' (2018) 128 Yale L J Forum 362.

[9] For example, as seen in 26 USC 541, Imposition of personal holding company tax. See Bittker and Eustice (ed. § 15.40) [personal holding company rules (secs. 541–47), accumulated earnings tax rules (secs. 531–37), foreign investment company rules (sec. 1246)].

[10] Melissa Redmiles and Jason Wenrich, 'A History of Controlled Foreign Corporations and the Foreign Tax Credit', in IRS, *Statistics of Income Bulletin* (Internal Revenue Service 2007) 133.

kinds of rules generally work by deeming certain types of income earned by a foreign corporation to have been paid out to a domestic shareholder as a dividend.[11] The act of deeming a resident taxpayer to have received an item of income such as a dividend removes the tax advantage that would otherwise occur if the taxpayer could avoid tax on their investment earnings by placing assets in the hands of foreign companies.[12] By way of example, the United States adopted personal holding company rules in 1934 but it did not enact controlled foreign corporation rules until 1962; it added passive foreign investment inclusion rules in 1986 as an expansion of these base protecting measures.[13]

The US adoption of its controlled foreign corporation regime is of note not only because it has had global influence, but also because legislative history demonstrates that the lawmakers of the time fully understood the foreseeable harm to the US tax system that would occur if taxpayers could escape US taxation simply by incorporating abroad.[14] It is clear that US lawmakers initially considered full pass-through taxation of all corporate income but they ultimately rejected this approach in favour of focusing their regime on specified types of foreign income, by appearances in direct response to pressure by US multinational firms.[15] Despite these pressures to abandon the project all together, the US legislature pressed ahead in creating deeming rules for highly mobile income streams because they understood that foreign incorporation presented opportunities for US taxpayers to defer, indefinitely in some cases, US tax on these gains. Since permanent deferral ultimately eliminates taxation all together, the effect of allowing such easy tax avoidance strategies to flourish would be to oversee a hollowing out of the US tax base.[16]

Over the years, US lawmakers have considered myriad ways to extend the rules to cover more foreign income, including, on occasion, so-called active

[11] As seen in 26 USC 951. Amounts included in gross income of United States shareholders; Income Tax Act, Canada, s 91(1), Amounts to be included in respect of share of foreign affiliate.

[12] Bruce F Davie and Bruce F Duncombe, *Public Finance* (Holt, Rinehart and Winston, 1972), 505 ('U.S. adopted controlled foreign corporation rules "to diminish the attractiveness of direct foreign investments in order to promote balance of payments stability"').

[13] A fourth regime specifically aimed at foreign personal holding companies was adopted in 1937 but repealed in 2004 as duplicative of the other regimes then in place.

[14] Vasujith Ram, 'Conceptualizing the History of Subpart F' (2018) Tax Notes, October 12315; National Foreign Trade Council, Inc., 'The NFTC Foreign Income Project: International Tax Policy for the 21st Century, Part One: A Reconsideration of Subpart F' (2001) 37–57; Joint Committee on the Economic Report, 'Federal Tax Policy for Economic Growth and Stability: Papers Submitted by Panelists Appearing Before the Subcommittee on Tax Policy' (1955); Nir Fishbien, 'From Switzerland With Love: Surrey's Papers and the Original Intent(s) of Subpart-F' (2018) 38(1) Va Tax Rev.

[15] Reuven S Avi-Yonah, 'U.S. Notice 98-11 and the Logic of Subpart F: A Comparative Perspective' (1998) Tax Notes Int'l, 8 June 1797; David R. Tillinghast, 'An Old Timer's Comment on Notice 98-11' (1998) Tax Notes, 30 March 1739.

[16] J Clifton Flemming Jr, Robert J Peroni, and Stephen E Shay, 'Worse than Exemption' (2009) 59 Emory L J 79.

business income earned through foreign corporate forms.[17] In turn, other states adopted similar regimes and made adjustments with the same goals in mind.[18] Expanding these regimes to more states and harmonizing some of their terms was the goal of Action 3 of the OECD BEPS initiative.[19]

In creating a backstop tax on foreign investment, controlled foreign corporation and other pass-through regimes effectively enable other states to tax at source first, under certain assumptions surrounding the creditability of foreign income taxes. Any foreign income not subject to pass-through taxation continues to escape residence state taxation either until repatriated or permanently, depending on the residence state's rules for active income.[20]

The Role of Creditability

The extent to which pass-through taxation facilitates the taxation of multinational income at source depends on the creditability of foreign taxes. If the residence states adopt pass-through taxation accompanied by a credit that is carefully designed to eliminate taxation only when duplicative, the tax base will likely move from residence to source states over time unless prevented by mutual agreement, that is, through a treaty. This is why, in the early days of the modern income tax in the United States, the foreign tax credit was characterized by some as a 'present of revenue to other countries.'[21] However, the overall distributive effect of foreign tax credits depends on the combination of their technical design and the relevant source state's resistance to tax competition.

The basic design of a foreign tax credit typically involves extending a dollar-for-dollar credit for foreign taxes paid against domestic taxes imposed on the same foreign-source income.[22] In most cases, the broad rule of creditability is

[17] Allison Christians, 'What the Baucus Plan Reveals About Tax Competition' (2013) Tax Notes Int'l, December.

[18] For example, Canada and Germany both followed the US example in 1972. Allan Lanthier, 'The Taxation of Foreign Affiliates' (1995) 43(5) Can Tax J 1603; Martin Weiss, 'Recent Developments in the German Tax Treatment of CFCs' (2015) European Taxation, September 439.

[19] OECD, *Action 3 Final Report: Designing Effective Controlled Foreign Company Rules* (OECD Publications 2015).

[20] For example, Canada exempts foreign active income earned in treaty countries in the form of an 'exempt surplus' rule, even when there is no tax at source and even when the income is itself passive but derives from active income earned elsewhere.

[21] Edwin R Seligman, *Double Taxation and International Fiscal Cooperation* (Macmillan Co. 1928) 132, 135.

[22] For example, in the United States § 901(b)(1) allows taxpayers a credit against foreign 'income, war profits, and excess profits taxes.'

accompanied by a definition that narrows what constitutes a 'creditable tax' in order to limit the otherwise boundless nature of the allowance. Thus, as a threshold matter, most residence states with foreign tax credit regimes seek to protect their own tax bases by ensuring that the foreign tax to be credited replicates the domestic tax and is not a different kind of tax or a fee disguised as an income tax.[23]

The neutralizing effect of creditability is undermined if foreign governments are able to help taxpayers 'soak up' foreign costs of all kinds (including things like mining license fees or permits for undertaking various actions) by casting them in the form of creditable income taxes. This fear has prompted residence state governments to adopt various safeguards, including countering the possibility that source states might provide disguised subsidies by imposing taxes to allow the taxpayer to claim the credit, only to later return the original tax to the taxpayer in the form of a rebate or refund.[24]

The design of foreign tax credit rules is therefore one of the keys to making tax at source possible. A foreign tax credit that is too generous will erode the residence state tax base and incentivize source states to engage in more tax competition, such as by adopting soak up taxes designed to take advantage of creditability elsewhere and rebates designed to return funds to taxpayers after another country has already given a credit. On the other hand, a foreign tax credit that is too strict will increase the sensitivity of firms to foreign taxes which will increase tax competition at source. Maintaining a workable credit system that does not fall into either of these traps is challenging, but affluent states have years of experience and domestic policy motivations to spend the necessary resources to do so.[25]

[23] For example, US Treasury Regulations to § 901 construct a test to determine whether a foreign levy is a creditable tax, determining whether the levy is indeed a 'tax' and if so, whether its predominant character is that of an income tax 'in the United States sense.' *Wada v. Commissioner* [1995] 69 TCM 2793 T.C. Memo. 1995-241. The definitional issue of when a foreign payment constitutes a tax for domestic law purposes permeates the discussion of the foreign tax credit and has proven very difficult for courts to reconcile in some cases. See, eg, Allison Christians, 'Reversal of Fortune: Did PPL Corporation Get a Foreign Tax Credit from the Wrong Government?' (2013) Lexis Fed Tax J Q 1 (discussing US Supreme Court decision *PPL Corp and Subsidiaries v Commissioner of Internal Revenue*, allowing the taxpayer to take a foreign tax credit in respect of a payment that the IRS denied because it was not a tax in the United States sense).

[24] For example, US Treasury Regulations seek to deny creditability for 'disguised subsidies,' defined in Regulation § 1.901-2(e)(3) and § 901(i) as 'tax payments' used by foreign governments to provide any direct or indirect benefit to the taxpayer, to a related party, or to any party to the transaction. The Regulation states that a 'subsidy' includes benefits in the form of a rebate, refund, credit, deduction, payment, discharge of an obligation, or any other method that is employed to confer a benefit.

[25] Elisabeth Owens, *The Foreign Tax Credit* (Harvard University Press 1961).

Effect on Tax Base Allocation

Pass-through taxation with carefully tailored foreign tax credits reduces tax competition for source states by making the expected tax on cross-border investment a zero sum game: so long as the shareholders' residence state taxes are reducible by that imposed at source, taxpayers are indifferent as to which state imposes the tax.[26] If residence states can properly calibrate their tax credit systems, taxing shareholders on deemed income inclusions in respect of foreign business, income earned through corporate forms would almost certainly increase the overall amount of tax ultimately paid on corporate profits. This is likely to occur because virtually all states in which shareholders of multinationals reside impose taxes on the earnings of their residents at relatively high and often progressive rates (whether under the domestic corporate or personal income tax regime).

In their position as the first state with the opportunity to tax in such a scenario, source states would likely move their own tax rates closer to the level expected to be imposed at residence. This shift is only possible, however, if existing tax treaties do not prevent tax at source by imposing rate caps or high thresholds to taxes on business profits—as most of the world's bilateral tax treaties do today. Motivating states to change terms that they currently view as favourable is a constant challenge. The Model Tax Convention developed by the United Nations provides direction since it calls for more source taxation through both higher withholding rates on passive items and lower thresholds to taxation of business profits.[27] This Model Tax Convention was first introduced in 1980 in response to urging by lower income states that the dominant tax treaty model was not appropriate for tax treaties involving non-reciprocal cross border activity; since then, the UN Model has consistently led the way in expanding tax at source, most recently with a proposed new provision for imposing withholding taxes on advertising fees paid to foreign firms.[28]

[26] Joel Slemrod, 'Location, (Real) Location, (Tax) Location: An Essay on Mobility's Place in Optimal Taxation' (2010) 63 Nat Tax J 854 ('in most cases a taxpayer is indifferent to which country taxes are remitted').

[27] United Nations, *Model Double Tax Convention between Developed and Developing Countries* (United Nations 2017) 318 viii.

[28] UN, *Model Tax Convention* (n 27) Article 12B.

Feasibility of the Reform

The recent rise of acceptance in the notion of global minimum taxes, such as the US GILTI regime and the OECD GloBE proposal have already moved the world closer to accepting the idea of more comprehensive pass-through taxation. The safeguards introduced to protect the tax base in residence states, while allowing for foreign tax creditability, provide some evidence that residence states are willing to enact some reforms that have the effect of making room for tax at source, whether or not that is their intention.

That said, every regime that seeks to look through the corporate form and impute income to owners is technically complicated and beleaguered by an imbalance of information between taxpayers and tax authorities. The only way to enforce such regimes is through detailed tax information collection and exchange between states, coupled by the development of sophisticated tax administrations that are capable of analysing the information, correctly identifying income streams, matching them with ultimate owners when they are tax residents, and reconciling actual income flows with previously taxed deemed income flows.[29] These can be extremely complex tasks that require the dedication of significant tax administration resources. Even highly developed tax administrations struggle to implement their own revenue safeguards. Still, states with sophisticated tax credit rules generally appear willing to expend the resources to maintain the integrity of their tax systems by funding the administrative resources needed to enforce even the most complex rule sets.

Instituting pass-through taxation would support the realization of a fair allocation of the benefits of cooperation in light of the duty of assistance if these challenges could be overcome, but only to the extent doing so would increase the total tax on corporate profits and also result in much of that tax being collected at source. By effectively creating the means for a backstop tax to arise by imputing current earnings to shareholders, pass-through taxation would theoretically create policy space to increase taxation at source, but the administrative challenges in actually carrying out the requisite tracing are likely to overwhelm tax administrations in many places. Still, if the world's major capital exporters moved to pass-through taxation, source states might find it easier to tax corporate profits with less risk of capital flight than they experience

[29] Hence foreign information gathering rules, such as those adopted by the United States in 1960, are prerequisites for effective controlled foreign corporation rules. Revenue Act of 1960 §6038, Pub. L. No. 86-780, 68A Stat. 286, 1014.

under today's status quo in which most active foreign income escapes taxation on a current, and sometimes permanent, basis.

4.3. Step Two: Increase Source-Based Tax Capacity

The second step toward making room for taxation at source is by accommodating source states that undertake to exercise their claims of entitlement over multinational income via taxation, whether by means of withholding tax on more types of outgoing income flows, or by reconfiguring existing allocation norms for affiliated groups and unincorporated branches. The latter may also require lowering thresholds to tax business profits at source. Each approach is discussed in turn.

Accommodating Withholding Taxes

Perhaps the most straightforward way for residence states to facilitate greater source-based taxation is to accept revised or new withholding taxes by source states. Withholding taxes are simply taxes imposed on specified income streams at a specified rate, typically without offset for expenses or losses. Imposing new withholding taxes is straightforward in the sense that doing so would follow a well-understood path and well-established precedent. Even so, there are some conceptual obstacles that might stand in the way of source states simply adopting new withholding taxes.

To understand both the opportunity and the potential obstacles to expanding withholding taxes at source, a bit of explanation about the nature and concept of these taxes is necessary. First, it is important to understand that in the international tax context, a source-base withholding tax on a given income stream is typically (not always) a final tax on a gross amount of income. This is in contrast to, for example, the withholding of income taxes that an employer might be obligated to carry out with respect to their employees, but as to which the employees may later file annual returns that allow the factoring in of various deductions and credits.

Being imposed on a gross basis, source-based withholding taxes were traditionally imposed at lower rates than the regular (often progressive) rates applied to net income. For example, when the United States first adopted a standard flat rate of 30 per cent on various US source income flows to foreign taxpayers, its regular progressive rate maxed out at twice that rate. When the regular rates on net income subsequently fell, the 30 per cent rate appeared to be high in comparison, but most taxpayers experience much lower rates owing to treaty-based withholding rate reductions. For example, in treaties based on the OECD Model, it is common to find source-based withholding rates to be capped at 15 per cent and lower, including all the way down to zero. The UN Model tax treaty typically calls for higher caps but the ultimate rate in a given treaty varies according to the terms agreed by the negotiating parties.

By advocating withholding taxes, we mean to suggest that with greater taxes at residence per Step 1 as we outlined above, source states could raise their rates on their existing withholding taxes but they could also consider adopting new forms of withholding taxes on different streams of income. Advocating for source states to raise the rates of their withholding taxes is relatively easy to defend in a world with residual income taxes at residence, and we would not be the first to propose this move for source states. However, advocating an expansion of the idea of withholding to more and different streams of income is more challenging. Doing so requires defending the idea that new withholding taxes ought to be considered income taxes in the same way as existing ones, so that they would be compatible with the foreign tax credit systems we described above as integral to the overall increase in the ability of source states to tax at source.

As such, when we advocate expanding the range of withholding taxes, the idea is to expand the types of gross-basis taxes on income flows that are eligible for foreign tax credits, so that the source tax does not act as a surcharge over and above the residual or backstop tax at residence. This requires some additional explanation.

Income that is subject to gross-basis withholding would typically be subject to net basis taxation (that is, subject to set off by associated expenses and losses) if the taxpayer was a resident; hence gross-basis withholding taxes are typically creditable in an income tax only if they are seen to stand 'in lieu of' net-basis income taxes (this is another reason for the historical decision to choose lower rates for gross-basis withholding taxes).[30] Adopting new withholding taxes might therefore require states to engage in some persuading of residence states that these new taxes are of a piece with existing (creditable) withholding taxes.

This raises the possibility that an existing treaty relationship might either facilitate or preclude the type of reform we advocate here, while the absence of

[30] Taxing on a net basis would be preferable but infeasible. Stephen E Shay, J Clifton Fleming, Jr,` and Robert J Peroni, '"What's Source Got to Do with It?"—Source Rules and International Taxation' (2002) 56 Tax L Rev 81.

a treaty might also either hurt or help the situation, depending on the differing views of the states whose foreign tax credit systems are at issue. For example, expanding the range of income types subject to withholding taxes could be relatively straightforward if there is no pre-existing treaty relationship since all that is required is that the expanded or new withholding tax be designed as an income tax, in the same manner as other withholding taxes.[31] However, doing so will undoubtedly clash with some of the common wisdom surrounding which kinds of gross-basis taxes ought to be viewed as in lieu of income taxes, such that foreign tax creditability can be assured. Conventional framing influences this analysis and if there is no treaty in place, then there is no ready procedure by which the affected states could resolve the tax coordination problem that would arise in the case of a disagreement as to the nature of the new tax.

The main difficulty in this regard lies in the notion that the categories of income tax withholding that are viewed as equivalent to income taxes comprise a closed list, to which new types of income cannot be added.[32] Thus in the historical lexicon of withholding taxes, we are accustomed to seeing five main entries across income tax systems: interest, dividends, rents, royalties, and capital gains. Being excluded from this list, any other tax imposed on a gross basis risks being viewed as an excise tax rather than an income tax (and may even prompt trade-based inquiries as a tariff, as has recently been seen in the case of so-called digital services taxes, discussed in more detail below). Yet several

[31] As, for example, in Canada Income Tax Act Part XIII, Tax on Income from Canada of Non-resident Persons; 26 USC 861, Income from sources within the United States. Shay, Fleming and Peroni 'Source Rules' (n 30) 112 note that 'There is no meaningful domestic law limitation on the level of source taxation in the absence of a treaty containing the usual nondiscrimination clause.' They later consider that clause and conclude that 'there is virtually unanimous agreement that . . . nonresidents are not in "the same circumstances" as [domestic] residents and, therefore, imposition of . . . flat-rate, gross-basis withholding tax on a nonresident's [domestic] source passive income does not violate the nondiscrimination Article.' (Shay, Fleming, and Peroni, 'Source Rules' (n 30) 113). In support of this argument, they cite, *inter alia*, American Law Institute, Federal Income Tax Project, *International Aspects of United States Income Taxation II, Proposals on United States Income Tax Treaties* (1992) 260–63; Model Tax Convention Explanation, Art 24, 1 Tax Treaties (CCH) I 214A ('the common underlying premise is that if the difference in treatment is directly related to a tax-relevant difference in the situations of the domestic and foreign persons being compared, that difference is not to be treated as discriminatory' under the nondiscrimination article); Peter Blessing, *Income Tax Treaties of the United States* (1996) 20-15 to 20-16 ('For certain purposes, such as subjecting foreign persons who derive dividends, interest, royalties, or certain other types of income not connected with a permanent establishment to a gross-basis tax coupled with a withholding requirement, it is universally acknowledged that the different tax regime is justified by the dissimilar circumstances of the recipient.'); and Robert A Green, 'The Troubled Rule of Nondiscrimination in Taxing Foreign Direct Investment' (1994) 26 L & Pol'y Int'l Bus 122–23 ('The nondiscrimination rule . . . requires neither that the nonresident be taxed on a net basis nor that the gross-basis withholding taxes be comparable to the net-basis tax.').

[32] Steven Dean, 'A Constitutional Moment in Cross-Border Taxation' (2020 working paper) (discussing classification and assignment as two primary goals of the international tax regime and exploring the limiting doctrine of numerus clausus as a restriction on expanding taxation at source).

factors mitigate against viewing the traditional list of five income-equivalent gross basis withholding taxes as eternally closed to new entries.

First, the idea of what constitutes income can change. For instance, for many years and in many places, capital gains were not always viewed as income in the classic sense of the term, since 'income' was traditionally defined as a flow of return to a corpus of investment that necessarily excludes the corpus itself.[33] The world has long since come to accept the notion that capital gains ought nevertheless to be considered income for income tax purposes, and there is no problem seeing the taxes on such gains as in lieu of income taxes, thus eligible for foreign tax credits. It should not therefore be surprising that other new categories of income have occasionally (if rarely) made their way into the withholding lexicon. Common additions to the list are management fees,[34] social insurance and retirement payouts,[35] and technical services fees, which are specifically included in the UN Model Income Tax Treaty at Article 12A (even though often resisted by relatively affluent states).[36]

Further, a conventional distinction between active and passive income both obscures and explains why taxing income flows on a gross basis is permissible in an income tax, which would otherwise typically require taxation to be applied only on net income.[37] Listed income types (excluding retirement benefits) are characterized as business income when earned by a taxpayer for whom the underlying activity is active rather than passive, where active is conventionally associated with continuous and regular activity of the taxpayer or a delegate.[38] For this reason, domestic statutes and treaties alike recognize that

[33] Capital gains were accordingly not defined as income for tax purposes in Canada until 1972, after a thorough study commissioned by the government concluded that to continue to exclude them from the definition was both unjustified and unworkable. Canada, *Royal Commission on Taxation, Report* (Queen's Printer 1966).

[34] As, for example, in ITA s. 212(1)((a).

[35] As, for example, in ITA s. 212(1)(h)-(l); 26 USC 871(a)(3); (f).

[36] Carl Estes, 'Tax Treaties' (1980) 14(3) Int'l Law 508.

[37] The requirement to tax net income goes to the notion that income taxation gets at the taxpayer's ability to pay, thus costs and losses must be taken in to account, in contrast to *ad valorem* taxes which are calculated on the fair market value of a given property or cash flow. Henry C Simons, *Personal Income Taxation: The Definition of Income as a Problem of Fiscal Policy* (University of Chicago Press 1938), 50; Robert M Haig, 'The Concept of Income-Economic and Legal Aspects' in Robert M Haig, *The Federal Income Tax* 1, 7 (Robert M. Haig ed, 1921), reprinted in Am Econ Ass'n, Readings in the Economics of Taxation 54 (Richard A Musgrave and Carl S Shoup eds, 1959); Georg van Schanz, 'Der Einkommensbegriff und die Einkommensteuergesetze' (1896) 13 Finanz-Archiv 1–87.

[38] Shay, Fleming, and Peroni, 'Source Rules' (n 30) 129 explain by way of reference to the seminal US Tax Court case of *Lewenhaupt v. Commissioner*, 20 T.C. 151, 163 (1953), aff'd, 221 F.2d 227, 227 (9th Cir. 1954), which involved a foreign individual that inherited some parcels of improved commercial real property in the United States, some of which he directed an agent to sell. Despite the minimal activity undertaken by the agent, the individual was held to be engaged in a trade or business in the United States, since his activities went beyond mere ownership into 'considerable, continuous, and regular' management for profit.

the category of active or business profits is defined by the nature of the activity and not the type of the income: business profits can include the five named income items but also many others. Once the activity exceeds a defined threshold to taxation, the business income thereby derived is subject to local reporting requirements, which require the taxpayer to take associated expenses and losses into account when computing taxable income. Passive income earned by a non-resident is often not subject to local filing but is achieved by imposing the obligation to report, withhold, and pay the tax onto the payor instead of the recipient. This is done out of administrative necessity where it is not realistic to impose the extensive reporting and filing obligations that would be necessary to tax on a net basis.[39]

A question that arises in the decision to invest abroad is therefore whether the contemplated activity is likely to exceed relevant thresholds thus giving rise to an obligation to calculate and pay tax to the source state. The interplay of active and passive forms of income can be seen in the ordering rule found in treaties reflecting the OECD Model Article 7(4), which states that when a taxpayer's business profits include items of income dealt with separately in other articles of the convention, those other articles apply.[40] As such, even if activity thresholds are not met, a source state may impose taxes on specified items of income.

As we will explore in more detail below, many (not all) tax treaties expressly include a provision for 'other income,' which means that the category of income that can be subject to withholding should not be considered closed.[41] Whether

[39] Shay, Fleming, and Peroni, 'Source Rules' (n 30) 121 explain that 'This internationally accepted system of having the payor withhold a gross basis tax at source addresses directly the inability of the source country to collect the tax imposed on income of a nonresident. The joint and several liability of the withholding agent for the tax to be withheld enables the [source state] to enforce source taxation over payments to those outside its jurisdiction.' They further explain that 'A fundamental reason for the difficulty in assigning income to a geographic source lies in the nature of the net income concept underlying the US federal income tax. The idealized Schanz-Haig-Simons definition of income as equaling consumption, plus, or minus, the change in the taxpayer's wealth between the beginning and the end of a year is an attribute of a person, not a place. Because a person is not divisible into geographic parts, the Schanz Haig-Simons net income concept can describe only a taxpayer's worldwide income. It cannot allocate that worldwide income among the various countries whose legal and economic infrastructures may have contributed to the production of the income.' (Shay, Fleming, and Peroni, 'Source Rules' (n 30) 137.) Similarly, the UN Model Tax Convention explains that '[m]any developing countries have limited administrative capacity and need a simple, reliable and efficient method to enforce tax imposed on income from services derived by non-residents. A withholding tax imposed on the gross amount of payments made by residents of a country, or non-residents with a permanent establishment or fixed base in the country, is well established as an effective method of collecting tax imposed on non-residents.' UN, *Model Tax Convention* (n 27) 329.

[40] OECD, *OECD Model Tax Convention on Income and on Capital* (2017) Article 7.

[41] David Ward and others, 'The Other Income Article of Income Tax Treaties' (1990) Can Tax J 38; C John Taylor, 'Some Distinctive Features of Australian Tax Treaty Practice: An Examination of their Origins and Interpretation' (2011) 9(3) J Tax Res 294.

and to what extent the relevant terms are subject to revision once a treaty has been ratified by both parties is a matter of debate. However, the use of the 'other income' category is only as useful as the allowance for source taxation provided by each treaty. While the UN Model explicitly allows for source-based taxation under the category of other income, the OECD Model Tax Convention does not follow suit, and this appears to be the dominant position. States with treaties following the OECD model may therefore face legal hurdles in subjecting various forms of income to withholding taxes under some or all of their existing treaty relationships.

Even then, however, the application of tax treaties is far from well-established because disputes about the reach, scope, and meaning of treaties are resolved through a diplomatic process that involves designated officials whose discretion to resolve matters with treaty partners is broad according to the terms of the treaty. As explained in the OECD Model Tax Convention, the designated treaty dispute resolution personnel—the so-called 'competent authorities' of the respective treaty partners—are authorized not only to endeavour to resolve 'any difficulties or doubts arising as to the interpretation or application of the Convention,' but they 'may also consult together for the elimination of double taxation in cases not provided for' in the treaty.[42] This is a very broad delegation of authority that in effect empowers the treaty partners to achieve ends not necessarily laid out in the treaty.[43]

The Vienna Convention on the Law of Treaties may act as a constraint on the ways in which competition authorities may interpret or apply tax treaties. However, there exist no definitive statutory interpretation standard which competent authorities are duty bound to follow. On this point, the OECD recently declared that tax treaties are to be interpreted using the so-called ambulatory approach to interpretation, even though the appropriateness of this doctrine is far from settled amongst legal scholars.[44] An ambulatory approach

[42] OECD, *Model Tax Convention* (n 40) Art 25.

[43] Allison Christians, 'How Nations Share' (2012) 87 Indiana L J 1407.

[44] Ulf Linderfalk and Maria Hilling, 'The Use of OECD Commentaries as Interpretative Aids—The Static/Ambulatory Approaches Debate Considered from the Perspective of International Law' (2015) 1 Nordic Tax J 34 (surveying the literature); Rebecca M Kysar, 'Interpreting Tax Treaties' (2015) 101 Iowa L Rev 1387 (advocating an ambulatory approach to fill tax treaty gaps as a result of policy learning as well as exogenous factors such as technological change); Lee-Ann Steenkamp, 'The Use of the OECD Model Tax Convention as an Interpretative Aid: The Static vs Ambulatory Approach Debate Considered from a South African Perspective' (2017) J Econ & Fin Sci 195; E Jansen van Rensburg, 'The Application and Interpretation by South African Courts of General Renvoi Clauses in South African Double Taxation Agreements' (2019) PER 1; Michael S Kirsch, 'The Limits of Administrative Guidance in the Interpretation of Tax Treaties' (2009) 87(6) Tex L Rev 1064; Juan Ángel Becerra, *Interpretation and Application of Tax Treaties in North America* (IBFD 2007); Klaus Vogel, 'The Influence of the OECD Commentaries on Tax Treaty Interpretation' (2000) Bulletin 612–16; J Avery Jones, 'The Effect of Changes in the OECD Commentaries after a Treaty Is Concluded' (2002) 56(3) Bull Int'l Fiscal Doc

says that a treaty should be interpreted according to the contemporary interpretation of its terms rather than by reference to laws in place at the time of ratification. Whether one agrees with the ambulatory approach or not, the OECD's approach confirms that a liberal interpretation of tax treaty terms is consistent with the interpretation principles laid out in the Vienna Convention.[45]

An ambulatory approach could help defend the expansion of withholding taxes at source against a categorical rejection on doctrinal grounds, because the notion would be that the relevant conceptions have changed in such a way that to continue to adhere to conventional definitions would be contrary to the broader intentions of the parties to the treaty. Wherever tax treaties appear amenable to accommodating the expansion of withholding taxes at source, cooperation by residence states is warranted in response to the duty to assist. However, even if a specific treaty is more rigidly constructed, there is a case for, essentially, nullification of treaty terms in order to fulfil the duty to assist. We will return to this idea in more detail below, as we explore the other approach to expanding taxation at source, namely, by expanding the opportunity for states to tax business profits. This requires reconfiguring profit allocation norms, which may also include expanding tax jurisdiction to include more business operations.

Accommodating Profit Reallocation

As we saw above, taxing business profits at source requires the taxpayer to either have a local corporate subsidiary, which is a resident for tax purposes, or to have sufficient business operations or activities to exceed a threshold, commonly defined by the presence of a permanent establishment.[46] Whether the taxpayer has a subsidiary or a branch operating through a permanent establishment, the extent to which the source state can tax is determined by reference to so-called 'arm's length' assumptions; transfer pricing, in the case of affiliated companies, and attribution to the permanent establishment, in the

102–04; David Ward, 'The Role of Commentaries on the OECD Model in the Tax Treaty Interpretation Process' (2006) 60(3) BFIT 97–102.

45 Becerra, *Interpretation and Application* (n 44) 35–40.

46 In some countries, the permanent establishment threshold is a treaty-based term only, and the domestic threshold is relatively lower. This is the case, for example, in the United States, where the domestic law threshold to the taxation of business profits consists of being 'engaged in a trade or business,' which effectively encompasses even the most modest of activity in the territory. Yariv Brauner and Allison Christians, 'U.S. Report,' in Guglielmo Maisto (ed), *The Meaning of 'Enterprise,' 'Business,' and 'Business Profits' under Tax Treaties and EU Tax Law* (IBFD 2011).

case of unincorporated branches. For ease in the discussion, we will examine this idea in the context of the transfer pricing norms applicable to related groups of companies, but the same principles apply broadly to the allocation of business income to non-corporate branch operations.[47]

Transfer pricing refers to the setting of prices between, and therefore the allocating of profits and losses among, related members of a group of associated companies.[48] The goal of transfer pricing rules is to divide revenues between states in a generally acceptable way.[49] States adopt transfer pricing rules unilaterally in order to ensure that multinationals do not use legal ownership and control structures among their separate entities to move profit out of the territory for tax purposes.[50]

The prices established within a controlled group attract scrutiny by tax administrators because the basic element of the free market that otherwise governs tax outcomes is missing. That element is the bedrock of fair market valuation upon which income taxation largely depends, namely, that free market prices are the product of non-compelled transactions among parties, each of which seeks to gain maximum advantage from the other.[51] These are also referred to as 'arm's length' market conditions—that is, the parties to the transaction are not in a cooperative or controlling relationship but stand at arms' length to one another as competitors, each aiming for the most advantageous terms they can extract from the other. Transfer pricing rules seek to conform the prices in transactions between separate but affiliated entities to those that would be expected to obtain in free market exchanges among non-affiliated market participants.[52]

[47] Robert Couzin, 'The OECD Project: Transfer Pricing Meets Permanent Establishment' (2005) 53(2) Can Tax J 401–07.

[48] OECD, *OECD Transfer Pricing Guidelines for Multinational Enterprises and Tax Administrations* (OECD Publishing 2017) ('Transfer prices are the prices at which an enterprise transfers physical goods and intangible property or provides services to associated enterprises').

[49] Yariv Brauner, 'Value in the Eye of the Beholder: The Valuation of Intangibles for Transfer Pricing Purposes' (2008) 28 Virg Tax Rev 83 ('an arm's length based transfer pricing regime, such as ours, permits relatively peaceful division of revenues between countries.').

[50] Some countries have detailed national transfer pricing laws and regulatory structures in place, while others do not. For example in Canada, ITA 247; in the United States, IRC 482; in the Netherlands, Corporate Tax Act Art. 8b(3), 29b-h; in South Africa, ITA s. 38.

[51] Income taxation depends on free market pricing because otherwise the responsibility to evaluate the value of transfers to various market participants for tax purposes would fall to the tax authority. Accordingly, market prices are generally deemed to constitute the relevant value for tax purposes unless there are circumstances surrounding the parties that indicate the possibility that taxpayers may act in concert to defeat taxation. This is why most advanced tax systems have a number of rules specifically designed to protect the tax base against manipulation by taxpayers who are related by virtue of family lines or legal connections.

[52] OECD, *Transfer Pricing Guidelines* (n 48) ('OECD member countries have chosen this separate entity approach as the most reasonable means for achieving equitable results and minimizing the risk of unrelieved double taxation . . . OECD member countries continue to endorse the arm's length principle

Transfer pricing rules are relevant to taxation at source because they contain the technical means by which active multinational income is ultimately assigned a source to one state or another. The basic rule of thumb is that a deduction from income in one entity demands an addition of income in another. Accordingly, a deduction taken at source, for example in the case of a payment incurred for services rendered by an affiliate in another state, reduces the tax base in the source state, while it creates tax base in the other state. If a state considers that a multinational has incorrectly priced transactions amongst its affiliated members, it is usually because the tax authority deems the profits declared in the state to be artificially low. The rationale might be that fees or prices paid out of the source state to foreign affiliates are too high, thus eroding the source tax base, or too low, thus eroding the residence base.

The opportunity for relatively affluent states to make room for more tax at source would arise if a source state were to increase its scrutiny of arms' length pricing, drawing more profits into the source base by recalculating the income of the local entity to either deny a deduction or change an inter-company price. Arm's length allocations can cause double taxation when one state interprets the standard to claim more profit than the taxpayer has initially allocated to it. When that happens, taxpayers typically look to coordinating rules to ensure that an increase in one state is offset by a decrease in the other, lest the group face an overall global profit for tax purposes that exceeds its economic profit. When a state requires such an adjustment, a corresponding adjustment is typically needed by the other state (or states) in which the group operates, in order to prevent the double tax.[53]

Corresponding adjustments are necessary to prevent double or multiple taxation, and therefore require international cooperation—a foreign tax credit will not likely help this situation because the underlying income will be categorized as domestic source by the crediting state. An international dispute arises either when the first state is unwilling to reverse its initial adjustment or the other state or states are unwilling to make the necessary adjustments. It is in the taxpayer's discretion to determine which course to pursue.[54]

The international tax community has accordingly adopted guidelines laying out the consensus views on appropriate methods to transform the combined

as embodied in the OECD Model Tax Convention (and in the bilateral conventions that legally bind treaty partners in this respect)').

[53] United States Treasury, *United States Model Income Tax Convention* 2016) Art. 9 (calling for a correlative adjustment when the two countries agree to an initial transfer pricing adjustment).

[54] Christians, 'How Nations Share' (n 43).

economic source of profit into distinct geographic sources of profit, so that primary taxing rights can be assigned to one state instead of others. This *de facto* harmonization across states occurs in the form of a set of 'Transfer Pricing Guidelines' propagated and continuously updated by the OECD.[55] Some seventy-five states treat the guidelines as enforceable, thirty-nine as instructive or interpretive but not binding, and thirty-three as not formally recognized but useful for analysis, while twenty-seven do not explicitly acknowledge any application.[56] As such, scholars tend to view the Transfer Pricing Guidelines as useful sources of legal emulation if not soft law.[57]

Despite its widespread use and its structural importance to the functioning of the international tax regime, observers have consistently decried the arm's length standard for being built on two interrelated structural faults: its inordinate complexity and its intractable malleability. These two faults, it is noted, permit sophisticated taxpayers to effectuate any outcome they desire while preventing coherent enforcement by many tax administrations. The effectiveness of enforcement is further imperilled by the worry that even if a government manages to deploy its enforcement tools effectively, the taxpayer will have recourse to other governments through treaty-based mutual agreement procedures.

Accordingly, to fulfil the duty to assist, relatively affluent residence states would first need to ensure that their own enforcement of the arm's length principle prevents taxpayers from creatively diverting profit to low tax jurisdictions. Second, relatively affluent states would need to deploy the malleability of the standard to make treaty-based corresponding adjustments whenever doing so would reallocate income to states in which subsistence rights deficits persist.

Effect on Income Allocation

To this point, we have established that a tax at residence acts as a backstop that makes room for tax at source. We then suggested two ways that source states could make use of this room: by either expanding their gross-basis withholding on specified income streams or revising their allocations of business

[55] OECD, *Model Tax Convention* (n 40) Article 5(7) for the separate entity approach, and Article 9 for the arm's length principle; OECD, *Transfer Pricing Guidelines* (n 48).

[56] Ernst & Young, 'Worldwide Transfer Pricing Reference Guide 2020'.

[57] M Calderón Carrero, 'The OECD Transfer Pricing Guidelines as a Source of Tax Law: Is Globalization Reaching the Tax Law?' (2007) 35(1) Intertax 4; Alberto Vega, 'International Governance through Soft Law: The Case of the OECD Transfer Pricing Guidelines' (2012) Working Paper of the Max Planck Institute for Tax Law and Public Finance No. 2012-05.

profits with transfer pricing adjustments (or both). We acknowledge that some readers will view both of these moves as going beyond existing norms and standards. Even if so, we think our proposed steps are broadly consistent with the OECD's efforts to re-examine international tax norms but we have argued that even if some adjudge our positions to go beyond those developments, doing so is warranted to fulfil the duty to assist. We argue that residence states ought therefore to cooperate with new source claims, even if expansive, when doing so would make it possible for states with populations suffering subsistence rights deficits to claim more tax revenues.

The effectiveness of these approaches may be dampened, if not eliminated, by the presence of intermediary states that do not cooperate in the same way. This is particularly problematic in the case of transfer pricing, where the presence of intermediaries is significant. By way of simplified example, we can imagine a corporate structure that involves three parties: a relatively affluent state as the state of residence of the corporate headquarters and the major shareholders; an intermediary company that is tax resident in a relatively affluent yet low tax state (at least, with respect to the functions attributable to the type of intermediary companies in question); and an operating company that is located in a state with a population that suffers from subsistence rights deficits.

All the transfer prices relevant to determining the extent to which the source state can tax are between the lowest tier company, which is located in that source state, and the intermediary company in a low tax jurisdiction. At the same time, the upper tier residence state will be scrutinizing the transactions between the company in its own jurisdiction and that in the intermediary state, for purposes of protecting its own tax base. If the intermediary state declines to accept its duty to assist the source state, then any effort by the source state to assign more profit to itself will create double taxation that will not be relieved by a corresponding adjustment, as the intermediary state resists this move. Meanwhile, the ultimate state of residence may also seek to reassign profit from the intermediary state to itself, which may make the intermediary state even more reluctant to cooperate with the source state, even if it accepted the duty to assist.

Unless the intermediary state both accepts the duty to assist and enlists the ultimate residence state in the task of ceding to the source state, multiple levels of uncoordinated conflict will ensue. Resolving such conflicts will be costly to the taxpayer, which potentially threatens the economic viability of investment in the source state.[58] The pressure on the source state to give up will be high in

[58] Chloe Burnett, 'International Tax Arbitration' (2007) 36 Austr Tax Rev 273 ('In terms both of frequency of cases and the amount of money at stake, the major international tax disputes have been over

this case. However, if major capital-exporting states were to adopt our first proposal of pass-through taxation with appropriate tax credits, the attractiveness of having companies located in low tax jurisdictions would already be lessened, thus potentially reducing the volume of conflicts.

Feasibility of the Reform

Unlike pass-through taxation, our argument that residence states should generally cede to source-based taxation when subsistence rights are at stake—even if they might otherwise view the source state claims as incompatible with prevailing norms and standards—may appear unjustified in terms of adherence to the rule of law. However, as we hinted above when introducing the legal analysis of the 'other income' provisions in tax treaties, an avenue of feasibility may be found in the admittedly arcane rules of treaty-based dispute resolution. In brief, states that accept they have a duty to assist could effectuate their cooperation by simply, as a matter of administrative discretion, deciding to allow duly authorized officials to cede the domestic tax in situations involving states with subsistence rights deficits, even if doing so would not be universally perceived as easily compatible with relevant legal doctrines. We find authority for this action in the administrative delegations laid out in tax treaties.

The provision at issue, briefly introduced above, is called the mutual agreement procedure, often shortened to its acronym MAP. Mutual agreement is a century-old diplomatic solution, a standard form of the informal diplomatic dispute resolution language that is used in most of the world's treaties.[59] The tax treaty mutual agreement procedure came into being in the early days of tax treaty history and it has become the industry standard through the OECD Model.

The standard mutual agreement provision states that 'Where a person considers that the actions of one or both of the Contracting States result or will result . . . in taxation not in accordance with the provisions of this Convention, it may, irrespective of the remedies provided by the domestic law of those States . . . present [the] case to the competent authority.'[60] This language does

transfer pricing, where a difference between what each tax authority, and the taxpayer, considers to be the arm's length price usually leads to a form of double taxation.').

[59] Virtually all treaties include a provision for informal diplomatic consultation as the primary method of dispute resolution. Barbara Koremenos, 'If Only Half of International Agreements Have Dispute Resolution Provisions, Which Half Needs Explaining?' (2007) 36 J Leg Stud 189, at 201.

[60] OECD, *Model Tax Convention* (n 40) Art 25.

not create a right for a taxpayer to sue a foreign government in the event of a perceived treaty violation;[61] instead, it creates the right to present the taxpayer's grievance to a treaty administrator, designated by the treaty as the competent authority. Once so presented, it is up to the competent authority, and not the taxpayer, to pursue the matter further.[62]

As such, treaty-based disputes arise because the governments, having previously agreed in principle upon the sharing of revenues between them, subsequently take opposing positions on a particular set of facts. But dispute resolution arises as a legal procedure only when the taxpayer notifies one or both of the treaty partners that one of them has imposed a tax in contravention of the treaty terms.

A taxpayer's goal in raising an international tax dispute is usually for the two governments to allocate the right to tax to one of the two jurisdictions, thereby eliminating the double imposition of tax.[63] In some cases, the dispute can be resolved if just one of the two governments acts, while in others, the governments will have to act in coordination by making corresponding adjustments. As such, there are several parties to an international tax dispute that have different stakes in the outcome, namely, the taxpayer and the multiple governments that have laid justifiable, if overlapping, jurisdictional claims. These parties have distinctly unique roles in the process of international tax dispute resolution.

International tax disputes are hence first and foremost inter-nation disputes, subject to the same administrative, political, and institutional issues that governments face in other transnational regulatory contexts.[64] The taxpayer initiates the resolution by bringing a claim to a competent authority, but it is the competent authorities alone that engage in resolution. The taxpayer is interested in having the governments resolve the problem, but once the claim has been laid, the taxpayer's role becomes one of observer, at best.[65]

Competent authorities process thousands of mutual agreement requests each year, the vast majority of which are resolved by closing agreements which

[61] Confirmed by US District Court in *Komet v Finland*, A F T R 2d (RIA) 1827 [2002] (dismissing a suit filed by a Finland company against the government of Finland pursuant to the US–Finland tax treaty, on the ground that Finland had not waived its sovereign immunity under the treaty).

[62] 'The competent authority shall endeavour, if the objection appears to it to be justified and if it is not itself able to arrive at a satisfactory solution, to resolve the case by mutual agreement with the competent authority of the other Contracting State, with a view to the avoidance of taxation which is not in accordance with the Convention.' US, *Model Tax Convention* (n 53) Art 25(2) and OECD, *Model Tax Convention* (n 40) Art 25 (2).

[63] Elisabeth Owens, 'United States Income Tax Treaties: Their Role in Relieving Double Taxation' (1963) 17 Rutgers L Rev 428.

[64] John Braithwaite and Peter Drahos, *Global Business Regulation* (Cambridge University Press 2000).

[65] Kerwin Chung and Richard McAlonan, 'Competently Negotiating the U.S. Competent Authority Process' (2007) 59 Tax Exec.

are confidential, limited to the taxpayer, and not typically accompanied by reasoned explanation.[66] Perhaps due to their pivotal role, the expertise of the competent authorities—not only in respect of subject matter but also with regard to geographic specialization—is viewed as 'extremely valuable'.[67] However, it is fully shielded from public view. Tax Analysts, a US publisher of tax news and reports, initiated a Freedom Of Information Act (FOIA) request in 2000 to compel the IRS to release these documents.[68] The IRS did not respond to the Tax Analysts' request, but almost immediately thereafter, the US Congress passed a statute ensuring the confidentiality of all competent authority requests, procedures, and outcomes and effectively preventing the FOIA request from going forward.[69]

In explaining the adoption of the US statute, the House Report stated that '[i]t is the understanding of the conferees that competent authority agreements (also referred to as mutual agreements) generally do not contain an explanation of the law or application of law to facts. Instead, such agreements are negotiated arrangements to resolve issues of double taxation.'[70] This can be problematic in the sense that the competent authority process is obscure and unaccountable to those other than the competent authorities themselves, but it is useful to explain why the competent authority process could be used immediately in fulfilling the duty to assist, without requiring any change in law.

Deploying the competent authority to this purpose may make some observers uneasy as it might appear to some to achieve policy ends only by subverting some imagined rule of law. Two observations serve to counter this worry. First, competent authorities already use their uneven bargaining powers to achieve policy goals in ways that are hard to track and quantify. Since competent authorities need not give reasons for their negotiated outcomes, there is simply no way to know how widespread or significant the phenomenon of geo-political

[66] See OECD Mutual agreement procedure statistics at <https://www.oecd.org/ctp/dispute/mutual-agreement-procedure-statistics.htm>.

[67] Chung and McAlonan, 'Competently Negotiating' (n 65) 257.

[68] Conference Report on HR 4577, Departments of Labor, Health and Human Services, and Education, and Related Agencies Appropriations Act, 2001 H12412 (House of Representatives—15 December 2000) (hereinafter House Report on HR 4577) ('A publisher of tax related material and commentary has made a FOIA request for the disclosure of competent authority agreements. The request has been pending since March 14, 2000. The IRS has not denied the request, nor has it produced any documents responsive to the request. At this time, no suit has been filed to compel disclosure of these documents, although such a suit may be brought in the future. The initial FOIA request of March 14, 2000, covered all competent authority agreements executed for the United States from January 1, 1990, to date. In response to a request from the Department of Treasury, by letter dated April 17, 2000, the FOIA request was narrowed to cover competent authority agreements executed between 1997 and 1999. The right to pursue the 1990 through 1996 agreements, however, was reserved.').

[69] 26 USC 6105.

[70] House Report on HR 4577 (n 68).

power is to the mutual agreement process, nor with what distributive effect. To the extent the obscurity of the process allows the geo-politically strong to exact concessions from those less so, the process cannot be supported as appropriate in standard rule of law terms in any event. But the process could be redeemed if it serves states in the fulfilment of the duty to assist.

More importantly, even if all competent authorities sought only to administer and implement the rule of law without any bias or resort to differential power structures, it is clear that treaty disputes rarely if ever can be said to have a single technically correct outcome. The reason that disputes arise, including in the definitions of terms, the interpretation of the inter-relationships of different treaty provisions, and the fact-specific exercise of profit allocation, invariably turns on ambiguity and vagueness in treaty and domestic law terms. Competent authorities are not bound to interpret the law of the treaty as they might in the context of a purely domestic application of a tax law to a specified taxpayer. They are authorized not only to negotiate a mutually acceptable outcome, but to do so using any criteria they mutually agree to use, and to do so without fear of scrutiny or overrule by the judiciary. There is, in short, simply no good reason why relatively affluent states should fail to use the competent authority process in furtherance of their duty to assist.

4.4. Conclusion

There is a strong case to be made that states have backup duties of justice to assist in the fulfilment of subsistence rights when facilitating international investment in states with populations facing deficits in such rights. The international tax system is currently structured in a way that ignores this duty. The animating theme of the discussion laid out above is that relatively affluent states are obliged to build institutions that maximize the ability to tax of states with subsistence rights deficits. To discharge this duty, these affluent states should work toward building an international tax system that embraces, rather than sidelining, well-known ways to enable and protect source-based taxes. This would help realize the moral imperatives of the entitlement principle, conditioned on the duty to assist, in legal terms.

Existing momentum is building in the international community regarding more effective taxation at source, albeit mostly for reasons having to do with how the status quo affects taxation by relatively more affluent states. This momentum suggests that since protecting the ability to tax at source is an increasingly universal goal, the broad ideas presented in this chapter are within reach in a way that they may not have been in the past, whether or not the underlying philosophical justifications are expressly recognized.

However, even if we are convinced that the duty to assist compels states to adopt the reforms we have suggested in this chapter, we recognize that it may be difficult for some readers to accept the idea of fully ceding residence taxation to enable taxation at source. For tax experts, especially, an unfamiliarity with the duty to assist and its broad implications may provide reason for doubt. But equally, deeply ingrained respect for a legal order built on technical rules a century in the making may cause some readers to reject the proposition as unprincipled in technical terms even if it is principled in normative ones. The next chapter therefore returns to the entitlement and equal benefit principles to explore their implications if the duty to assist is rejected as a legitimate constraint.

5

The Burden of Subsistence Rights Deficits

There may be those who reject the existence of a duty of assist as defended in Chapter 3 or deny its implications for the terms of fair tax cooperation. This chapter therefore considers the implications of the entitlement and equal benefit principles in the case that the widespread existence of subsistence rights deficits does not trigger duties of assistance for relatively affluent, well-ordered states (or, if it does trigger those duties, they are not appropriately performed by the measures we suggested in the previous chapter).

The focus for this discussion is again the conception of the human right to subsistence, which we defended in Chapter 3 as the source of backup duties on the part of relatively affluent states. In this chapter, we proceed on the assumption that there exist no such backup duties and that states are either solely responsible for fulfilling subsistence rights within their own territories or they must be assisted with capacity or institution building, but not with wealth transfers.

The basic question in this chapter is therefore how to conceive of fair cooperation between states when at least one of them has a population facing subsistence rights deficits (assuming that such cooperation is morally permitted). We analyse what the entitlement principle and the requirement of fair cooperation entail in the presence of subsistence rights deficits in cooperating states in this case. The aim is to show that even if the duty to assist burdened or negligent states with wealth transfers is rejected, the existence of subsistence rights deficits is nevertheless key to determining what constitutes a fair allocation of the benefits and burdens of cross-border cooperation.

The chapter begins by revisiting the principles of entitlement and fair cooperation. We introduce the idea that subsistence rights deficits create both costs and benefits for those engaging in cross-border investment, and that they do so in vastly different measures. We then argue that to ignore these costs and benefits in determining what constitutes a fair allocation of investment gains, mitigated as that allocation is through taxation, is to deny relatively less affluent states the equal share of the cooperative surplus to which they are entitled. Further, we argue that this denial may even deny relatively less affluent

Tax Cooperation in an Unjust World. Allison Christians and Laurens van Apeldoorn, Oxford University Press. © Allison Christians and Laurens van Apeldoorn 2021. DOI: 10.1093/oso/9780192848673.003.0006

states the share of investment returns they would be expected to reap under autarky, thus compounding the injustice. We then establish the feasibility of quantifying the costs and benefits of subsistence rights deficits in conventional market terms, and therefore conventional tax terms. The chapter concludes that even in the absence of a duty to assist, since relatively more affluent states are not entitled to more than an equal share of the cooperative surplus from cross-border investment, the costs and benefits of subsistence rights deficits ought to be incorporated into the fabric of the international tax regime.

5.1. The Equal Benefit and Entitlement Principles Reconsidered

The entitlement principle, as noted, holds that states are entitled to the wealth of their territory, while the equal benefit principle holds that when states co-operate with each other for their mutual benefit, each is entitled to an equal share of the (net) cooperative surplus thus created. In this chapter and the next, we proceed on the assumption that states lack a duty of justice to assist in financing the Sustainable Development Goals abroad, even to the extent that they are understood as necessary and instrumental to securing subsistence rights. This assumption is appropriate if such a duty of assistance does not exist: states may still have moral reasons to relieve human suffering and it would be good and praiseworthy if they were to do so, but these duties would be humanitarian in nature rather than duties of justice. As such, the decision to assist others would not affect states' entitlement to their wealth. The assumption is also appropriate if a duty of assistance does exist, but contrary to our arguments above, cannot effectively be discharged by making additional resources available to states with populations facing subsistence rights deficits. The duty to assist would then have to be performed in other ways, for instance, through political pressure or assisting in capacity and institution building.

Proceeding under these assumptions, the implication is that both principles hold in cooperating with burdened or negligent states. States have an unqualified entitlement to the wealth of their territory, at least in the absence of establishing international schemes of mutually beneficial cooperation (and bracketing other possible injustices, for instance those that might give rise to rectificatory duties). The equal benefit principle applies to the cooperation of states that otherwise have an unqualified entitlement to the wealth of their territory: when engaging in mutually beneficial cooperation they must determine the cooperative surplus and split it evenly among them.

Assuming that it is morally permissible to engage in mutually beneficial forms of cooperation with states whose populations face subsistence rights deficits, the question arises how we should interpret and apply the equal benefit principle in such cases. Is the presence of subsistence rights deficits a factor to be considered in determining what counts as a fair allocation of the cooperative surplus? In this chapter we argue that it does. We will make two claims as a result. First, subsistence rights deficits that are implicated in cooperation must be treated as burdens of cooperation, to be accounted for in the determination of an equitable allocation of the benefits and burdens of cooperation. Second, they must be treated as such regardless of whether they are caused by the cooperative practice in question or are pre-existing.

We will suggest that subsistence rights deficits as burdens of cooperation can be understood in terms of the economic costs of preventing or rectifying them. The intuitive plausibility of this idea can be brought out by considering that having subsistence rights deficits implicated in a cooperative scheme produces benefits to other participants in the form of higher returns than they would have had, if subsistence rights had been fulfilled. We understand these benefits in terms of the costs saved by not expending resources to prevent subsistence rights from being violated or the resources that would be necessary to rectify them.

In the allocation of the benefits and burdens, the state in which the implicated subsistence rights defects are located must be compensated for those burdens before the remaining (or surplus) benefits can be allocated between the cooperating states. The reason why the state must be compensated, instead of partially or wholly bearing the that burden itself, lies ultimately in the requirement that participants in a cooperative scheme do not benefit from injustice. This means that even if relatively affluent states lack a duty to assist in financing the policies and measures needed to address subsistence rights deficits in other states, relatively affluent states may not benefit from extant rights deficits. In what follows, we develop these lines of argument by applying them to international cooperation on cross-border investment.

Subsistence Rights Deficits and Cross-Border Investment

Cooperation on international investment in many ways implicates the extant subsistence rights deficits introduced in Chapter 3. Implicated are those rights deficits that are first, directly or indirectly, caused by investment and the production that gives rise to cross-border income, and second, those that are involved in such investment and production (regardless of whether they are caused by it—that is, they could be pre-existing).

An example of rights deficits *caused* by cross-border investment would be a foreign-owned company that directly or indirectly (such as through a local contractor) employs workers in hazardous conditions, leaving them systematically vulnerable to occupational accidents causing illness and death. This would happen if, for instance, the foreign-funded investment introduced the use of dangerous chemicals that exposed workers to health risks, introduced effluents to local water supplies, or overused local resources with broader economic and environmental impacts. The claim of causation rests in the observation that in the absence of the company's arrival, workers might have had a lower subsistence wage but they would not have worked in conditions that are routinely life-threatening, or at least, not in the particular conditions created by the particular employer, and communities might have had fewer economic prospects, but they would not have suffered the particular economic and environmental damage introduced by the foreign investment.

An example of rights deficits *involved* in—but not caused by—cross-border investment would be a foreign-owned company that pays its workers less than a living wage, preventing them from maintaining a minimally decent life, yet improving their conditions relative to what existed prior to the arrival of the foreign investment. This situation is encompassed in Nicholas Kristof's commonly repeated observation that 'the central challenge in the poorest countries is not that sweatshops exploit too many people, but that they don't exploit enough'.[1] Kristoff made this claim by comparing sweatshop labour to the alternative of scouring garbage dumps for recyclables, in light of which 'a job in a sweatshop is a cherished dream, an escalator out of poverty.' Kristoff's observation follows that of other economists such as Paul Krugman, who opined a decade earlier that 'bad jobs at bad wages are better than no jobs at all'.[2] The investment and production in question involves subsistence rights deficits, since it uses labour that is not paid a living wage, yet the investment cannot be said to have caused the rights deficits since, in its absence, the same or worse deficits would also have been present. We discuss these distinct cases in turn.

[1] Nicholas Kristof, 'Where Sweatshops Are a Dream' New York Times (New York, 14 January 2009).

[2] Paul Krugman, 'In Praise of Cheap Labor: Bad Jobs at Bad Wages Are Better Than No Jobs at All' Slate (21 March 1997).

Subsistence Rights Deficits Caused by Investment

The case for including subsistence rights deficits as burdens in the assessment of what constitutes fair cooperation is perhaps clearest when the rights deficits are directly caused by foreign investment that originates in a relatively affluent state. The deficits caused by such investment should be viewed as causal in the sense that in the absence of the investment, these specific subsistence rights deficits would not have occurred. If domestic factors had been employed in domestic production, these particular subsistence rights deficits would not have occurred, so in this respect, the state has been made worse off as the result of cooperation. According to the entitlement principle, states are at minimum entitled to the returns they would have had had their inputs been employed in fully domestic production, besides an equal share of the surplus resulting from the shift to international production. The new burden on subsistence rights created by the cross-border investment entails that the source state is entitled to compensation.

It does not matter if the source state is responsible for the existence of these subsistence rights deficits (for example, because it did not impose adequate labour or environmental protections). It is true that the source state may actively fail to prevent these deficits, for example by upholding a deficient regulatory framework, and is responsible for that failing. Yet, this does not entail that the source state must therefore bear the costs as if they were a purely domestic matter. The economic costs of these subsistence rights deficits are no different than other costs that must be included in the assessment of the benefits and burdens of cooperation. If they are not compensated, phenomena that constitute costs to the source state in terms of a diminution of its national endowment will flow to the residence state in the form of additional gains (even if the gains of cooperation are otherwise fairly shared).

To illustrate with a hypothetical, return to the example of the foreign-owned company that employs workers in hazardous conditions, leaving them systematically vulnerable to occupational accidents causing illness and death. This might happen, for example, if a company manufactures consumer goods using useful but dangerous chemical processes that are hazardous to human health if used without protection or disposed of incorrectly.[3] We might assume that in the (relatively affluent) residence state, such chemicals would be subject

[3] This is common in the textile dyeing and finishing treatment processes, for example. Rita Kant, 'Textile Dyeing Industry an Environmental Hazard' (2012) 4(1) Nat Sci 22, 23 (examining environmental and personal impacts of such processes and noting that World Bank estimates that 17 to 20 per cent of industrial water pollution comes from textile dyeing and finishing treatment given to fabric).

to regulations that either banned their use entirely or allowed their use only under strict requirements, such as to provide employees with protective gear and medical attention when necessary and to ensure proper disposal of waste so to protect surrounding communities.[4] Or we might even assume that the negative impact of the chemicals is not yet widely understood or well established in scientific studies, but industry norms and concerns about litigation risk prevents companies from exposing workers and communities in affluent states to the possible health risks. Wishing to use the chemicals in its processes but effectively unable to do so in a cost-effective manner (or at all) in such states, the company looks to implement the desired process in another state.

Assume further that the necessary regulations are simply absent or unenforceable in that other state, while the industry standards are such that the use of hazardous chemicals is an accepted business practice.[5] The lack of regulation might be due to lack of administrative resources and capacity to draft and enforce the same laws as in the more affluent state, or it might be because these particular chemicals were not in use in the state prior to their introduction by the foreign-owned company, so lawmakers are not aware of the need to regulate. Conversely, it might be because the source state fully recognizes the aim of the company to save itself the cost of undertaking the necessary protections, and makes a political decision that imposing the necessary regulations might drive away the investment to a different jurisdiction that makes a different trade-off.[6]

On these facts, in the absence of the incoming investment in the means of production, the particular harms of these chemical processes would not arise in the source state.[7] Once the foreign investment is accepted, these harms do arise. If the source state cannot regulate effectively, the company imposing this cost does so in a way that cannot be appropriate. But even if the failure to regulate is a conscious choice by a source state competing to attract foreign investment, as we introduced in Chapter 1, this is not an independent political choice. It is instead the choice to forego the benefits of international investment

[4] This is not always the case, and when it is not, the state is responsible for the rights deficits thereby caused.

[5] D-H Han, MS Park, 'Survey of Awareness About Hazardous Chemicals of Residents Living Near Chemical Plants in South Korea' (2018) 56 Ind Health 285–91; Sharrel Rebello and others, 'Hazardous Minerals Mining: Challenges and Solutions' (2021)402 J Hazardous Materials 402.

[6] Mohan Munasinghe, 'Is Environmental Degradation an Inevitable Consequence of Economic Growth: Tunneling Through the Environmental Kuznets Curve' (1999) 29(1) Ecol Econ 89–109; J Martinez-Alier, 'The Environment as a Luxury Good or "Too Poor to Be Green"?' (2005) 13(1) Ecol Econ 1–10.

[7] Rebello and others, 'Hazardous Minerals Mining' (n 5) 2 establishes that even naturally occurring minerals may be hazardous but extraction processes add more hazardous chemicals to the environment.

(by imposing costs that discourage investment in the face of competition from other possible production sites), or facilitate investment on unfair terms (by refraining from imposing rules that ensure that the benefits of the investment are fairly shared).

Investment in the Context of Pre-Existing Rights Deficits

The case is perhaps less straightforward where the rights deficits were not caused by international investment but the income produced through that investment nevertheless involves such deficits. The idea is that in the absence of international cooperation, the subsistence rights deficits would also have been present, and the international investment merely steps into a situation not of its own making. In this case, the economic costs of subsistence rights deficits cannot be considered a direct or indirect cost of cooperation, since the source state would have faced these burdens regardless of whether it had cooperated in facilitating international investment and production. Yet even then, if the burdens of the implicated subsistence rights deficits for the source state are not accounted for, an apparently fair distribution of the returns among cooperating states would lead to an unjust enrichment of the residence state.

In making this argument, we treat the economic costs of rectifying subsistence rights deficits that are implicated in international investment and production as equivalent to the reduced costs of production, which translates to correspondingly increased gains. By way of example, consider the comparison that Kristoff made between the employment conditions in a factory with inadequate labour and environmental protections and the conditions faced by those without any employment, who were forced by circumstance to endure even more harsh and hazardous conditions. For our purposes, the costs of rectifying subsistence rights deficits are those that would be necessary to further improve the lot of the workers now employed in a factory and guarantee them a minimally decent life. These are costs that the company can avoid paying precisely because of where in the world the activity is taking place.

If these foregone costs are ignored in determining the cooperative surplus, then the benefit of failing to rectify the subsistence rights deficits implicated in the investment is partly or wholly allocated to the residence state. This is unjust. If two states cooperate by facilitating international investment and production but this cooperation implicates individuals facing subsistence rights deficits, and if the benefits of that cooperation are equally shared without taking those deficits into account, then the capital-exporting state is a beneficiary of a wrong. It receives returns that were only possible by virtue of cooperation under those conditions.

Benefiting from an injustice is itself unjust, and 'innocent beneficiaries of wrongdoing should relinquish benefits which they wrongly received.'[8] Thus, even if, as Kristof has it, the investment makes some people marginally better off than they might be in its absence, this fact does not suffice to support the conclusion that the residence state is entitled to the returns thereby created.

One might argue that it is not the source state but the individuals whose subsistence rights are not met that have the right to be compensated for the failure to rectify these deficits. If the source state could reasonably put in place legislation that would prevent subsistence rights deficits but fails to do so, the benefits of the investment predominantly accrue to others. There is a related worry that if taking subsistence rights deficits into account results in a redistribution to the source state, this might have the perverse effect of preserving or even worsening existing domestic injustices.

In response, we observe that taking the costs of subsistence rights deficits into account in calculating cooperative surplus gains does not relieve the source state of trying to fulfil these rights. Source states continue to have these obligations, as virtually all have recognized by committing to various rights recognizing instruments including the UDHR and the 2030 Agenda. Where accounting for the costs of subsistence rights deficits would have the effect of making more resources available to them, source states would be obliged to use the additional gains to redress the injustices within its borders.

However, the capital-exporting state has no claim of right to enjoy the gains arising from subsistence rights deficits in other states. From the perspective of such capital-exporting states, a given source state's right to account for subsistence rights deficits is independent of its rectification efforts. Any gains that arise from unmet subsistence rights belong either to the source state or its residents, but they cannot belong to the capital-exporting state. To claim otherwise would be to argue that relatively affluent states are entitled to benefit from the ongoing conditions present in states with subsistence rights deficits. Besides being unjustified, the claim would serve to incentivize relatively affluent states to do little to tackle the causes of those conditions. This incentive would be particularly problematic in the case of states that are purposeful in neglecting their obligations to rectify subsistence rights deficits.

[8] Robert Goodin and Christian Barry, 'Benefiting from the Wrongdoing of Others' (2014) 31(4) J Applied Phil 363; Daniel Butt, 'On Benefiting from Injustice (2007) 37(1) Can J Phil 129. For a qualified critique, see Bashshar Haydar and Gerard Øverland, 'The Normative Implications of Benefiting from Injustice' (2014) 31(4) J Applied Phil 349.

5.2. The Permissibility of Cooperation

We assumed above that it is morally permissible to engage in mutually beneficial cooperation with states whose populations face subsistence rights deficits, but having considered the troubling problem that there are economic gains to be had so long as these deficits continue, we need to revisit that assumption. It may be impossible for states' cooperation to facilitate international investment to be fully 'fair' or 'just' if it implicates subsistence rights deficits. For the source state, the correct response to the presence of significant injustices may not be to consider them burdens of cooperation and therefore demanding of compensation, but rather to correct them and prevent them from happening in the future. For the residence state, the correct response may seem to be to avoid establishing investment relations in the first place, so as to avoid becoming implicated in subsistence rights deficits.[9]

Cooperation with Burdened, Negligent, and Outlaw States

Rawls suggests as much with regard to what he calls 'outlaw states,' states that are militarily aggressive and/or habitually and actively violate the human rights of their people. The best course of action could be to exclude such states from cooperative schemes as an incentive for domestic institutional reform: political pressure may have to be 'backed up by the firm denial of economic and other assistance, or the refusal to admit outlaw regimes as members in good standing in mutually beneficial cooperative practices.'[10] Perhaps precisely such threats and sanctions would form a feasible and effective way to discharge a duty (if there is such a duty) to assist populations suffering from subsistence rights violations that are inflicted by their own governments.

The main point of this argument must be accepted: a cooperative venture that implicates subsistence rights deficits cannot be fully fair or just. Nevertheless, it

[9] See, eg, Pope Francis: Speech at World Meeting of Popular Movements, 10 July 2015, <http://www.archivioradiovaticana.va/storico/2015/07/10/pope_francis_speech_at_world_meeting_of_popular_movements/en-1157291>. ('Colonialism, both old and new, which reduces poor countries to mere providers of raw material and cheap labor, engenders violence, poverty, forced migrations and all the evils which go hand in hand with these, precisely because, by placing the periphery at the service of the center, it denies those countries the right to an integral development. That is inequality, and inequality generates a violence which no police, military, or intelligence resources can control.')

[10] John Rawls, *The Law of Peoples, with The Idea of Public Reason Revisited* (Harvard University Press 1999) 93. In the footnote accompanying this quote, Rawls suggests an hypothetical example of a society with institutionalized slavery.

is not certain that this policy of non-engagement is most appropriate for what we called burdened or negligent states.

Recall from our discussion in Chapter 3 that burdened states are those that lack the capacity to robustly secure the subsistence rights of their populations, while negligent states have that capacity but fail to exercise it. As we understand them, negligent states are not necessarily outlaw states. Some would welcome the improvement of the position of the poor within their borders and would not actively obstruct such improvements, but they nevertheless fail to adequately address the injustices. There is reason to think that including many burdened and even negligent states in a cooperative practice may further the goal of subsistence rights fulfilment.

This is particularly clear in the case of burdened states. For these states, exclusion from mutually beneficial economic cooperation is likely to prevent them from accumulating the wealth they need to tackle the injustices within their borders. There is perhaps more room for disagreement about the best course of action in relation to negligent states, but there, too, a policy of non-engagement may well ultimately hurt those facing subsistence rights deficits more than it helps them.

It is likely that the vast majority of states today with populations facing subsistence rights deficits and the significant financing needs as accounted in the context of the 2030 Agenda, are best characterized as suffering from both lack of capacity and lack of political will in various degrees, making cooperation with them a morally defensible policy. As we argued in Chapter 3, many lower-income states face significant challenges to robustly securing subsistence rights and attaining the Sustainable Development Goals more broadly. In this context, foreign investment is an important source of capital accumulation.

A source state can reasonably determine that the benefits of welcoming international investment and production are more important than—or even justify—the introduction or persistence of subsistence rights deficits, since it may be the only viable way to induce greater economic growth leading to reductions of human rights deficits elsewhere or in the future. A state may therefore neglect to properly regulate important aspects of the activity funded by foreign investment, including labour compensation and minimum wage legislation, workplace health and safety regulation, and environmental protections.[11]

[11] United Nations, 'Extraction Fuels Rights Violations and Racial Subordination—UN expert' (OHCHR 8 July 2019) <https://www.ohchr.org/EN/NewsEvents/Pages/DisplayNews.aspx?NewsID=24801> (citing report by Special Rapporteur E Tendayi Achiume stating that multinational firms engaging in the extractive industry in poor countries are experiencing significant profits at the expense of populations that continue to be 'subject to gross human rights violations, including violations of the right to life; rights to

The reasoning would be that putting in place and enforcing stricter regulations would make the state less appealing as an investment location, which would only prolong the poverty of its population and underdevelopment of its economy. As Krugman observed, 'as long as you have no realistic alternative to industrialization based on low wages, to oppose it means that you are willing to deny desperately poor people the best chance they have of progress.'[12] Kristoff echoed this sentiment when he stated that 'sweatshops are only a symptom of poverty, not a cause, and banning them closes off one route out of poverty'.[13] A similar point could be made about environmental legislation.

If there is indeed a moral case for the acceptance of subsistence rights deficits for such consequentialist reasons, then fairness requires that the benefits and burdens (including the economic costs of the implicated injustices) be fairly shared between the cooperating states. It is true that the source state may be willing to bear the burden of remaining uncompensated for the costs of these subsistence rights deficits facing its own population—since autarky is assumed to be worse. But what a state may be willing to accept given the available alternatives is not equivalent to what is in fairness required.

Cooperation in Light of Regulatory Competition

The existence of competition on environmental and labour regulations lends support to the judgement that lower-income states may be forced to accept domestic injustices in order to induce foreign capital inflows, although the evidence is mixed.[14] In the context of environmental legislation, the issue is often referred to as the 'pollution haven hypothesis': the expectation is that firms locate pollution-heavy activities and industries in those states where weak regulatory regimes allow them to externalize the costs of pollution abatement. Some studies find no evidence for this hypothesis, and see little or no effect of environmental standards on the investment decisions of firms.[15] This result

racial equality and to be free from discrimination; to health and a healthy environment; to water; to free speech and assembly; to participate in political processes; and to just and favorable working conditions').

[12] Krugman, 'In Praise of Cheap Labor' (n 2).

[13] Kristof, 'Where Sweatshops Are a Dream' (n 1).

[14] McKinsey Global Institute, *Globalisation in Transition: The Future of Trade and Value Chains* (McKinsey and Company 2019) 8 (stating that labour arbitrage is still the basis for at least 18 per cent of foreign investment).

[15] Eg, Beata Smarzynska Javorcik and Shang-Jin Wei, 'Pollution Havens and Foreign Direct Investment: Dirty Secret or Popular Myth?' (2004) 3(2) Contributions to Econ Anal & Pol'y 21

can be explained as the result of the fact that pollution-abatement costs are generally minor compared to other production costs, such as wages.[16] The cost savings that can be attained by moving to pollution havens may therefore be limited, and unlikely to be offset by the costs of relocating production facilities.[17] Additionally, factors such as the distance to market and infrastructure quality have been identified as much more important drivers for investment decisions.[18]

However, the potential for cost-savings depends on the industry, and for some industries the environmental compliance expenditures can be significant.[19] There is evidence that in environmentally hazardous industries, for which the costs of pollution control are generally significantly higher than average, firms have tended to relocate to states with less strict regulations.[20] Two recent studies, based on large sector-level data sets of the outward investment of US and Dutch multinational firms, show significant effects. The first study demonstrates that for 'the developing and transition countries in the top 20th percentile of US multinational production growth, approximately 32 per cent of their growth can be attributed to falling relative levels of environmental stringency and enforcement.'[21] The second study shows that both regulation and enforcement of environmental policies are inversely correlated with investment inflows in several sectors, including pollution-heavy sectors such as natural resources extraction, refining and construction.[22] This is a particularly

(concluding that host country environmental standards have very little impact on FDI inflows both in terms of volume and in terms of composition).

[16] Jennifer Clapp, *Toxic Exports: The Transfer of Hazardous Wastes from Rich to Poor Countries* (Cornell University Press 2001) 106–07.

[17] Eric Neumayer, 'Pollution Havens: An Analysis Of Policy Options for Dealing with an Elusive Phenomenon' (2001) 10(2) J Env & Dev 147, 162 (citing average pollution abatement expenditures as a percentage of GDP below 2 per cent).

[18] David Wheeler, 'Beyond Pollution Havens, Global Environmental Politics' (2002) 2(2) Global Envtl Pol 1, 5; G Eskeland and A Harrison, 'Moving to Greener Pastures? Multinationals and the Pollution-Haven Hypothesis' (1997) World Bank Policy Research Department Working Paper No. 1744.

[19] For instance, in 1996, pollution abatement accounted for 42 per cent of total new expenditures in petroleum and coal production in the US. See Neumayer, 'Pollution Havens' (n 17) 162.

[20] Clapp, *Toxic Exports* (n 16) 106–07; H Jeffrey Leonard, *Pollution and the Struggle for the World Product* (Cambridge University Press 1988) 111; Ingo Walter, 'Environmentally Induced Industrial Relocation to Developing Countries' in Seymour Rubin and Thomas Graham (eds), *Environment and Trade: The Relation of International Trade and Environmental Policy* (Frances Pinter 1982).

[21] Derek K Kellenberg, 'An Empirical Investigation of the Pollution Haven Effect with Strategic Environment and Trade Policy' (2009) 78(2) J Int'l Econ 243.

[22] Steven Poelhekke and Frederick Van Den Ploeg, 'Green Havens and Pollution Havens' (2005) 38(7) World Econ 1159, at 1171 (noting that 'in the sectors natural resources extraction and refining, construction, retail, food processing, beverages and tobacco, and utilities a more stringent environmental policy in the host country significantly deters FDI.').

notable result since these industries are capital-intensive with large fixed costs, for which relocation is generally expensive.

The evidence is similarly mixed for the existence of regulatory competition on labour standards. Some studies find evidence that lower labour costs are associated with additional investment inflows, which is indicative of competition between states to attract capital and the possibility of a 'race to the bottom.'[23] There is also evidence that labour standards between states are positively correlated, indicative of competitive dynamics, with reductions in one state giving rise to reductions in another.[24] Yet, other studies do not find evidence for downward regulatory competition for investment. Indeed, several studies show a positive correlation between foreign direct investment and labour standards in a cross-section of states.[25]

While perhaps inconclusive, these studies provide evidence that states looking to attract foreign investment are under pressure to provide relatively more lax environmental and labour regulation and enforcement, as they would risk losing capital inflows if they were to implement stronger regulations.

From the observations made so far in this chapter, we conclude that in most cases it is morally permissible for relatively affluent states to engage in mutually beneficial cooperation with states whose populations face subsistence rights deficits, but it is not morally permissible for the former to benefit from the continuation of those deficits. To prevent this outcome, we will argue that the costs of continued subsistence rights deficits must be taken into account in the determination of cooperative surplus. Doing so would accomplish two goals. First, it would more clearly reveal as unjust the status quo international tax norms, standards, and rules that currently distribute the cooperative surplus. Second, it would provide the rationale and the means to change the tax distribution

[23] William Olney, 'A Race to the Bottom, Employment Protection and Foreign Direct Investment' (2013) 91(2) J Int'l Econ 191, 203 ('employment protection rules have a significant negative impact on FDI. In addition, employment protection rules have a more negative impact on the relatively mobile types of FDI. Specifically, employment protection legislation in the host country has small impact on horizontal FDI, a more substantial negative impact on export-platform FDI, and a large, negative impact on vertical FDI'). See also Keith Head, John Ries, and Deborah Swenson, 'Attracting Foreign Manufacturing: Investment Promotion and Agglomeration' (1999) 29(2) Reg Sci & Urban Econ 197–218; Franz Traxler and Birgit Woitech, 'Transnational Investment and National Labour Market Regimes: A Case of "Regime Shopping"?' (2000) 6(2) Euro J Indus Rel 141–59.

[24] Krishna Vadlamannati and Ronald Davies, 'A Race to the Bottom in Labour Standards? An Empirical Investigation' (2013) 103 J Dev Econ 1.

[25] Dani Rodrik, 'Labour Standards in International Trade: Do They Matter and What Do We Do About Them' (1996) Oversees Development Council. David Kucera, 'Core Labour Standards and Foreign Direct Investment' (2002) 141 Int'l Lab Rev 1–2 finds a positive correlation between FDI and labour standards in a cross-section of countries. Also Bradley Setzler and Felix Tintelnot, 'The Effects of Foreign Multinationals on Workers and Firms in the United States' (2019) NBER Working Paper No. 26149.

rules in order to get closer to a world in which states benefit equally from their cooperation with each other to facilitate international investment.

5.3. Calculating the Costs of Subsistence Rights Deficits

In examining subsistence rights deficits above, we proceeded on the assumption that the costs of rectifying subsistence rights deficits implicated in international investment are equivalent to the reduced costs of production, which translates to the correspondingly increased investment gains that form the corpus of cooperative surplus as we defined it in Chapter 1. We argued in the abstract that these costs must be included in determining the fair allocation of the benefits and burdens of cooperation. Eligible are all costs associated with rectifying subsistence rights deficits that are implicated in international investment.

In the discussion that follows, we will seek to move from this abstract imperative to understanding how such costs can be recognized and calculated. We first briefly explain the general idea that cost savings are a common source of gain for investors. We then focus on two kinds of cost savings associated with ongoing subsistence rights deficits: those associated with labour practices, which we divide into inadequate compensation and inadequate health and safety practices, and those associated with environmental pollution, meaning damage to air, land, or water.[26] Identifying these cost savings as contributors to cooperative surplus not only reveals the true scope and magnitude of what states stand to gain or lose from their cooperation with each other, but it is also a necessary step to understanding how the international tax system does or could serve the imperative that each state must benefit equally from such cooperation.

Cost Saving as a Source of Gain

When subsistence rights are not protected in a state, investors may have opportunities to avoid bearing costs they would otherwise face, for example in their home state. The foregone costs, or costs saved by taking advantage of those opportunities, are relevant to the measurement of their gains.[27] This is a simple

[26] Others could include land, water, and energy use.

[27] Allison Christians and Laurens van Apeldoorn, 'Taxing Income Where Value is Created' (2018) 22(1) Fla Tax Rev 1.

idea but its implications for understanding cooperative surplus are relatively unexamined, so a brief explanation is warranted. In the discussion that follows, we use the terms 'return,' 'gain,' 'profit,' and 'income' interchangeably. In any given income tax system, each of these terms is a technical term with specified meanings but conceptually they get at the same idea, namely, the increase in wealth that is achieved as a result of pursuing a given activity by expending capital or labour or a mix of them.

It is perhaps easiest to understand the relationship between foregone costs and available gains by examining how the logic of supply chain analysis normally measures value added by cost saving.[28] Manufacturing in particular has progressed through multiple stages of increasing profit by reducing costs. For example, in the automotive industry, following the lead of the Toyota Production System developed in Japan, the US-based Lean Manufacturing approach identified seven key sources of waste: excess production, inventory, transportation, processing, scrap, motion, and waiting.[29] Warehouse management systems likewise add value by ensuring products are delivered within a facility to an exact location at a precise time, thus eliminating excess storage, handling, and risk of damage. Waste elimination is similarly the preoccupation of supply chain management systems involving process planning,[30] transportation, and other factors.[31] The main premise of lean manufacturing, warehouse management, and other supply chain waste elimination mechanisms across industries is that even though manufacturing generally adds value to

[28] For a useful introduction see Donna Everatt, Terence Tsai, and Bor-shiuan Cheng, *The Acer Group's China Manufacturing Decisions*, Ivey Case Series #9A99M009 (Richard Ivey School of Business, University of Western Ontario 1999) (laying out the visualization of the global value chain of a computer according to Acer CEO Stan Shih).

[29] 'Toyota Production System: Maximising Production Efficiency Through the Elimination of Waste' (Toyota) (explaining the system, stating that it 'was developed during the second half of the 20th century and . . . has been studied, adapted and put to use worldwide, not just by manufacturers, but by all types of businesses that want to make their performance more efficient.'); William M Feld, *Lean Manufacturing: Tools, Techniques, and How To Use Them* (CRC Press 2000); Alireza Anvari and others, 'A Study On Total Quality Management and Lean Manufacturing: Through Lean Thinking Approach' (2011) 12(9) World Appl Sci J 1585.

[30] For example, Materials Requirement Planning (MRP) software coordinates customer demand over a given amount of time with internal production requirements over the same period of time. An MRP system breaks down a finished good into its components and creates a demand plan over time taking onto account raw materials, inventory, and necessary processes. The technology enables manufacturing companies to analyse their ability to meet customer demands in light of current production machine and labour capacity, thus maximizing output and minimizing wasteful measures. See, eg, Robert F Jacobs, 'Enterprise Resource Planning (ERP): A Brief History' (2007) 25(2) J Operations Mgmt 357.

[31] Transportation management systems provide a means to optimize freight options based on selected criteria, including the availability of appropriate carriers at a given time, traceability and duration of delivery, and size (parcel shipment (eg, via UPS and FedEX), 'less than truck load', or full truck load). A transportation management system will notify the carrier that there is a pick up at the facility, communicating to all relevant parties the shipment size, the carrier, the duration for delivery, and real-time tracking information.

raw materials, production is devalued whenever costs that could be eliminated, are not.

Accordingly, firms constantly seek to identify opportunities to reduce their costs, and there is an entire industry dedicated to delivering such cost savings by estimating the potential of various changes to the given supply chain, over and above simply paying less for various resources.[32] Some of these changes involve sourcing cheaper inputs (depending on quality trade-offs) and cheaper processes (such as by putting processes in destinations where labour is cheaper or major overhead costs are subsidized) while others involve reducing regulatory burdens.[33] The logic is simple: an eliminated cost translates to more potential for gain. Of course it is true that firms may not capture all of the gain—some might accrue to consumers in the form of reduced prices, while others might accrue to other members of society as positive spillovers (as we first discussed in Chapter 1). But as a rule of thumb, cutting costs is a common and uncontroversial profit-maximizing strategy.

That said, the logic of cost elimination as a value driver leads to the inevitable conclusion that many supply chain cost-cutting decisions potentially involve trading on a lack of substance rights in a given destination. We examine a series of base cases in the discussion that follows.

Costs Saved by Underpaying Labour

We start by examining a popular source of cost saving, namely the search for cheaper labour. The cost of subsistence rights deficits in the context of labour practices concerns primarily the monetary value of underpaying workers (whether as employees or as independent providers of services) in ways that prevent them from receiving a wage necessary to sustain minimally decent lives. When an employer or contractor pays a worker less than this amount, and when the community in which the worker lives does not make up the difference through public spending to meet subsistence rights, the worker will suffer from unmet subsistence needs.[34] When this happens, one could say

[32] See, eg, High Jump, Infor, SAP, JDA Software, etc.

[33] This may be less well documented in the supply chain literature, but it is well understood by political actors around the world who routinely use rhetoric around regulatory burdens to make political promises surrounding jobs and growth. Most such promises are articulated without the benefit of empirical support, and most go unchallenged both ex ante and ex post.

[34] It is immaterial whether the worker is underpaid directly by the foreign-owned firm or indirectly, through contractual arrangements with local firms and service providers. As has been thoroughly documented in the literature, many foreign-owned firms use garmented business models rather than directly controlling those who provide them labour. For a review, see Bart Los, Marcel P Timmer, and

that the worker bears the economic cost of their own unfulfilled subsistence rights, passing the cost savings of securing those rights on to their employer or contractor.

The magnitude of this shift of value from the world's poorest workers and their communities to those that employ them is by all accounts monumental. As one possible indicator of the size of the issue, we return to the International Labour Organization estimates we first encountered in Chapter 3 when discussing the scope of subsistence rights deficits. We observed that more than 630 million workers in developing and emerging economies live in working poverty, that is, below the World Bank poverty line of less than USD $3.20 purchasing power parity a day.[35] As noted, this poverty line is at best a conservative depiction of what is required to meet basic human needs, but it provides a starting point for analysis.

Most if not all of these workers are likely paid less than a living wage. A living wage is an amount that allows workers, in the context of the public services available in their specific location and circumstances, to meet basic nutritional, housing, education, transportation, health care, and other essential needs.[36] The costs of occupational illness and death must be included in determining a living wage if the likelihood of accidents is so significant and pervasive that they constitute or contribute to subsistence rights deficits. Such costs include lost income and medical expenses to the extent that these costs are borne by the workers or the society at large (rather than the employer).

Calculating the difference between what workers are actually paid and what they would be paid if their subsistence rights were met provides some evidence of the total costs saved by underpaying labour. As a reminder, these costs are potentially transferred to investors as the source of their profitability in employing or contracting such workers.[37]

Gaaitzen J de Vries, 'How Global Are Global Value Chains? A New Approach to Measure International Fragmentation' (2015) 55(1) J Reg Sci 66–92.

[35] ILO, *World Employment and Social Outlook: Trends 2020* (International Labour Organisation 2020) 13.

[36] Martha Anker and Richard Anker, 'A Shared Approach to Estimating Living Wages: Short Description of Agreed Methodology' (Global Living Wage Coalition 2013) 2 (Counting as a living wage, '[r]emuneration received for a standard work week by a worker in a particular place sufficient to afford a decent standard of living of the worker and her or his family. Elements of a decent standard of living include food, water, housing, education, healthcare, transport, clothing and other essential needs including provision for unexpected events.').

[37] Diane Elson and Ruth Pearson, 'Nimble Fingers Make Cheap Workers: An Analysis of Women's Employment in Third World Export Manufacturing' (1981) 7(1) Fem Rev 87–10 (analysing the increase in profits that can be extracted from female labour due to low wages).

Such calculations are available and in widespread use. Recent efforts by a number of academics and non-governmental organizations have shown that it is possible to develop robust country- and region-specific living wage benchmarks that provide evidence of what wage would be needed to meet basic needs. Two of these benchmarks in particular are worth noting. The first of these is adopted by the ISEAL Alliance, a global association for sustainability standards, and six standard-setting organizations, including Fairtrade International, UTZ Certified, and Forestry Stewardship Council (FSC), together known as the Global Living Wage Coalition. Their reports on individual states and specific industries include detailed estimates of the local living wage as well as an estimation of the prevailing wages (wages paid to the majority of workers).

The Global Living Wage Coalition estimates the cost of a decent standard of living using a method developed by Martha Anker and Richard Anker in *Living Wages Around the World: Manual for Measurement.*[38] Broadly speaking, the 'Anker method' of measuring living wages is calculated by reference to an assessment of the local cost of a low-cost diet, adapted to local circumstances and based on World Health Organization guidelines, the local cost of acceptable housing using international (UN-HABITAT) and national standards for decency, and the cost of other essential expenses for basic healthcare, education, and transport. These costs are determined using local data collection and other available data sources. The Anker method emphasizes its conservative assumptions, transparency, and detailed documentation to ensure a credible estimation. The resulting data is used to determine the living costs for a typical family size with the typical number of full-time equivalent workers per family.

The Anker method determines whether workers receive a living wage by drawing on interviews and government data. Overtime pay, non-guaranteed productivity bonuses and allowances, and mandatory deductions from pay, such as taxes and social insurance payments, are excluded. In-kind benefits such as lunches and transportation to and from the workplace are included. This allows for the calculation of the 'wage gap' between the prevailing wages of workers and the wages they would need to earn to afford a minimally decent standard of living for themselves and their families.

A second influential living wage benchmark has been developed by the Asia Wage Floor Alliance, consisting of trade unions and labour rights activists in

[38] Richard Anker and Martha Anker, *Living Wages Around the World: Manual for Measurement* (Edward Elgar Publishing 2017).

Asia and elsewhere.[39] The alliance presents its campaign primarily as a collective bargaining strategy for workers in the Asian garment industry. It is designed to tackle the threat that wage increases in one of the garment producing states lead to a relocation of production to other states in the region.[40] The calculation of the living wage is therefore less tailored to specific geographical locations, the aim instead being to identify a wage floor that will guarantee a living wage for workers in the entire region. This is reflected in the methodology, which is less data driven than the Anker method. For instance, it extrapolates non-food costs from the cost of the estimated price of a food basket, and assumes that a family consists of two adults and two children rather than calculating average family size from government sources.[41] While the Asia Wage Floor is generally somewhat higher than living wages calculated according to the Anker method, it is included as point of reference in the reports of the Global Living Wage Coalition, the Fair Labor Association, and others.

Assessment of wages around the world using these benchmarks demonstrate that workers in many industries in low-income states face wage gaps, with prevailing wages often falling significantly short of living wages. Using the Anker method, the Global Living Wage Coalition estimates, for instance, that the living wage is 24 per cent higher than prevailing wages of workers in the seafood processing industry in rural Vietnam,[42] 34 per cent higher than the prevailing wages of garment workers in urban Vietnam,[43] and 45 per cent higher than the prevailing wages of sports balls stitchers in urban Sialkot, Pakistan.[44]

The Global Living Wage Coalition identified some of the largest wage gaps in Bangladesh and Ethiopia. In the flower industry in Ethiopia, the living wage was estimated to be up to three times higher than prevailing wages, which were close to the World Bank extreme poverty line.[45] In Dhaka, the capital and

[39] Asia Wage Floor Alliance, <https://asia.floorwage.org/> ('The Asia Floor Wage Alliance (AFWA) was founded in 2007 as an Asian labour-led global labour and social alliance across garment producing countries (such as Bangladesh, Cambodia, India, Indonesia, Pakistan and Sri Lanka) and consumer regions (USA and Europe) for addressing poverty level wages, gender discrimination, and freedom of association in global garment production networks.').

[40] Helen I Safa, 'Runaway Shops and Female Employment: The Search for Cheap Labor' (1981) 7(2) Signs J Women Cult & Soc 418–33.

[41] J Merk, 'Stitching a Decent Wage Across Borders: The Asia Floor Wage Proposal' (2009) Asia Floor Wage Alliance, 48ff.

[42] Global Living Wage Coalition, 'Living Wage Report: Rural Vietnam' (Global Living Wage Coalition 2017) 44.

[43] Global Living Wage Coalition, 'Living Wage Report: Urban Vietnam' (Global Living Wage Coalition 2016) 55.

[44] Asad Sayeed and Kabeer Dawani, 'Living Wage Report: Urban and Rural Pakistan' (Global Living Wage Coalition 2017) 33.

[45] AT Melese, 'Living Wage Report: Non-Metropolitan Urban Ethiopia' (Global Living Wage Coalition 2015) 43–44.

largest city of Bangladesh, the living wage for garment workers was calculated to be twice as high as the prevailing wages.[46] Most of these workers earn less than the Work Bank poverty line and the Bangladesh urban poverty line during normal working hours, a fact corroborated by the Fair Labor Association.[47] Comparing prevailing wages to what a living wage would comprise demonstrates conclusively that the workers in certain industries and locations, such as the seafood processing industry in Vietnam and the garment factories in Bangladesh, accept wages that do not allow them to provide a minimally decent standard of living for themselves and their families.

These examples of wage gaps between prevailing wages and living wages provide measurable instances of subsistence rights deficits but they also provide evidence of just how much cost savings are enjoyed by employers of such workers. Anyone that benefits from labour that is provided at less than a living wage, whether as the direct employer or contractor or through contractual arrangements, can be seen to have benefited in the amount of the cost differential between the wages paid and that required to sustain life. The cost saved by underpaying workers ultimately contributes to profitability, whether or not accessing low-cost labour was one of the main purposes for the investment in the relevant location.

Costs Saved by Failing to Curb Health Hazards

Closely related to the costs saved by underpaying workers are those saved by failing to take measures to prevent or mitigate health hazards in workplaces. The International Labour Organization has estimated that 2.3 million people annually worldwide die from work-related causes and a further 317 million are injured as the result of occupational accidents and diseases.[48] Although there is limited data on occupational health risks in less affluent states, researchers note a shift with a gradual reduction of occupational injuries and fatalities in relatively more affluent states, with simultaneous increases in 'industrially progressing countries', in particular in Asia.[49] As one commentator observes,

[46] ME Khan and others, 'Living Wage Report: Dhaka, Bangladesh and Satellite Cities' (Global Living Wage Coalition 2016) 45.

[47] Fair Labor Association, 'Toward Fair Compensation in Global Supply Chains' (Business & Human Rights Gateway 2016) 26–30.

[48] ILO, *Estimating the Economic Costs of Occupational Injuries and Illnesses in Developing Countries: Essential Information for Decision-Makers* (International Labour Organization 2012).

[49] Jukka Takala and others, 'Global Estimates of the Burden of Injury and Illness at Work in 2012' (2014) 11(5) J Occ & Envtl Hyg 326, 329.

'[t]he experience of developed countries with the costs of occupational health is that a very substantial financial burden is being shifted to the industrializing countries through the process of globalization.'[50] This is due to working conditions being on average far worse in less affluent states.

Relevant factors include a greater number of individuals in informal sector employment, some with perversely appealing titles such as 'artisanal mining,'[51] and the industrial composition of the economy with the greater reliance of less affluent states on agriculture, which remains a 'distinctly hazardous' industry.[52] Moreover, in many states the economic burden of occupational illness and death is likely to be borne by workers and their families owing to a lack of adequate public spending to prevent or mitigate these harms.[53] A report on government compensation schemes for occupational injuries in southern African concludes that many 'fall short of providing a minimum standard'.[54] Among the reported problems are inadequate inflation indexing for compensatory pay-outs, as well as 'inadequate resources for enforcement, poor compliance, reduced revenues, and administrative expenses which are high as a percentage of contribution incomes.'[55]

These failures leave injured workers and the families of victims of occupational fatalities to bear the costs associated with the harm itself as well as the consequent loss of work. Workers in the least affluent states are particularly vulnerable to occupational risks, due to antiquated production facilities and lack of effective health and safety regulation and monitoring.[56]

Employers and contractors will bear some of the costs of occupational injuries and illnesses, for instance in the form of lower labour productivity and additional education and training expenses. Yet a substantial part of total costs is likely to be externalized or borne by the affected workers themselves, and the communities in which they live.[57]

[50] Joseph LaDou, 'International Occupational Health' (2003) 206(4/5) Int'l J Hyg & Envtl Health, 303–13, 304.

[51] Paul Cordy and others, 'Characterization, Mapping, and Mitigation of Mercury Vapour Emissions From Artisanal Mining Gold Shops' (2013) 125 Envtl Res 82–91; Elias Charles and others, 'A Cross-Sectional Survey on Knowledge and Perceptions of Health Risks Associated with Arsenic and Mercury Contamination From Artisanal Gold Mining in Tanzania' (2013) 13(1) BMC Pub Health 1–8; Myriam M Elenge and Christophe De Brouwer, 'Identification of Hazards in the Workplaces of Artisanal Mining in Katanga' (2011) 24(1) Int'l J Occ Med & Env Health 57–66.

[52] ILO, *Estimating the Economic Costs of Occupational Injuries* (n 48) 29–31.

[53] ILO, *Estimating the Economic Costs of Occupational Injuries* (n 48) 32.

[54] Elaine Fultz and Bodhi Pieris, 'Compensation for Employment Injuries in Southern Africa: An Overview of Schemes and Proposals For Reform' (1999) 138(2) Int'l Lab Rev 171.

[55] Fulz and Pieris 'Compensation for Employment Injuries' (n 54) 188.

[56] Ahasan M Rabiul and Timo Partanen, 'Occupational Health and Safety in the Least Developed Countries—A Simple Case of Neglect' (2001) 11(2) J Epidemiol 74–80.

[57] ILO, *Estimating the Economic Costs of Occupational Injuries* (n 48) 9.

Do occupational health risks constitute subsistence rights deficits? Rights, as Shue argues, provide a justified demand that the actual enjoyment of the right is 'socially guaranteed against standard threats.'[58] This does not mean that the right has 'been fulfilled only if it is impossible for anyone to be deprived of it or only if no one is ever deprived of it. The standard can only be some reasonable level of guarantee.'[59] Determining what counts as a reasonable level of guarantee, and accordingly what counts as being adequately protected from 'standard threats' to the enjoyment of a right, may depend on the circumstances of the case.

As such, a business that fails to internalize the costs associated with creating unsafe or unhealthy working conditions can be seen to have benefited in the amount of the cost differential between risk prevention and mitigation measures taken and those that could have been taken. Some of these costs may be determined by reference to industry- and location-specific analysis.[60] As it was in the case of underpaying labour, the costs saved by externalizing preventable health and safety deficits ultimately contribute to profitability.

Costs Saved by Polluting

A third major source of cost savings for investors in relatively less affluent states are those associated with complying with environmental protection standards in other locations. There is a very strong correlation between, on the one hand, the stringency of the environmental regulation and its enforcement and, on the other hand, per capita income of the state, such that the wealthier states become the better they prevent pollution from occurring within their borders.[61] Explanations for this correlation are diverse, but they include the policy priorities of less affluent states, which must focus first on providing basic services

[58] Henry Shue, *Basic Rights* (2nd edn, Princeton University Press 1996) 13.

[59] Shue, *Basic Rights* (n 58) 17.

[60] See, eg, Eugenio Pellicer and others, 'A Method to Estimate Occupational Health and Safety Costs in Construction Projects' (2014) 18(7) KSCE J Civ Engin 1955–65; Georgeta Buica and others, 'Occupational Health and Safety Management in Construction Sector—The Cost of Work Accidents' (2017) 18(S1) Calitatea 35; Delfina GG Ramos, Pedro Arezes, and Paulo Afonso 'Economic Analysis of Occupational Risk Prevention: A Case Study in a Textile Company' in Steenbergen and others (eds), *Safety, Reliability and Risk Analysis: Beyond the Horizon* (Taylor & Francis Group 2014) 1473–78; Martha I Riaño-Casallas and Emile Tompa, 'Cost-Benefit Analysis of Investment in Occupational Health and Safety in Colombian Companies' (2018) 61(11) Am J Ind Med 893–900; Bernard Brody, Yves Letourneau, and Andre Poirier, 'An Indirect Cost Theory of Work Accident Prevention' (1990) 13(4) J Occ Acc 255–70; Jos Verbeek, Marjo Pulliainen, and Eila Kankaanpää, 'A Systematic Review of Occupational Safety and Health Business Cases' (2009) 35(6) Scand J Work Env & Health 403–12.

[61] Susmita Dasgupta and others, 'Environmental Regulation and Development: A Cross-Country Empirical Analysis' (2001) 29(2) Oxford Dev Stud 173.

including education and healthcare to their populations, and their lack of administrative capacity to monitor and enforce existing regulations.[62] This translates into an inverse correlation between pollution intensity and negative health effects, and per capita income.[63]

A *Lancet* study calls pollution 'one of the great existential challenges of the Anthropocene epoch' and has shown that in 2015, pollution was responsible for a staggering nine million premature deaths worldwide, 92 per cent of which occurred in low- and middle-income states.[64] Indeed, in the worst affected states, pollution was responsible for one in four of all deaths.[65] The report also warns that several forms of pollution associated with industrial activities such as mining and electricity generation are still increasing, especially in industrializing low-income and middle-income states. These conclusions are supported by a World Bank report on air pollution, which estimates that in 2013, over five million people died prematurely from air pollution.[66] In both low-income and lower-middle-income states, pollution is the third most prevalent cause of death (with 10 per cent and 11 per cent of attributable deaths respectively).[67] These deaths directly impact the productivity of states and lead to significant lost labour income, $225 billion globally that year.[68]

The impact of pollution in terms of producing subsistence rights deficits is clear, not only in relation to these mortality rates but also when it comes to illness. Deaths or illnesses, as a result of being exposed to pollution that may be prevented by introducing and enforcing more stringent environmental regulations, constitute subsistence rights deficits. A recent report to the UN Human Rights Council on human rights obligations relating to the environment, notes that international human rights bodies have 'applied human rights law to environmental issues by 'greening' existing human rights, including the rights to

[62] David Wheeler, 'Beyond Pollution Havens, Global Environmental Politics' (2002) 2(2) Global Envtl Pol 1–10 2; see also Will Steffen and others, 'Planetary Boundaries: Guiding Human Development on a Changing Planet' (2015) 347(6223) Science (explaining that 'early industrial societies often used local waterways and airsheds as dumping grounds for their waste and effluent from industrial processes,' eventually leading to 'the introduction of local or regional boundaries or constraints on what could be emitted to and extracted from the environment (eg, chemicals that pollute airsheds or waterways) and on how much the environment could be changed by direct human modification (land-use/cover change in natural ecosystems').

[63] Wheeler, 'Beyond Pollution Havens' (n 62) 3.

[64] Philip J Landrigan and others, 'The Lancet Commission on Pollution And Health' (2017) 391(10119) Lancet Comm 462, 466.

[65] Landrigan and others, 'The Lancet Commission' (n 64) 475.

[66] World Bank, *The Cost of Air Pollution: Strengthening the Economic Case for Action* (World Bank 2016) 1.

[67] World Bank, *The Cost of Air Pollution* (n 66) 3, 1.

[68] World Bank, *The Cost of Air Pollution* (n 66) xiii, 1.

life and health.'[69] It further notes that '[a] safe, clean, healthy and sustainable environment is necessary for the full enjoyment of human rights, including the rights to life, to the highest attainable standard of physical and mental health, to an adequate standard of living, to adequate food, to safe drinking water and sanitation.'[70]

In the same manner as economic costs of under-compensating workers can be computed, the costs associated with causing or benefiting from environmental and social destruction in a geographic location may be quantified.[71] In particular, certain externalized environmental costs are well known to produce price distortions in addition to incentivizing irresponsible behaviour, with immediate health effects on workers and surrounding communities. Other externalized costs may be less well documented or understood, but equally impactful.[72]

Some of the relevant costs may be quantifiable through 'life cycle assessments,' which seek to measure the full cost of the production of goods and services including resourcing, processing, distribution, use, and disposal.[73] Most life cycle assessment to date focuses on ecological impacts but more recent studies expand the analysis to social and economic impacts as well.[74] Many of the life cycle assessments focused on ecological impact are quantitative in nature, thus providing a resource for pricing the difference between a production line that internalizes versus one that externalizes such costs.

Most life cycle assessments focus on the externalities in specific industries or jurisdictions.[75] For example, some recent location and industry specific life

[69] Report of the Special Rapporteur on the issue of human rights obligations relating to the enjoyment of a safe, clean, healthy and sustainable environment, UN Human Rights Council, Thirty-seventh session, 26 February–23 March 2018, 4.

[70] Ibid, 7.

[71] Seminal work by Marilyn Waring established that failing to count the cost of environmental damage constitutes a fundamental economic mistake. Marilyn Waring, *If Women Counted: A New Feminist Economics* (Harper & Row 1988); *see also* Marilyn Waring, *Counting for Nothing: What Men Value and What Women are Worth* (Heritage 1999). A more recent affirmation of this work can be found in Mariana Mazzucato, *The Value of Everything: Making and Taking in the Global Economy* (PublicAffairs 2018).

[72] James Fava and others (eds), *SETAC Workshop Report, A Conceptual Framework for Life Cycle Impact Assessment* (SETAC Press 1993).

[73] ISO, *14040:2006 Environmental Management—Life Cycle Assessment—Principles and Framework* (2nd edn, International Organization for Standardization 2006); John Vail Farr and Isaac Faber, *Engineering Economics of Life Cycle Cost Analysis* (Taylor & Francis 2018).

[74] Walter Klöpffer and Birgit Grahl, *Life Cycle Assessment (LCA): A Guide to Best Practice* (Wiley 2014) 1–2 (citing the ISO 14040 and other standards and explaining that standard life cycle assessment focuses on ecological impacts and not economic or social impacts); Subramanian Senthilkannan Muthu (ed), *Social Life Cycle Assessment: An Insight* (Springer 2015)(explaining that environmental life cycle assessment is well developed and widely used, while social assessment, a complementary approach, is less so).

[75] See, eg, PWC, 'Life Cycle Assessment and Forest Products: A White Paper' (2010) (stating that '[w]herever possible LCA practitioners use existing data contained in databases rather than create new data. There are public Life Cycle Inventory (LCI) databases, which are typically free, and private

cycle assessments include studies of sugarcane, sugar and ethanol production in Thailand;[76] electric vehicles in Brazil;[77] oilseed crop rotation in the Pacific Northwest;[78] and cut roses in Ecuador and the Netherlands.[79] Others examine externalized costs involved in specific products, such as construction waste;[80] plastic and glass used to make milk bottles;[81] and the energy demands of information and communication technology.[82] Life cycle assessment is not limited to consumer products, however. It also encompasses, *inter alia*, assessments of the externalized costs of providing advertising services[83] and, more recently, digital services.[84]

In additional to the assessments developed in scholarly research, firms undertake life cycle assessments to determine the costs unique to their specific supply chains and processes, though these internal studies may not easily scale to industries or nations.[85] In addition, many life cycle assessments are semi-quantitative in nature, using a scoring system to rate a product cycle on

databases that typically charge fees. The quality of the data in the databases varies both within and between databases. The potential impact on the results is often studied by sensitivity analyses on the key inputs and outputs.'). An example of a public life cycle inventory database is the 'National Renewable Energy Laboratory, U.S. Life Cycle Inventory (LCI) Database' (2012) which measures energy and material flows into and out of the environment in US-based production processes.

[76] Wanchat Sawaengsak and others, 'Development of a Social Impact Assessment Method and Application to a Case Study of Sugarcane, Sugar, and Ethanol in Thailand' (2019) 24 Int'l J Life Cycle Assess 2054.

[77] Jorge Enrique Velandia Vargas and others, 'Life Cycle Assessment of Electric Vehicles and Buses in Brazil: Effects of Local Manufacturing, Mass Reduction, and Energy Consumption Evolution' (2019) 24 Int'l J Life Cycle Assess 1878.

[78] Sharath Kumar Ankathi and others, 'Life Cycle Assessment of Oilseed Crops Produced in Rotation with Dryland Cereals in the Inland Pacific Northwest' (2019) 24 Int'l J Life Cycle Assess 627.

[79] J Franze and A Ciroth, 'A Comparison of Cut Roses from Ecuador and the Netherlands' (2011) 16 Int'l J Life Cycle Assess 366–79.

[80] Sylvain Guignot and others, 'Recycling Construction and Demolition Wastes as Building Materials: A Life Cycle Assessment' (2020) 19(6) J Ind Ecol 1030.

[81] Roberta Stefanini and others, 'Plastic or Glass: A New Environmental Assessment with a Marine Litter Indicator for the Comparison of Pasteurized Milk Bottles' (2021) 26 Int'l J Life Cycle Assess 767–84.

[82] Bernard Aebischer and Lorenz Hilty, 'The Energy Demand of ICT: A Historical Perspective and Current Methodological Challenges' in Lorenz Hilty and Bernard Aebischer (eds), *ICT Innovations for Sustainability* (Springer 2015) 71–103.

[83] Elaine Croft McKenzie and Pablo Luis Durango-Cohen, 'An Input-Output Approach for the Efficient Design of Sustainable Goods and Services' (2010) 15 Int'l J Life Cycle Assess 946–61 (proposing a method of assessing the life cycle costs of print and digital advertising).

[84] René Itten and others, 'Digital Transformation—Life Cycle Assessment of Digital Services, Multifunctional Devices and Cloud Computing' (2020]) 25 Int'l J Life Cycle Assess 2093–98 (finding that 'the digital carbon footprint is now increasing by about 8 per cent a year because digital "volumes" (i.e. devices, network traffic, computing instances and stored data) are growing exponentially').

[85] See, eg, UNEP, *Guidelines for Social Life Cycle Assessment of Products* (United Nations Environment Programme 2009) 57 (affirming that social life cycle assessments are very costly and time-consuming); PWC, 'Life Cycle Assessment' (n 75) 11 ('LCA is an assessment tool that requires a large amount of data and data analysis.').

the basis of various indicators.[86] This type of assessment may be informative to a firm assessing its own practices for internal purposes, but it does not necessarily yield specific information about the cost firms save by failing to change their practices accordingly.[87] Qualitative or score-based assessments may be difficult to translate into specific price adjustments without some additional work, but there is some evidence that such analyses may soon be more widely available, as researchers are beginning to work with firms to develop best practices and standards for broader applicability.[88]

As in the case of saving costs related to labour standards, a firm that fails to internalize the costs associated with its contribution to pollution levels can be seen to have benefited in the amount of the cost differential between pollution-curbing or mitigating measures taken and those that could have been taken. In the same way that saving costs by underpaying labour and failing to curb health and safety risks produces profit, the cost saved by externalizing the costs of pollution ultimately contributes to the firm's profitability.

5.4. Conclusion

We have established that saving costs by taking advantage of subsistence rights deficits produces benefits that can and must be accounted for in the division of cooperative surplus, and we have given some examples of why and how such costs savings can be quantified. We conclude by considering the implications of this analysis for the entitlement and equal benefits principles we have been advancing throughout the book.

Both the argument about the requirement of fair cooperation presented in this chapter and that based on the duty to assist presented earlier in this book seek to establish that the entitlement and equal benefit principles are in some

[86] These types of life cycle assessments use a 'scale-based' approach to characterize various 'performance reference points.' See, eg, Juliane Franze and Andreas Ciroth Franz, *LCA of an Ecolabeled Notebook: Consideration of Social and Environmental Impacts along the Entire Life Cycle* (GreenDeltaTC GmbH 2011), Federal Public Planning Service Sustainable Development, Brussels (developing a scoring system using six performance levels: very good; good; satisfactory; inadequate; poor; and very poor performance levels, and six impact levels: positive; lightly positive; indifferent; lightly negative; negative; and very negative effect).

[87] See, eg, UNEP, *Guidelines* (n 85) 25.

[88] See, eg, TruePrice <https://trueprice.org> ('a social enterprise with the mission to realize sustainable products that are affordable to all by enabling consumers to see and voluntarily pay the true price of products they buy'); True Price, 'A roadmap for true pricing: Vision paper-consultation draft' (June 2019). (Using life cycle analysis to build externalized costs into the price of consumer goods, using LCA: ISO 14040 and ISO 14044 [2006]; World Business Council for Sustainable Development (WBCSD) [2016]; Natural Capital Coalition [2016]; Greenhouse Gas Protocol [2011].)

circumstances impacted by the existence and persistence of subsistence rights deficits within cooperating states. In the earlier chapters, we determined that in cross-border cooperation among relatively more affluent states and states with populations experiencing subsistence rights deficits, the duty to assist required the former to lend assistance to the latter by addressing, to the extent feasible, global institutional terms affecting the taxation of exported capital that would make it feasible for source states to tax. Our prescription was for residence states to create space for source states to tax, effectively by all available means.

The solutions proposed to this end in Chapter 4 include measures broadly in line with some past and ongoing international tax practices or at least recognizable in some contemporary momentum shifts, especially when viewed in light of the OECD's work on curbing base erosion and profit shifting. To the extent these measures would be broadly accepted in international tax consensus terms even if the underlying principle is not generally embraced, they would presumably also further the requirement of fair cooperation laid out in this chapter.

To the extent the measures we raise in connection with the duty to assist would not enjoy international agreement and implementation, however, the requirement of fair cooperation carries a distinct implication: that to the extent possible, residence states should accept the valuation of avoided costs associated with the persistence of subsistence rights deficits for tax purposes, such that these costs can be counted in ways that affect the distribution of profits among the various states involved in cross-border investment and production.

Assume the existence of a source tax that ensures that the source state receives the national income they would have had, had their inputs been employed in fully domestic production, and second, an equal share of the value of the surplus resulting from the shift to international production. This tax would appear to allow the state to enjoy the returns to which it is entitled, by receiving an equal share in the surplus of productive gains created by economic cooperation. Yet it does not insofar as the costs of subsistence rights deficits implicated in the investment and production are ignored.

The implication is therefore as follows: if subsistence rights deficits occur in a source state, that state is entitled to the profits derived from the resulting cost savings before any remaining surplus is divided among the cooperating states. Claiming the relevant profit amount would be possible by, for instance, increasing the rate of the source tax in some amount that is economically related to the deficit in question. Such a tax would have the effect of shifting more of the investment returns to the source state to compensate for the associated costs. The conclusion to be drawn is that even if the duty to assist in alleviating subsistence rights deficits does not justify a relocation of tax revenues *per se*, the persistence of these deficits must be taken into account when applying the entitlement and equal benefit principles. This may be accomplished by devising methods to measure and take into account for tax purposes the costs of specified subsistence deficits. Accordingly, the next chapter outlines possible approaches and examines their feasibility.

6
Tax Cooperation Without a Duty of Assistance

So far we have seen that the costs of subsistence rights deficits impact the prospects for achieving returns on cross-border investment and accordingly, the fair sharing of the burdens and benefits of cooperation. Even if states do not have duties of justice to assist those suffering from subsistence rights deficits, it is clear that the existence of such deficits is an economic factor that impacts the expected profitability of cross-border investment, and therefore affects how we understand the entitlement and equal benefit principles.

While international cooperation that creates or trades on subsistence rights deficits cannot be fully just or fair, we recognize that cross-border investment carries on against the backdrop of such suffering, and will do so for the foreseeable future. We also take it as a given that some states may be unwilling to alter their current international tax practices unless enough are convinced that such change is both warranted and likely to be accepted by other states. There is a good chance that even then, geo-politically powerful states will exert their will regardless of any particular policy stance. These factors persuade us that any proposals we make should be both normatively justified and technically consistent with the foundational norms of income taxation, rather than advocating for a radical departure of those norms that renders implementation improbable.

Accordingly, this chapter aims to demonstrate that accounting for the cost of subsistence rights deficits is already possible and indeed is on occasion already undertaken under existing well-accepted tax norms and standards. In doing so, we aim to show that some existing international tax norms could be adjusted to accommodate more source taxation, in the same spirit and along the same lines as those we introduced in Chapter 4 when thinking about ways residence states could facilitate greater taxation at source. We examine how international cooperation with the proposed adjustments could be facilitated using existing tax law precedents and practices as well as conventional international coordination regimes. We raise and answer some of the

Tax Cooperation in an Unjust World. Allison Christians and Laurens van Apeldoorn, Oxford University Press. © Allison Christians and Laurens van Apeldoorn 2021. DOI: 10.1093/oso/9780192848673.003.0007

likely critiques of the proposed approaches, and conclude that, as we saw in Chapter 4, current trends in multilateral policy negotiations may be creating the necessary momentum to achieve a fairer sharing of the cooperative surplus derived from cross-border investment, in line with the entitlement and equal benefit principles.

6.1. Accounting for Costs in the Vocabulary of Source

Chapter 5 established that fair cooperation requires taking into account the costs associated with subsistence rights deficits, and explored some of the main ways in which such costs can be calculated. The challenge ahead is to explain why such costs warrant an adjustment of multilateral profit to one state or another for tax purposes, as well as how such an adjustment could be made, consistent with prevailing international tax norms and standards.

A preliminary challenge is that, as we first saw in Chapter 4, the international tax system allocates profit among jurisdictions by assigning a single source to each element that goes into a taxpayer's income calculation—each expense, loss, receipt, and so on. States can and do disagree on the sources of various income and deduction items, but if they do not resolve their differences, the risk is that either double taxation or tax competition will arise. As such, when we say that we seek to account for the cost of subsistence rights deficits within international tax rules, what we mean is that we seek to assign more income to the state that we identify as the source of the income because it is the territory in which the costs to rectify the relevant subsistence rights were avoided. Reassigning the source of an item of income in this way has the effect of altering the ultimate distribution of taxing rights between all of the states that are involved in a given cross-border investment.

The rationale of such reassignment is that the sources of the various forms of cost savings we documented in the previous chapter are the various interrelated conditions associated with subsistence rights deficits. This is a basic intuition that is on occasion acknowledged by courts, when deliberating the proper allocation of profits across jurisdictions. For example, *Sundstrand Corporation v The Commissioner*, a 1991 US tax court case, examined the cost savings associated with the taxpayer's decision to expand operations outside the United States and acknowledged that the reduction of wages was a source of the company's overall profit.[1] Similarly, in *Eli Lilly & Co. v Commissioner*,

[1] *Sundstrand Corp v Commissioner* [1991] 96 TC 226. Similarly, see *National Semiconductor Corporation v Commissioner* [1994] 67 TCM 2849 ('labor cost savings was the impetus for US

a 1985 US tax court case, the Court explained that the taxpayer's decision to relocate chemical and pharmaceutical manufacturing facilities to Puerto Rico created additional profit on account of, *inter alia*, the lower labour costs available in Puerto Rico.[2]

In the vocabulary of tax law, the conditions that permit subsistence rights to go unmet are the source of the cost savings thereby available for investors. As such, the economic source of the costs saved by underpaying labour is the systemic deprivation of subsistence rights that forces individuals to work for less than a living wage and without adequate social and environmental protections.[3] Tax law is perfectly capable of assigning value to hours of uncompensated labour and externalized costs of social and environmental damage, in the same way as it handles resource-saving manufacturing and transportation designs and processes. The identification and valuation of intangibles, including supplier-based intangibles, provide a ready precedent and guide. For example, in the United States, these kinds of intangibles are accounted for as 'the value resulting from the future acquisition . . . of business, of goods or services that will be sold or used by the taxpayer', pursuant to favourable relationships or contracts.[4] Failing to connect these things to the concept of source in the tax system in effect rewards relatively affluent states for policies that enable systematic exploitation of people and resources in other states. As we saw in Chapter 5, this is not justified. The tax system should therefore reassign profits that

semiconductor manufacturers to locate assembly operations in the Far East. Wages there were low, and the labor force was reliable, disciplined, and comparatively well educated. The Far East also had low transportation costs and favorable labor laws, customs procedures, US tariff provisions and investment incentives, including tax holidays').

[2] *Eli Lilly & Co. v Commissioner* [1985] 84 TC 996, aff'd in part, rev'd in part and remanded, 856 F.2d 855 (7th Cir. 1988).

[3] Adam Rosenzweig, 'Defining a Country's "Fair Share" of Taxes' (2015) 42 Fla St L Rev 373 (proposing an allocation of cooperative surplus according to what would produce an efficient allocation of public spending). Rosenzweig's proposed method would also allocate cooperative surplus to lower-income countries but not by way of existing standards or institutions. See also WHO, *Closing the Gap in a Generation: Health Equity Through Action on the Social Determinants of Health: Commission on Social Determinants of Health Final Report* (World Health Organization 2008) 73 (stating that 'The increasing power of large transnational corporations and international institutions to determine the labour policy agenda has led to a disempowerment of workers, unions, and those seeking work and a growth in health-damaging working arrangements and conditions. In high-income countries, there has been a growth in job insecurity and precarious employment arrangements [such as informal work, temporary work, part-time work, and piecework], job losses, and a weakening of regulatory protections. Most of the world's workforce, particularly in low- and middle-income countries, operates within the informal economy, which by its nature is precarious and characterized by a lack of statutory regulation to protect working conditions, wages, occupational health and safety, and injury insurance').

[4] U.S. Treas. Reg. 1.167-2(b)(7).

are associated with subsistence rights deficits. We examine two possible approaches below.

6.2. Two Methods to Account for Cost Savings Via Sourcing Rules

In Chapter 4, we explored the two main methods of taxation at source, namely gross-basis withholding taxes, typically but not exclusively on passive income flows, and net-basis taxes on income earned by local subsidiaries and branch operations, which are taxed by states according to conventional profit allocation norms. In examining how residence taxes could make room for greater source taxation to fulfil the duty to assist, we sought to align our proposals with existing tax norms and standards where possible, but allowed that deviations would be permissible if necessary to fulfil the duty to assist. We now return to the two approaches through the lens of the cost savings associated with ongoing subsistence rights deficits. Since the argument is that accounting for these costs is requisite to ensuring that states benefit equally from the cooperative surplus created by their coordination, here the goal is to demonstrate the feasibility of incorporating measurable cost savings into existing rule sets, with fidelity to commonly accepted tax principles as the priority.

Expand the Range of Withholding Taxes

In Chapter 4, we noted that residence states commonly support a fairly rigid, but not wholly exclusive, set of familiar gross basis taxes on income flows (by recognizing gross basis taxes as *in lieu of* income taxes and therefore eligible for foreign tax credits). We now seek to revisit that analysis by considering some less conventional kinds of income flows from which some states are already beginning to claim more than they did in the past, as well as some kinds of income flows that states could consider adding to the list. We then examine how these income flows can be said to reflect in some measure the concept of cost savings derived from subsistence rights deficits as we have laid it out above.

Two types of income flow, namely technical services fees and digital advertising fees, are particularly relevant to this analysis. First, because some states already subject technical services fees to separate withholding taxes or are considering doing so. Second, because both income flows are implicitly grounded in the notion that these states contribute to income earned by cross-border investors in ways that are not adequately recognized in the status quo rules, such that the lack of source taxation on such income flows represents an unequal sharing of the benefits of coordination.[5]

Withholding on technical services fees became an enduring, if not universally embraced, feature of the international tax landscape when it was added as new Article 12A to the UN Model Tax Convention in 2017.[6] The term technical services is defined in the Commentary to the UN Model Tax Convention to mean 'payments for services of a managerial, technical or consultancy nature.'[7] The Commentary explains that an additional treaty-based withholding provision for technical services fees was necessary to overcome the problem of base erosion and profit shifting. The problem to be solved was that technological change had enabled taxpayers to maintain a significant economic presence in the state from which they could earn business profit without exceeding traditional physical tax jurisdiction thresholds, or, if they were present in the state, could use the payment of such fees to shift the tax base from the source state to another, presumably lower tax, jurisdiction.[8]

The UN Model Tax Convention is aimed at solving coordination problems for lower-income states, so it is perhaps not surprising that the Commentary further explains that a second impetus for the addition of this provision is the lack of resources in some states, which prevents them from effectively addressing the profit-shifting problem. The Commentary notes in particular that such states 'are disproportionately importers of technical services and often lack the administrative capacity to control or limit such base erosion and profit shifting through anti-avoidance rules in their domestic law and tax treaties.'[9] This situation, it is noted, creates a parity problem between foreign service

[5] Stephen E Shay, J Clifton Fleming, Jr, and Robert J Peroni, '"What's Source Got to Do with It?"—Source Rules and International Taxation' (2002) 56 Tax L Rev 91 frame the rationale in benefit theory terms, and point to 'market access exploitation' as the benefit being conferred.

[6] The addition was initiated in 2011, when the UN Committee of Experts on International Cooperation in Tax Matters established a subcommittee to study the possibility of expanding source taxation on income derived from providing technical services where the taxpayer avoids exceeding the relevant statutory or treaty-based permanent establishment threshold. UN Committee, Fifth Session (19–23 October 2009), Note Provided by the Coordinator of the Subcommittee on Article 14 and the Tax Treatment of Services, E/C.18/2009/CRP.4, para 1 [2009] and UN Committee, Fifth Session (19–23 October 2009), E/2009/45 (SUPP)—E/C.18/2009/6 (SUPP), para 25 [2009]. See also Michael Lennard, 'Update on the United Nations Tax Committee Developments,' (2014) 20(1) Asia-Pac Tax Bull 20.

[7] United Nations, *Model Double Tax Convention between Developed and Developing Countries* (United Nations 2017) 318.

[8] UN, *Model Tax Convention* (n 7) 318 ('With the rapid changes in modern economies, particularly with respect to cross-border services, it is now possible for an enterprise resident in one State to be substantially involved in another State's economy without a permanent establishment or fixed base in that State and without any substantial physical presence in that State.'); UN, *Model Tax Convention* (n 7) 321 ('Within a multinational group, fees for technical services may sometimes be used to shift profits from a profitable group company resident and operating in one country to another group company resident in a low-tax country.').

[9] UN, *Model Tax Convention* (n 7) 322.

providers and their domestic counterparts.[10] Commentators generally view withholding on technical services as in line with general principles, even if they oppose such taxes on grounds of uncertainty or competitiveness.[11]

More recently, the UN Tax Committee used the technical services withholding tax provision framework in introducing a digital advertising fee corollary, in the form of a proposed Article 12B, entitled Income from Automated Digital Services.[12] If adopted, this article would impose source-based taxes on foreign providers of 'automated digital services,' either via a gross-based withholding tax or on a net basis using an apportionment formula. In the proposed text, income from automated digital services is defined to mean payment for a 'service provided on the internet or an electronic network requiring minimal human involvement from the service provider,' excluding fees for technical services covered under Article 12A.[13] The provision is likely to receive similar analysis as that directed at technical services.[14]

The principle of equal benefit provides a rationale for the UN's approach. In the case of firms that do not have a local presence in the form of business operations or a labour force, the possibility that investors might be profiting directly by underpaying workers or offloading pollution costs to communities is absent. Yet, just as in any other cross-border investment, involving a jurisdiction that suffers subsistence rights deficits, providers of digital and technical services derive profit by accessing a market that is impacted by such deficits on a grand scale. If they do not benefit directly by offloading those costs, they benefit indirectly by transacting with others that benefit from the kinds of costs savings described in Chapter 5. As such, withholding taxes on these fees might be necessary to ensure that residence states do not benefit from ongoing subsistence rights deficits in the source state.

An advantage to using withholding taxes is that the actual cost savings need not be measured, precisely because withholding taxes are imposed as a flat rate on a gross amount. In devising its provision for a technical services withholding tax, the United Nations in particular noted that the rate ought to match

[10] UN, *Model Tax Convention* (n 7) 322. This echoes the argument presented in Shay, Fleming, and Peroni, 'Source Rules' (n 5) 91.

[11] Franziska Sixdorf and Sebastian Leitsch, 'Taxation of Technical Services under the New Article 12A of the UN Model—Improved Taxation or a Step in the Wrong Direction?' (2017) Euro Tax'n 234; Tatiana Falcao and Bob Michel, 'Scope and Interpretation of Article 12A: Assessing the Impact of the New Fees for Technical Services Article' (2018) no. 4 Brit Tax Rev 422–40.

[12] United Nations, *Tax Treatments for Payments for Digital Services* (United Nations 2019).

[13] UN, *Proposed Article 12B* (n 12) 1.

[14] Some major capital exporting states, in particular the United States, have expressed resistance to both forms of withholding, and some commentators consider them to be discriminatory in trade law terms. See, eg, Catherine A Brown, 'Taxation and the Cross-Border Trade in Services: Rethinking Non-Discrimination Obligations' (2018) 21(2) Fla Tax Rev 715–61.

that applied to royalties, for the reason that there is some ambiguity between the concepts of technical services fees and royalties.[15] Digital services taxes of various kinds may create the same ambiguity, so the logic extends to these kinds of taxes as well. Since gross basis taxes on technical and digital services fees are demonstrably feasible and help ensure that source states receive an equal benefit from cross-border investment, it would be reasonable to consider other income flows paid out to foreign investors that are currently not taxed at source and design more withholding taxes as necessary.

That said, a more targeted approach is possible when the taxpayer is present in the jurisdiction through a subsidiary or branch operations that exceed the tax jurisdiction thresholds. In that case, calculating specific cost savings associated with subsistence rights deficits is possible, as the next part demonstrates.

Reconfigure Profit Allocation to Account for Cost Savings

As we saw in Chapter 4, when business is conducted through a local subsidiary or permanent establishment, the extent to which the source state can tax is determined by reference to so-called 'arm's length' assumptions: transfer pricing, in the case of affiliated companies, and attribution to the permanent establishment, in the case of unincorporated branches. When we first discussed profit allocation, we called for residence states to fulfil the duty to assist in the realization of subsistence rights by fully cooperating with expanded taxation efforts by source states, including in cases where there was some doubt that doing so would strictly adhere to the conventional arm's length norm.

However, even in the absence of the duty to assist, the measurable costs of subsistence rights deficits should be accounted for in the profit allocation exercise as a matter of accurately assessing the full benefits of cooperation that are to be shared equally among the coordinating parties. To do so requires a translation of the costs and benefits associated with subsistence rights deficits into the transfer pricing terms we initially saw in Chapter 4.

This is possible to the extent that cost savings can be converted to a price or premium (discount) factor[16] that can be incorporated by means of a transfer price adjustment under generally accepted standards, which is to say, without

[15] UN, *Model Tax Convention* (n 7) 319–20.

[16] The premium or discount (depending on one's view of the circumstances) would be applied as a percentage increase by a government as a price adjustment, even where the given price would otherwise fall within the acceptable range of comparable prices, as described in more detail below.

inflating the overall profit of firms.[17] The method proposed to price the cost savings attributable to development may be characterized as a form of 'location savings,' sometimes referred to as 'location specific advantage,' a term of art whose growing popularity may be traced to its use by China and India.[18]

In brief, location savings refers to 'cost savings attributable to operating in a particular market.'[19] Location savings achieved as a result of subsistence rights deficits might possibly be imagined as a single, market-wide intangible to which profit should be attributed, beyond any existing assets or activities, or it could be calculated as a price adjustment for each specific transaction of the taxpayer. The former would require locating an aggregate metric to serve as a proxy for actual cost savings, while the latter would require itemizing the measurable costs associated with each transaction.

An aggregate location savings factor could be derived from studies undertaken by researchers who measure the cost of attaining various aspects of the Sustainable Development Goals, generally expressed as a percentage of national GDP.[20] Early estimates derived from global or regional needs assessments, but current work is country-specific, albeit limited to certain of the easily quantified parts of the 2030 Agenda.[21]

[17] The exercise is thus purely distributional in nature when applied via transfer pricing or its corollary, income associated with a permanent establishment, so long as all countries cooperate to prevent double taxation as provided in tax treaties and domestic legislation. OECD, *OECD Transfer Pricing Guidelines for Multinational Enterprises and Tax Administrations* (OECD Publishing 2017).

[18] Jinyan Li, 'Location-Specific Advantages: A Rising Disruptive Factor in Transfer Pricing' (2017) 71(5) BFIT 259; Martin Hearson and Wilson Prichard, 'China's Challenge to International Tax Rules and the Implications for Global Economic Governance' (2018) 94(6) Int'l Affairs 1287–1307; Claire Peng, 'A Rethink of Location-Specific Advantages with an Analysis of the Chinese Approach' (2017) 24(6) Int'l Transfer Pricing J 482–502.

[19] OECD, *Transfer Pricing Guidelines* (n 17) s D.6.1 (adding in section 9.126 that 'Location savings can be derived by an MNE group that relocates some of its activities to a place where costs (such as labour costs, real estate costs, etc.) are lower than in the location where the activities were initially performed').

[20] See, eg, United Nations, Sustainable Development Solutions Network (explaining that the network is 'working with leading organizations, government agencies, international institutions and businesses around the world to support the financing of Agenda 2030' with a primary focus on private sector contributions to meeting the Sustainable Development Goals, 'particularly in Africa, financing the One Belt One Road Initiative, and the creation of municipal bond markets in the developing world'); Global Partnership for Sustainable Development Data, 'Financing SDG Data Needs: What Does It Cost?'; see also UNESCAP, 'Expert Group Meeting on How Much Do Ambitions Cost? Investment Needs for Achieving the Sustainable Development Goals in Asia and the Pacific' (14–15 November 2018) ('for governments to plan, budget and mobilize funds more effectively, they could benefit from a comprehensive assessment of the investment requirements. While there are selected sectoral estimates, for instance, in poverty-related social sectors or in economic infrastructure, we do not yet have a full picture of SDG investment requirements, which would also need to account for synergies and integrated scenarios.').

[21] Guido Schmidt-Traub, 'Investment Needs to Achieve the Sustainable Development Goals: Understanding the Billions and Trillions' (2015) SDSN Working Paper Version 2; Guido Schmidt-Traub and Jeffrey Sachs, 'Financing Sustainable Development: Implementing the SDGs through Effective Investment Strategies and Partnerships' (2015) SDSN Working Paper.

These studies provide a starting point for analysis. If the amount of investment needed to achieve the Sustainable Development Goals of particular states can be determined, a simple calculation may be used to determine a location saving involved in transacting in each jurisdiction, in tax terms. That is, for each state, there is an objective, economically discoverable cost to achieve the Sustainable Development Goals; this cost represents, in the aggregate, all of the costs savings associated with subsistence rights deficits in a state.[22] The measurement could be used to formulate the location savings which potentially alters the transfer pricing allocation.[23]

The simplest approach would be to take a state's aggregate annual development need and apply it to its annual GDP to produce a flat rate. By estimate, between 4 and 14 per cent of national GDP will be needed in lower-middle and low-income states, respectively.[24] Thus, for example, if it was determined that a state with an annual GDP of $10 million needed to spend $1 million per year to achieve the Sustainable Development Goals, the flat rate would be 10%. This rate would be applied to all prices within the jurisdiction unless it could be tailored to specified sectors depending on their contribution to GDP or their contribution to specific problems (such as environmental impact).[25]

The rationale of applying a premium rate is that the amount of spending needed to achieve subsistence rights represents some measure of the market-wide development-based discounts that provide firms with cost savings, including those we explored above. In the absence of a more accurate economic measure, the overall spending need is an, albeit imperfect, approximation of the location-based cost savings attributable to subsistence rights deficits. Using this metric, a tax authority would be justified, in both normative and legal terms, in making a universal price adjustment using the prescribed percentage.

[22] As discussed in Chapter 3, the Sustainable Development Goals encompass some rights that may not be strictly associated with subsistence, so this method potentially overstates the cost savings relevant to the analysis. This is a risk inherent to using proxies, with the positive trade-off being greater certainty and simplicity.

[23] Peng, 'Location-Specific Advantages' (n 18).

[24] Guido Schmidt-Traub, 'Investment Needs to Achieve the Sustainable Development Goals—Understanding the Billions and Trillions' (2015) UN SDSN Working Paper Version 2..

[25] The Chinese approach would not simply apply the gross rate to stated prices but instead would determine the profit ratio that would have been available to the investor had the investment been made in a jurisdiction without the identified location savings, as compared to the profit ratio achieved from the actual transaction, and then apply the profit markup differential accordingly. The method involves four steps that are explained in China's 'Country practice' section of the UN Transfer Pricing Manual and demonstrated with an example. United Nations, *Practical Manual on Transfer Pricing* (United Nations 2017) 568–72. Hearson and Prichard, 'China's Challenge' (n 18) 1288 view China's overall approach as a 'subtle but potentially profound challenge to OECD orthodoxy' that seeks to appear in 'solidarity with developing countries' but is in fact intended to shape international tax policy to increase China's share of revenues at the expense of other countries, thus mirroring the longstanding US approach to international tax policy.

The normative coherence of the position is as laid out above, and the legal coherence derives from the OECD and UN transfer pricing standards that we encountered earlier.

That said, the aggregate method may not be wholly satisfactory. First, an economic argument could be made that imposing a price adjustment of a flat rate will ultimately raise only a fractional increase in taxation and certainly not the indicated percentage of the GDP, so the price adjustment does not in fact match the solution to the problem. More fundamentally, a second argument is that imposing a price adjustment of a flat rate is not sufficiently precise in conventional pricing terms, not least because perhaps every state could make a similar location savings argument, rendering 'accurate' profit allocation an impossibility. In response to these concerns, a more precise measurement of costs savings could be done on an item-by-item basis.

This brings us to our second approach, namely: a series of cost savings adjustments that would reflect the externalized costs of production in states with subsistence rights deficits. These adjustments would be accomplished by internalizing such costs on a case-by-case basis using independent economic analysis for each factor relevant to the scrutinized case, in just the same way as standard supply chain analysis explains the costs involved in eliminating other kinds of costs. This method tracks international standards for allocating global profit across states, that is, as reflected in OECD and UN transfer pricing standards.[26]

These standards embody a process by which a multinational firm demonstrates to each relevant tax authority, via contemporary documentation, that its stated income in each jurisdiction should be respected for tax purposes. It should be so respected when the inter-company transactions that produced the income reflect what would be expected between unrelated parties acting in their own interests in fair market conditions (in tax terms, acting at arm's length). Firms explain their income calculations by reference to the price, cost, margin, or profit associated with the underlying transactions, depending on which transfer pricing method is applied. Some states require firms to use specified methods in a specified order of preference, or require certain methods be used by certain firms or in certain sectors, while others simply require the firm to choose the method that best reflects economic reality.

Given their policy dominance, it is easiest to examine our proposed approach through the lens of the OECD Transfer Pricing Guidelines, though

[26] OECD, *Transfer Pricing Guidelines* (n 17); UN, *Transfer Pricing Manual* (n 25). This alignment has benefits and drawbacks, which are also discussed below.

an analysis of the UN Transfer Pricing Manual would yield similar results, as would an analysis under the US regime upon which both sets of standards are built.[27] In broad strokes, the Transfer Pricing Guidelines undertake a four-step process to ensure related party prices reflect fair market value.[28] The first step is to identify the taxpayer's stated price for a given transaction. The second is to compare the stated price against a range of cases in the market that are comparable and involve unrelated parties. If the stated price falls outside the range of the comparable prices, the third step is to make appropriate allowances for factors that affect either the stated price or one or more of the comparable prices.[29] Finally, if the stated price is still outside the given range of prices, the fourth step is to adjust the stated price to reflect the price that would be agreed between unrelated parties in fair market conditions.[30]

A cost savings analysis would begin at the second step of this analysis, namely, in the search for 'comparable' prices involving unrelated parties. The challenge at this stage is that all relevant prices are distorted by the same economic condition, namely, ongoing subsistence rights deficits. In a conventional search for comparable prices, these market-wide distortions are typically allowed to stand without notice or challenge. This perpetuates the conditions that produce the distortion: since comparable A is wrong, a similarly priced B will necessarily be wrong as well, and therefore so would be prices C through Z, whether they are the taxpayer's stated price or a comparable. Using available relevant economic data, all comparable prices would therefore need to be adjusted to reflect what would be expected if the market was not distorted by subsistence rights deficits.

The living wage analysis and life cycle assessments described in Chapter 5 provide tools that might be applied to this task.[31] The first analysis focuses on labour. The premise is that where workers are systematically paid wages lower than that demonstrably required to sustain life, stated prices cannot reflect fair market value since in a fair market, unexploited workers would clearly not accept such

[27] The US rules are contained in regulations to IRC § 482, at 26 CFR 1.482-0 et seq.

[28] OECD, *Transfer Pricing Guidelines* (n 17). For ease in navigating the proposed approach, all possible transfer pricing methods are encompassed within the term 'profit' in the discussion that follows such that the term includes, for these purposes, 'cost', 'margin', or 'profit', as the case may be, in relation to the relevant rule in the Transfer Pricing Guidelines.

[29] For example, adjustments may be made to account for different levels and forms of risk and economic conditions that differently affects controlled versus uncontrolled taxpayers. OECD, *Transfer Pricing Guidelines* (n 17) s 1.33–1.40.

[30] OECD, *Transfer Pricing Guidelines* (n 17) s 4.4.

[31] In addition to the two sources described herein, costs savings could be associated with a number of other sustainable development goal targets, including for example the externalities associated with organized criminal control of global supply chains.

conditions.[32] Since wages distorted by subsistence rights deficits translate into prices that do not reflect fair market value, profit allocation for tax purposes is accordingly distorted. Instead of properly allocating profit to the cost saved by underpaying workers, firms will attribute their increased profit to other sources of value in their value chains, especially intangibles whose value is in the eye of the beholder.[33]

To correct this error, the existing economic models would be drawn upon to provide a more accurate allocation. This gap provides the taxing authority with evidence of the necessary counterfactual to stated prices. The gap thus revealed can be characterized for tax purposes as an uncompensated portion of labour. This is a cost saving that can be attributed in globally accepted source terms to the jurisdiction where the work took place, since the source of wages is typically the location where 'the employment is exercised.'[34] The costs saved in the jurisdiction thus acknowledged as a source of income, an adjustment for tax purposes to the price of goods transferred among related parties is warranted. This adjustment does not directly change the wages paid to labour or create phantom profit to the firm.[35] Instead, its sole purpose is to more accurately allocate the firm's global profit to its corresponding elements of the supply chain instead of allocating the profits derived from such uncounted costs to other intangibles such as design, branding, goodwill, and the like.

6.3. Objections and Alternatives

A main objection to the proposed approaches, especially in the area of profit reallocation, is likely to be that our suggestions are impractical on account of their technical complexity. This objection is warranted but it extends to the international tax system as a whole and transfer pricing in particular. The idea of transfer pricing might be conceptually coherent in some theoretical sense but as a system, it is inordinately complex to achieve in practice.[36] Determining

[32] Allison Christians and Laurens van Apeldoorn, 'Taxing Income Where Value Is Created' (2018) 22(1) Fla Tax Rev 1.

[33] Yariv Brauner, 'Value in the Eye of the Beholder: The Valuation of Intangibles for Transfer Pricing Purposes' (2008) 28 Virg Tax Rev 83; Michael Lennard, 'Act of Creation: The OECD/G20 Test of "Value Creation" as a Basis for Taxing Rights and Its Relevance to Developing Countries' (2018) 25 Transnat'l Corp 55; Jonathan D Putnam, *The Value of International Patent Rights* (PhD Dissertation, Yale University 1997); Dominique Guellec and Bruno van Pottelsberghe, 'Applications, Grants and the Value of Patent' (2000) 69(1) Econ Letters 109; Markus Reitzig, 'What Determines Patent Value?: Insights from the Semiconductor Industry' (2003) 32 Research Pol 13.

[34] OECD, *OECD Model Tax Convention on Income and on Capital* (2017) Article 15; UN, *Model Tax Convention* (n 7) Article 15.

[35] That said, the articulation of the gap and its consequences may (should) prompt future regulation.

[36] UN, *Transfer Pricing Manual* (n 25) 8 ('Countries with less sophisticated tax systems and administrations have run the risk of absorbing the effect of stronger enforcement of transfer pricing

what price two related parties would probably pay each other if they were not related is necessarily speculative and depends on highly specific facts and circumstances with innumerable applicable variables, exceptions, and conditions.[37] These factors have animated voluminous criticism of the use of arm's length pricing norms over the years.[38] They have also animated several cycles of negotiation over consensus rule sets, as taxpayers and governments continuously seek certainty in their dealings with each other.[39] Transfer pricing often defies the resources of states that try to enforce it, while yielding too few revenues for some states even when enforced.[40] Numerous researchers and nongovernmental organizations have therefore proposed moving away from transfer pricing to adopt a wholly different international tax system for corporate income, namely unitary taxation with formulary apportionment.[41]

in developed countries and in effect paying at least some of the MNEs' tax costs in those countries'); European Commission, 'Transfer Pricing and Developing Countries Final Report' (2011) Euro Comm 9 ('Developing countries often lack the necessary legal framework to enforce TP and sanction non-compliance and misconduct . . . Furthermore, it is widely accepted that applying TP requires skill and judgment by both taxpayers and tax authorities. Especially regarding TP expertise, developing countries often face difficulties due to information gaps. Local tax administrations may fail to collect necessary information due to the absence of documentation requirements, be unable to enforce such requirements or lack the capacity to process and evaluate such information. Additionally, there is the problem of human resource gaps, meaning that the few TP or large-taxpayer experts that there are within tax administrations may leave the organization because of changes in governing structures or more competitive employment opportunities in the business environment'); Caroline Silberztein, 'Transfer Pricing: A Challenge for Developing Countries' (2009–2010) 29 OECD Observer 31 ('Developing economies are keenly aware of the challenges posed by transfer pricing. Their goal is the same as for OECD countries: protecting their tax base while not hampering foreign direct investment and cross-border trade.').

[37] Alan J Auerbach, 'Measuring the Impact of Tax Reform' (1996) 49(4) Nat'l J Tax Reform 665 ('The inability of economic research to provide clear and precise information about the economic impact of tax policies has long frustrated policy-makers.').

[38] Clifton Fleming, Robert Peroni, and Stephen Shay, 'Getting Serious about Cross-Border Earnings Stripping: Establishing an Analytical Framework' (2015) 93 N Car L Rev 673; E J Bartelsman and R M W J Beetsma, 'Why Pay More? Corporate Tax Avoidance Through Transfer Pricing in OECD Countries' (2003) 87(9–10) J Pub Econ 2225; S C Borkowski, 'The Transfer Pricing Concerns of Developed and Developing Countries' (1997) 32(3) Int'l J Acctng 321.

[39] Thomas C Pearson, 'Preparing Multinational Companies for Transfer Pricing Audits of Intangibles' (2006) 2(2) Int'l L & Mgmt Rev 159, 192 (noting that many companies enter into advanced pricing agreements with tax authorities for the purpose of 'tax certainty rather than tax savings'); IMF, *Tax Certainty: IMF/OECD Report for the G20 Finance Ministers* (OECD 2017) 30 ('Uncertainty about each type of tax is generally reported as more important than the level of the tax itself—a result which can only be taken as symptomatic of the importance respondents attach to the issue.').

[40] Sol Picciotto, 'Problems of Transfer Pricing and Possibilities for Simplification' (2018) ICTD Working Paper 86; Michael Durst, 'Limitations of the BEPS Reforms: Looking beyond Corporate Taxation for Revenue Gains' (2015) ICTD Working Paper 40; A Cobham and D McNair, 'The Role of Rich Countries in Development: The Case for Reforms' in T Hopper and others (eds), *Handbook of Accounting and Development* (Edward Elgar 2012); Eduardo Baistrocchi, 'The Transfer Pricing Problem: A Global Proposal for Simplification' (2006) Tax Law Summer 2006.

[41] See, eg, Jinyan Li, 'Global Profit Split: An Evolutionary Approach to International Income Allocation' (2002) 50(3) Can Tax J 824–83; Sol Picciotto, 'Is the International Tax System Fit for Purpose, Especially for Developing Countries?' (2013) ICTD Working Paper 13; A Agúndez-García, 'The Delineation and Apportionment of an EU Consolidated Tax Base for Multi-jurisdictional

Under a unitary system, headquarters companies would calculate their profits on a worldwide basis and this global profit amount would be apportioned according to a formula to be decided *ex ante* through global consensus. Most often, the proposed formula is based on the US state model, which allocates taxable profits among jurisdictions according to the relative values of assets, sales, and payroll in each jurisdiction.[42] However, owing in part to the enduring problem posed by things like hard-to-value intangibles,[43] some call for the formula to rest on a single factor, namely sales.[44]

A move to unitary taxation has the potential to be an improvement over the current transfer pricing system, but a move to conventional formulary apportionment based on sales, assets, and payroll is not. Since a formula that measures relative sales, assets, and payroll tracks the same economic logic as that which drives the transfer pricing analysis, the potential gains to adoption might be neutral or positive for relatively affluent states but they are modest and may even be negative for many less affluent ones.[45] In particular, given disparate levels of consumption, unitary taxation based solely on sales will clearly benefit

Corporate Income Taxation: A Review of Issues and Options' (2006) European Commission Taxation Papers No. 9/06; R Avi-Yonah, K Clausing, and M Durst, 'Allocating Business Profits for Tax Purposes: A Proposal to Adopt a Formulary Profit Split' (2009) 9(5) Fla Tax Rev 497; RS Avi-Yonah and KA Clausing, 'Reforming Corporate Taxation in a Global Economy: A Proposal to Adopt Formulary Apportionment' (2007) Brookings Discussion Paper, 2007-08; C Fuest, T Hemmelgarn, and F Ramb, 'How Would the Introduction of an EU-wide Formula Apportionment Affect the Distribution and Size of the Corporate Tax Base? An Analysis Based on German Multinationals' (2007) 14 Int'l Tax & Pub Fin 605; C Fuest and others, 'Profit Shifting and 'Aggressive' Tax Planning by Multinational Firms: Issues and Options for Reform' (2013); Among nongovernmental organizations this has been a major campaign by the Tax Justice Network, Oxfam, the International Commission for the Reform of International Corporate Taxation, and the International Center for Tax and Development, among others. These are all relatively recent calls for reform, but the idea of unitary taxation with formulary apportionment has a long history. See, eg, Bret Wells and Cym Lowell, 'Income Tax Treaty Policy in the 21st Century: Residence vs. Source' (2013) 5(1) Colum J Law; Joann Weiner, 'Formulary Apportionment and Group Taxation in the European Union: Insights from the United States and Canada' (2005) Working Paper No. 8: Joann Weiner, 'An Economist's View of Income Allocation under the Arm's Length Standard and under Formulary Apportionment' (2010) The State and Local Taxpayer. Symposium Edition 25.

42 For a discussion, see Marco Runkel and Guttorm Schjelderup, 'The Choice of Apportionment Factors under Formula Apportionment' (2007) CESifo Working Paper Series, No. 2072.

43 Brauner, 'Valuation of Intangibles' (n 33) 104.

44 See, eg, Reuven S Avi-Yonah and others, 'Allocating Business Profits for Tax Purposes: A Proposal to Adopt a Formulary Profit Split' (2009) 9(5) Fla Tax Rev 498.

45 Valpy Fitzgerald and Tommaso Faccio, 'Sharing the Corporate Tax Base: Equitable Taxing of Multinationals and the Choice of Formulary Apportionment' (2018) 25(2) Transnat'l Corp 67 (using public data released by Vodaphone to study the likely impacts of adopting formulary apportionment and finding that lower income countries are not expected to materially benefit from the change unless the apportionment factors are designed specifically to reflect their contributions); Alexander Ezenagu, 'Faltering Blocks in the Arguments against Unitary Taxation and the Formulary Apportionment Approach to Income Allocation' (2017) 17 Asper Int'l Bus & Trade Law.

relatively affluent states at the significant expense of less affluent ones.[46] The risk is that virtually any formula based on conventional sourcing factors will continue to assign most multinational profits to relatively affluent states and conduit or intermediary (low tax) states, and very little to less affluent states.[47]

No matter which form of profit allocation is chosen, if it assigns profit according to conventional source categories in conventional ways, it will not take into account the externalized costs of ongoing subsistence rights deficits described in previous chapters. If profits are continuously allocated to the states with significant wealth and resources that can reinvest them productively, these states are enabled to continuously improve the very conditions that allow them to claim more profits for tax purposes in the future. Switching profit allocation systems while relying on prevailing source definitions will not help states break out of this cycle.

For this reason, some proponents of a switch to formulary apportionment propose various tweaks to the formula, such as that employees be counted as units rather than in terms of their pay,[48] or that most intellectual property assets be excluded. The intuition with respect to intellectual property is that eliminating these assets from the formula will prevent companies from accomplishing with formulary apportionment what they currently accomplish via transfer pricing, namely, strategically locating such property in low-tax jurisdictions. The intuition with respect to payroll is that since workers are paid little in less affluent states and much more in more affluent ones, an apportionment based on worker pay would inevitably skew toward the latter.[49] Conversely, having a higher number of workers in less affluent states than in relatively more affluent ones (for example 100 factory workers to one CEO), would help skew the apportionment to less affluent states.[50]

These tweaks might face feasibility challenges on grounds that they deviate too far from the conventional norms and standards in order to reach a more equitable outcome. Even if justified, such a move would clearly require *ex ante* multilateral cooperation since it is incompatible with the existing system and

[46] IMF, *IMF Policy Paper: Corporate Taxation in the Global Economy* (IMF Publications 2019) 33 (Predicting that 'advanced economies are more likely to gain revenue if apportionment is by value added, payroll, or sales.').

[47] Christians and Van Apeldoorn, 'Value Creation' (n 32).

[48] Fitzgerald and Faccio, 'Formulary Apportionment' (n 45).

[49] Fitzgerald and Faccio, 'Formulary Apportionment' (n 45).

[50] IMF, *IMF Policy Paper: Corporate Taxation in the Global Economy* (IMF Publications 2019) 33. This assumes that there are in fact more employees in poorer countries. Whether that is true now, advances in mechanization suggest that it might not be true in the future. See, eg, Ian Goldin, 'Will AI Kill Developing World Growth?' *BBC News* (18 April 2019). Moreover, some economists predict that an increase in tax burdens will hasten mechanization thus reducing employment.

involves a political choice to take into account different development levels when formulating global tax norms.[51] Adoption by any one state is expected to create systemically irreconcilable taxation outcomes, since other states would reject the approach as inconsistent not only with the agreed standard but also with the core concept of income taxation as embedded in the world's over 3,000 bilateral treaties.[52] Even though the adoption of unitary taxation is arguably an acceptable interpretation of the arm's length standard expressed in such treaties,[53] consensus is often viewed as a pre-requisite to its adoption in order to avoid double (or multiple) levels of taxation.[54]

6.4. Conclusion

In contrast to formulary apportionment as an alternative approach to revisit the allocation of multinational income across states, the approaches we have laid out in this chapter are in major respects consistent with the foundational norms and standards of the international tax system in place today, even if they may seem to depart from some common international tax practices in some respects. Expanding withholding taxation to cover new and different types of income as we initially suggested in Chapter 4 and expanded in this chapter may be controversial to some but doing so conceptually aligns our approach with existing withholding taxes, thus engaging with a well-understood and well-accepted method of source-based taxation.

Similarly, pricing in cost savings related to subsistence rights deficits might seem unusual or even radical to some readers, but the rationales and methods for taking cost savings into account are already embedded in the fabric of prevailing international tax norms and standards. As we saw in Chapter 4, having worked with these prevailing practices, our approach also works within existing

[51] World Bank, *Taxation & SDGs First Global Conference of the Platform for Collaboration on Tax* (World Bank 2018) 18 (acknowledging that '[m]ajor changes to tax-policy regimes are politically difficult, so it takes time to develop consensus among policy-makers.').

[52] Tarcisio Magalhaes, 'The OECD Multilateral Instrument: Challenge or Opportunity of Multilateralism?' in Johanna Wheeler (ed), *The Aftermath of BEPS* (IBFD 2020)(arguing that a Conference of the Parties could theoretically be used to promote any major changes to the international tax regime, including adopting methods or formulas that assign more revenue to low-income states).

[53] Li, 'Global Profit Split' (n 41) 838 ('A strong argument can be made that article 9 does not compel or plainly imply the required use of comparable pricing methodologies to the exclusion of formula-based methods. There is reported agreement among tax experts that the arm's length principle and formulary apportionment should not be viewed as polar extremes; rather, they should be viewed as part of a continuum of methods, ranging from CUP to predetermined formulas.').

[54] See, eg, Joann Weiner, 'Formulary Apportionment and Group Taxation in the European Union: Insights from the United States and Canada' (2005) European Commission Directorate General Taxation and Customs Union Working Paper No. 8.

institutions and processes for resolving uncertainty and disputes among states in the face of mismatched interpretations among states, namely in the form of treaty-based mutual agreement procedures.

For these reasons, we conclude that the proposals we have described above are both technically and politically feasible to implement. That said, it is possible that a more radical departure from prevailing international tax norms and standards is warranted in the face of the enormous scale of subsistence rights deficits we see in the world today. If so, the approaches we have outlined above will ultimately be too modest for the task.

Conclusion

This book is called 'tax cooperation in an unjust world' because we have considered the implications of the existence of persistent and widespread subsistence rights deficits on what, on a plausible account of international justice, counts as fair cooperation in international taxation. This account of international justice is the society-of-states model of international justice, as defended most famously by John Rawls. Within the philosophical literature it is hardly universally accepted, but it has two specific features that make it an appealing theory for our purposes.

The first of these is that the society-of-states model appears to be the prevailing framework within which debates in legal scholarship and among policymakers concerning international tax cooperation are conducted today. In particular there appears a widespread acceptance of the idea that states have an entitlement to the wealth of their territory.

A good example of this tendency can be found in recent policy developments surrounding tax avoidance by highly visible multinational companies. In a multilateral effort to counter these practices, the OECD called for 'a realignment of taxation and relevant substance'[1] to restore the capacity of states to exercise their 'legitimate right to tax the profits of a taxpayer based upon income and expenses that can reasonably be considered to arise within their territory.'[2] The language of legitimacy, rights, and reasonableness invokes the concern that states are being deprived of something to which they are entitled, even if the line where one state's entitlement ends and another begins remains blurry in such phrasings.[3]

The sentiment is further, even if more obscurely, expressed in the compelling mantra that profits should be taxed 'where economic activities take place and value is created.'[4] In making these claims, the OECD seems to accept,

[1] OECD, *Addressing Base Erosion and Profit Shifting* (OECD Publishing 2015) 13.

[2] OECD, *OECD Transfer Pricing Guidelines for Multinational Enterprises and Tax Administrations* (OECD Publishing 2017) 15, 55.

[3] That is, the returns attributable to the productive use of local economic factors leave the state as earnings to the foreign investor, as described above.

[4] OECD, *Aligning Transfer Pricing Outcomes with Value Creation, Actions 8-10 - 2015 Final Reports* (OECD Publishing 2015) 3.

Tax Cooperation in an Unjust World. Allison Christians and Laurens van Apeldoorn, Oxford University Press. © Allison Christians and Laurens van Apeldoorn 2021. DOI: 10.1093/oso/9780192848673.003.0008

implicitly, the entitlement of states to the wealth in their territory, and perhaps even to a fair share of the benefits created by international tax cooperation. The society-of-states model of international justice accordingly displays a large measure of congruence with much of the existing debates on international tax reform, which should ensure that our arguments speak to the participants of those debates, even if not all will accept our conclusions.

Second, compared to many other positions in the philosophical literature on international justice, the society-of-states model has relatively conservative implications about the requirement of cross-border wealth redistribution. This is perhaps most clearly visible in its commitment to the entitlement principle: states have (barring certain exceptions) an unqualified entitlement to the wealth of their territory. Even in the face of significant global wealth inequality, proponents of the society of states model accept this entitlement as long as states are capable of securing for themselves (minimally) just domestic institutions. Under such conditions, states lack duties of justice to ameliorate inequality across borders. Rather, they by and large honour their duties of international justice merely by observing a policy of non-interference in relation to other states. In this book, we have aimed to show that the international tax system today is unjust and must be reformed even if one departs from such a conservative theory. Proponents of this theory will generally be reticent to consider the distributive effects of international institutions like the international tax system as we have done. Those holding more radical philosophical views concerning international justice will need less convincing in this regard.

Our argumentative strategy has thus been to show that a relatively conservative theory of international justice, and one that is widely accepted in academic and policy debates on international tax reform (even if implicitly), allows one to draw far-reaching conclusions regarding the need to reform the international tax system.

We have done so by first identifying two principles of justice applicable to tax cooperation—the equal benefit and entitlement principles—concerning the distribution of wealth between states that interact and cooperate in a globalized economy. These principles hold, in brief, that states are entitled to the wealth of their territory and that they must equally share in the (net) benefits of cooperation. Tax cooperation is part of a cooperative practice whereby states facilitate international capital mobility and investment with the aim of mutually pursuing welfare gains. International tax policy can both facilitate and hinder such potentially welfare-enhancing cross-border investment. It can facilitate such investment if the coordination of tax policy across states facilitates the efficient allocation of worldwide capital, in particular by preventing double (non-)taxation. It can hinder such investment if double taxation renders international investment prohibitively costly, or if double non-taxation incentivizes individuals or companies to invest in locations that do not give rise to overall welfare gains. If tax cooperation gives rise to a cooperative surplus, the equal benefit principle holds that it must be shared equally among the cooperating states.

We then examined the reasons why currently, cooperating states do not equally share in the benefits of cooperative surplus, pointing to tax competition and peer pressure as two main impediments to this goal. We demonstrated that states' entitlement to tax has long been thwarted by common tax practices that have been fostered and even encouraged by the world's most affluent states. We established that changing course requires these affluent states be first to alter their approach. Pointing to current shifts in tolerance for tax competition that have uniquely opened up the possibility of structural change for the first time in many decades, we made the case for tax reforms that would facilitate taxation in states that heretofore have been discouraged from doing so by competitive pressures and internationally accepted norms.

The important assumption in reaching this conclusion, however, is that states are, in fact, entitled to the wealth of their territory. States have a right to share equally in the benefits of cooperation only if the cooperative surplus is created by employing the national endowments to which they are entitled, as reflected in the entitlement principle. This assumption, we have argued, is false in the unjust world we find ourselves in today. The grim fact is that a vast number of people across the globe face subsistence rights deficits, a subsistence right being a moral right to secure clean air, food, water, clothing, shelter, basic healthcare, physical security, and the opportunity to provide for oneself the means to subsistence through work in favourable conditions. These are the basic needs that any person at the very minimum may demand the fulfilment of, allowing them a minimally adequate standard of living. Yet, many, perhaps as many as two billion, today see their subsistence rights unfulfilled. We have argued that this fact upends the entitlement principle and by extension the idea that any (net) benefits of tax cooperation should be shared equally among the cooperating states.

We have put the argument in terms of a duty relatively wealthy and well-ordered states have to assist in fulfilling those subsistence rights. This is a duty, we have argued, that almost certainly exists in relation to burdened states, that is, states that are incapable of adequately addressing the human rights deficits of their populations by themselves. It most likely also applies in relation to negligent states, that is, states that have the capacity, but because of political or other reasons nevertheless fail to guarantee the subsistence rights of their populations. We reach this conclusion by taking seriously the observation by Henry Shue, that subsistence rights are correlated with a complex set of duties, at least some of which concern the protection of individuals from the effects of potential non-compliance of others.[5] These duties, given the society-of-states model, fall primarily on states to create and uphold institutions that effectively protect the subsistence rights of all, including from threats to those rights by their own governments.

The duty of assistance overrides the claims states can make to the wealth of their territory on the basis of the entitlement principle. We put this position, which has important implications, in terms of the 'conditionality' of the entitlement principle: the applicability of the entitlement principle is conditional on states having honoured their duty of assistance. It depends on the truth of a moral and a factual claim. The moral claim is that the duty of assistance is a duty of justice (rather than a humanitarian duty). As a duty of justice, it is logically prior to the establishment of a just distribution of holdings between states. Or put differently, in so far as states fail to honour the duty of assistance and this duty requires they cede some of their wealth to another country, the relevant wealth cannot be said to be 'theirs' to begin with. It is rather, as Brian Barry puts it, as much the other country's 'as it is now normally thought that what a country produces belongs to that country.'[6] The plausibility of this moral claim is ultimately grounded in considering the stringency of the demands that individuals can make on others that their subsistence rights are fulfilled so that they can at least live a minimally decent life.

The factual claim is that the duty of assistance can and must indeed be honoured by redistributing wealth to the burdened or negligent states in question. It is almost certainly false to say that a transfer of wealth is by itself sufficient to address subsistence rights deficits. The quality of domestic socio-economic and political institutions as well as the 'political culture, the political virtues and civic society of the country,' as Rawls already realized, have significant causal effects when it comes to the effectiveness of any wealth transfer.[7] However, we have suggested that it is most probably equally false to think that subsistence rights deficits can be addressed without making any additional resources available to struggling societies. In support of this contention, we have cited the

[5] Henry Shue, *Basic Rights* (2nd edn, Princeton University Press 1996) 62.

[6] Brian Barry, 'Humanity and Justice in Global Perspective' in J Roland Pennock and John W Chapman (eds), *Ethics, Economics, and the Law* (New York University Press 1982) 248.

[7] John Rawls, *The Law of Peoples, with The Idea of Public Reason Revisited* (Harvard University Press 1999) 108.

many international organizations such as the IMF and the World Bank that worry about the public financing gaps faced by governments in many low-income states, not least in the context of the Sustainable Development Goals.

The truth of this argument significantly affects what counts as fair cooperation in international taxation. Since the equal benefit principle is premised on the entitlement principle, and the applicability of the entitlement principle is conditional on states having honoured their duty of assistance, the duty of assistance takes precedence in determining how the international tax system should be fairly organized. We have suggested that this can be achieved by making room for taxation in the states in which subsistence deficits arise. This can be achieved through a number of policy instruments, of which we highlight two main choices. The first of these is expanding pass-through taxation of multinational income by capital-exporting states, which would allow for greater tax at source by raising the expected minimum tax level sought by multinationals from its current rate of zero to a positive minimum rate. The second of these is expanding the tolerance of capital-exporting states to source-based taxation through prevailing tax standards, in particular those related to withholding taxes on cash flows paid to foreign investors and those found in arm's length transfer pricing and related profit allocation regimes. We see precedents for both approaches in current law and think that contemporary trends point toward increasing acceptance for these and related approaches to increasing taxation at source.

We submit that these international tax policy reforms are feasible and required as a matter of justice if one accepts the society-of-states model of international justice. However, we realize that not all readers may be convinced of the existence of a duty of assistance (or the gloss we have put on it). They could deny it is a duty of justice, such that it does not affect the entitlements of states, even if they act in a morally blameworthy fashion insofar as they fail to honour this duty. Or they could question the efficacy of international tax reforms that result in an increased tax capacity for low-income states with populations facing human rights deficits, in the absence of other forms of capacity building and development support.

This is why we also consider the implications of the extant subsistence rights deficits in the application of the two principles of tax cooperation identified in the first chapter, if one denies the existence of a duty of assistance or if one denies the duty can be discharged by making available additional financing to burdened or negligent states. This argument is based on accepting the reality of the economic (not moral) costs of these subsistence rights deficits in determining what counts as an equal share of the benefits of tax cooperation. The economic costs of subsistence rights deficits can be understood as the price of rectifying or preventing them. International capital mobility and investment, facilitated by international tax cooperation, potentially leads to welfare gains that must be shared fairly between the cooperating states. We have argued that in calculating the (net) benefits of cooperation, the costs of subsistence rights deficits that are implicated in the production of those benefits should be counted, and the states where these costs are borne should be compensated.

This argument is compelling for subsistence rights deficits that are caused by the economic activities that result from the capital investment, in the sense that these deficits would not have occurred had the investment not taken place. If domestic factors had been employed in domestic production, these particular subsistence rights deficits would not have occurred, so in this respect the state has been made worse off as the result of cooperation. These subsistence rights deficits therefore clearly include costs that should be priced and included in the determination of the (net) benefits of cooperation. The case is perhaps less compelling for pre-existing subsistence rights deficits that are implicated in, but not caused by, cross-border investment and production. Although these subsistence rights deficits are not caused by cooperation (they would also have occurred if states had not cooperated) they should nevertheless be considered costs of cooperation for the following reason: in the absence of doing so, (some) of the benefits in the form of cost savings will be allocated to the other cooperating states, such that they would benefit from the existing subsistence rights deficits abroad. We submit that states lack the right to benefit in this way from injustices.

For these reasons, the costs of rectifying existing human rights deficits that are both caused and implicated in cross-border investment and production ought to be included in the assessment of what constitutes a fair division of the benefits and burdens of coordination. Injustices implicated in international investment should be conceived as burdens of cooperation which implies that the state in question must be compensated for those harms before the remaining (or surplus) benefits are allocated between the cooperating states.

In international tax policy, it is possible to account for these costs. The framework already exists in the transfer pricing and profit allocation regimes explored earlier in the context of making room for greater taxation at source. In particular, advancements in economic analysis of the externalized costs of human and environmental exploitation provide the means to more completely account for the true costs and benefits produced through cross-border cooperation so as to ensure a more accurate assessment of whether benefits are in fact equally shared. Again, we see precedent in contemporary legal frameworks as well as political momentum to implement the kinds of reforms we envision.

This book ends with an urgent call for action. It is unjust for those in relatively affluent states to remain complacent in the face of suffering from which we financially benefit. It is egregiously unjust for us to continue to demand a share of the benefits of international cooperation while denying the same to others because they lack the ability to influence the international institutions that embrace and enforce our unjustified claims while ignoring theirs. The need for urgency is only confirmed, and the means for action furthered, by the ongoing efforts of the international community to redefine the international tax system to achieve more fairness among states. A reckoning with the parameters and implications of the equal benefit and entitlement principles must be seen as an urgent priority in this process, lest the mistakes of the past continue into the future.

Cases

Lewenhaupt v Commissioner, 20 T.C. 151, 163 (1953), aff'd, 221 F.2d 227, 227 (9th Cir. 1954).

Eli Lilly & Co. v Commissioner [1985] 84 TC 996, aff'd in part, rev'd in part and remanded, 856 F.2d 855 (7th Cir. 1988).

Sundstrand Corp v Commissioner [1991] 96 TC 226.

National Semiconductor Corporation v Commissioner [1994] 67 TCM 2849.

Bibliography

B. Aebischer and L.M. Hilty, 'The Energy Demand of ICT: A Historical Perspective and Current Methodological Challenges' in L.M. Hilty and B. Aebischer (eds), *Advances in Intelligent Systems and Computing: Vol. 310. ICT Innovations for Sustainability* (Springer 2015) 71–103. https://doi.org/10.1007/978-3-319-09228-7_4.

Manuel Agosin and Roberto Machado, 'Foreign Investment in Developing Countries: Does It Crowd in Domestic Investment?' [2005] 33(2) Oxford Dev Stud 149.

A. Agúndez-García, 'The Delineation and Apportionment of an EU Consolidated Tax Base for Multi-jurisdictional Corporate Income Taxation: A Review of Issues and Options' [2006] European Commission Taxation Papers No. 9/06.

M. Rabiul Ahasan and Timo Partanen, 'Occupational Health and Safety in the Least Developed Countries—A Simple Case of Neglect' [2001] 11(2) J Epidemiol 74–80.

Ehtisham Ahmad and Nicholas Stern, 'Taxation for Developing Countries' in Hollis Chenery and T. N. Srinivasan (eds), *Handbook of Development Economics* (Vol. 2, Elsevier 1989), 1005–92.

Bernardin Akitoby et al., 'Tax Revenue Mobilization Episodes in Emerging Markets and Low-Income Countries: Lessons from a New Dataset' [2018] International Monetary Fund 7.

Fathi Ali, Norbert Fiess, and Ronald MacDonald, 'Climbing to the Top? Foreign Direct Investment and Property Rights' [2011] 49(1) Econ Inquiry 289.

Laura Alfaro, Chanda Areendam, Sebnem Kalemli-Ozcan, and Selin Sayek, 'FDI and Economic Growth: The Role of Financial Markets' [2000] Harvard Business School Working Paper 01-083.

Sabina Alkire and James Foster, 'Counting and Multidimensional Poverty Measurement' [2011] 95(7–8) J Pub Econ 476.

Philip Alston, 'The Parlous State of Poverty Eradication' Report of the UN Special Rapporteur on Extreme Poverty and Human Rights, A/HRC/44/40 (United Nations, 2 July 2020).

Rosanne Altshuler and Harry Grubert, 'The Three Parties in the Race to the Bottom: Host Governments, Home Governments and Multinational Companies' [2005] 7 Fla Tax Rev 137.

Sharath Kumar Ankathi et al., 'Life Cycle Assessment of Oilseed Crops Produced in Rotation with Dryland Cereals in the Inland Pacific Northwest' [2019] 24 Int'l J Life Cycle Assess 627.

Richard Anker 'Estimating a Living Wage: A Methodological Review' [2011] Conditions of Work and Employment Series No. 29 <https://ideas.repec.org/p/ilo/ilowps/994663133402676.html> accessed 31 August 2020.

Robert Anker and Martha Anker, 'A Shared Approach to Estimating Living Wages: Short Description of Agreed Methodology' (Global Living Wage Coalition 2013).

Robert Anker and Martha Anker, *Living Wages Around the World: Manual for Measurement* (Edward Elgar Publishing 2017).

Alireza Anvari et al., 'A Study on Total Quality Management and Lean Manufacturing: Through Lean Thinking Approach' [2011] 12(9) World Appl Sci J 1585.

Laurens van Apeldoorn, 'BEPS, Tax Sovereignty and Global Justice' [2018] 21(4) Crit Rev Int'l Soc & Pol Phil 478.

Laurens van Apeldoorn, 'A Sceptic's Guide to Justice in International Tax Policy' [2019] 32(2) Can J L & Juris 499–512.

Rachel Arthur, 'The Future of Fashion: 10 Wearable Tech Brands You Need to Know' Forbes, 30 June 2016.

Festud Aukonobera, 'Uganda' in M. Lang, Pasquale Pistone, and Josef Schuch (eds), *The Impact of the OECD and UN Model Conventions on Bilateral Tax Treaties* (Cambridge University Press 2012).

Alan J. Auerbach, 'Measuring the Impact of Tax Reform' [1996] 49(4) Nat'l J Tax Reform 665.

John Avery Jones, 'The Effect of Changes in the OECD Commentaries after a Treaty is Concluded' [2002] 56(3) Bull Int'l Fisc Doc.

Reuven S. Avi-Yonah, 'Corporate Taxation and Corporate Social Responsibility' [2014] 11(1) NYU J L Bus 1.

Reuven S. Avi-Yonah, 'U.S. Notice 98-11 and the Logic of Subpart F: A Comparative Perspective' [8 June 1998] 16 Tax Notes Int'l 1797–801.

Reuven Avi-Yonah, *International Tax as International Law: An Analysis of the International Tax Regime* (Cambridge University Press 2007).

Reuven S. Avi-Yonah, 'The Great Recession and the International Tax Regime' Kluwer International Tax Blog, 23 April 2019, <http://kluwertaxblog.com/2019/04/23/the-great-recession-and-the-international-tax-regime/> accessed 31 August 2020.

R.S. Avi-Yonah and K.A. Clausing, 'Reforming Corporate Taxation in a Global Economy: A Proposal to Adopt Formulary Apportionment' Brookings Discussion Paper, 2007–08.

R. Avi-Yonah, K. Clausing and M. Durst, 'Allocating Business Profits for Tax Purposes: A Proposal to Adopt a Formulary Profit Split' [2009] 9(5) Fla Tax Rev 497.

Eduardo Baistrocchi, 'The Transfer Pricing Problem: A Global Proposal for Simplification' [2006] 59(4) Tax Law 941–80.

Vudayagi Balasubramanyam, Mohammed Salisu, and David Sapsford, 'Foreign Direct Investment as an Engine of Growth' [1999] 8(1) J Int'l Trade & Econ Dev 27 <https://www.tandfonline.com/doi/abs/10.1080/09638199900000003> accessed 31 August 2020.

E Baldacci, B. Clements, S. Gupta, and Q. Cui, 'Social Spending, Human Capital, and Growth in Developing Countries: Implications for Achieving the MDGs' [2004] IMF Working Paper WP/04/217 <www.imf.org/en/Publications/WP/Issues/2016/12/31/Social-Spending-Human-Capital-and-Growth-in-Developing-Countries-Implications-for-Achieving-17781> accessed 31 August 2020.

Steven Bank, 'A Capital Lock-In Theory of the Corporate Income Tax' [2006] 94(4) Geo L J.

Brian Barry, 'Humanity and Justice in Global Perspective' in J. Roland Pennock and John W. Chapman (eds), *Ethics, Economics, and the Law* (New York University Press 1982) 219–52.

E.J. Bartelsman and R.M.W.J. Beetsma, 'Why Pay More? Corporate Tax Avoidance Through Transfer Pricing in OECD Countries' [2003] 87(9–10) J Pub Econ 2225.

Juan Angel Becerra, 'Interpretation and Application of Tax Treaties in North America' (IBFD 2007).

David Beetham, 'What Future for Economic and Social Rights?' [1995] 43(1) Pol Stud 41–60.

Charles Beitz, *Political Theory and International Relations* (Princeton University Press 1999).

Maria De Beneto, 'Corruption and Controls' [2015] 17(4) Eur J L Reform 479.

Curtis Berger, 'W(h)ither Partnership Taxation?' [1991] 47(1) Tax L Rev 105–72.

Timothy Besley and Torsten Person, 'Why Do Developing Countries Tax So Little?' [2014] 28(4) J Econ Perspectives 112.

Jagdish Bhagwati, 'The Capital Myth: The Difference Between Trade in Widgets and Dollars' [1998] 77(3) Foreign Aff 7.

Nancy Birdsall, 'Who You Callin' Middle Class: A Plea to the Development Community' Center for Global Development 18 April 2014 <https://www.cgdev.org/blog/who-you-callin%E2%80%99-middle-class-plea-development-community>.

Magnus Blomstrom and Ari Kokko, 'Multinational Corporations and Spillovers' [1994] 12(3) J Econ Surv 247–77.

D. Bloom and D. Canning 'Population Health and Economic Growth' World Bank Working Paper 47588 <http://documents.worldbank.org/curated/en/599491468151504321/Population-health-and-economic-growth> accessed 31 August 2020.

Eduardo R. Borenzstein, Jose De Gregorio, and Jong-Wha Lee, 'How Does Foreign Direct Investment Affect Growth?' [1998] 45(1) J Int'l Econ 115–35.

S.C. Borkowski, 'The Transfer Pricing Concerns of Developed and Developing Countries' [1997] 32(3) Int'l J Acctng 321.

Dorine Boumans et al., 'Expected Effects of the US Tax Reform on Other Countries: Global and Local Survey Evidence' [2019] CESIfo Working Paper No. 7491.

Yariv Brauner, 'An International Tax Regime in Crystallization' [2003] 56 Tax L Rev 259.

Yariv Brauner, 'Value in the Eye of the Beholder: The Valuation of Intangibles for Transfer Pricing Purposes' [2008] 28 Virg Tax Rev 83.

Yariv Brauner and Allison Christians, 'U.S. Report' in Guglielmo Maisto (ed.), The Meaning of 'Enterprise,' 'Business,' and 'Business Profits' under Tax Treaties and EU Tax Law (IBFD 2011) 575–610.

C. Briceño-Garmendia, A. Estache, and N. Shafik, 'Infrastructure Services in Developing Countries: Access, Quality, Costs and Policy Reform' [2004] World Bank Policy Research Working Paper 3468, 5 <http://documents.worldbank.org/curated/en/476891468782346365/Infrastructure-services-in-developing-countries-access-quality-costs-and-policy-reform> accessed 31 August 2020.

Bernard Brody, Yves Letourneau, and Andre Poirier, 'An Indirect Cost Theory of Work Accident Prevention' [1990] 13(4) J Occ Acc 255–70.

Kim Brooks, 'Canada's Evolving Tax Treaty Policy Toward Low-Income Countries' in Arthur Cockfield (ed.), *Globalization and Its Tax Discontents: Tax Policy and International Investments* (University of Toronto Press 2010) 189–211.

Catherine A. Brown, 'Taxation and the Cross-Border Trade in Services: Rethinking Non-Discrimination Obligations' [2018] 21(2) Fla Tax Rev 715–61.

Georgeta Buica et al., 'Occupational Health and Safety Management in Construction Sector—The Cost of Work Accidents' [2017] 18(S1) Calitatea 35.

Chloe Burnett, 'International Tax Arbitration' [2007] 36 Austr Tax Rev 273.

Daniel Butt, 'On Benefiting from Injustice' [2007] 37(1) Can J Phil 129.

M. Calderón Carrero, 'The OECD Transfer Pricing Guidelines as a Source of Tax Law: Is Globalization Reaching the Tax Law?' [2007] 35(1) Intertax 4.

C. Calderón and L. Servén, 'The Effects of Infrastructure Development on Growth and Income Distribution' [2004] Policy Research Working Paper Series no. 3400, 26. <https://papers.ssrn.com/sol3/papers.cfm?abstract_id=625277> accessed 31 August 2020.

Canada, *Royal Commission on Taxation, Report* (Queen's Printer 1966).

Richard Caves, Multinational Enterprises and Economic Analysis (Cambridge University Press 1982).

Elias Charles, et al., 'A Cross-Sectional Survey on Knowledge and Perceptions of Health Risks Associated with Arsenic and Mercury Contamination from Artisanal Gold Mining in Tanzania' [2013] 13(1) BMC Pub Health.

Richard Chisik and Ronald Davies, 'Asymmetric FDI and Tax-Treaty Bargaining: Theory and Evidence' [2004] 88(6) J Pub Econ 1119.

Allison Christians, 'Tax Treaties for Investment and Aid to Sub-Saharan Africa: A Case Study' [2006] 71(2) Brook L Rev 639.

Allison Christians, 'Hard Law and Soft Law in International Taxation' [2007] 25 Wisc J Int'l L 325.

Allison Christians, 'Networks, Norms, and National Tax Policy' [2010] 9 Wash U Glob Stud L Rev 1–37.

Allison Christians, 'Global Trends and Constraints on Tax Policy in the Least Developed Countries' [2010] 42(2) UBC L Rev 239.

Allison Christians, 'How Nations Share' [2012] 87 Indiana L J 1407.

Allison Christians, 'Drawing the Boundaries of Tax Justice' in Kim Brooks (ed.), *The Quest for Tax Reform Continues: The Royal Commission on Taxation Fifty Years Later* (Carswell 2013) 53–79.

Allison Christians, 'Reversal of Fortune: Did PPL Corporation Get a Foreign Tax Credit from the Wrong Government?' [2013] Lexis Fed Tax J Q 1.

Allison Christians, 'What the Baucus Plan Reveals About Tax Competition' [December 2013] Tax Notes Int'l 72.

Allison Christians, 'BEPS and the New International Tax Order' [2016] 1 BYU L Rev 603.

Allison Christians and Stephen Shay, *Assessing BEPS: Origins, Standards and Responses* (Int'l Fisc. Assoc. Cahier 102A, 2017).

Allison Christians and Laurens van Apeldoorn, 'Taxing Income Where Value is Created' [2018] 22(1) Fla Tax Rev 1.

Kerwin Chung and Richard McAlonan, 'Competently Negotiating the U.S. Competent Authority Process' [2007] 59 Tax Exec.

Jennifer Clapp, *Toxic Exports: The Transfer of Hazardous Wastes from Rich to Poor Countries* (Cornell University Press 2001).

A. Cobham and D. McNair, 'The Role of Rich Countries in Development: The Case for Reforms' in T. Hopper, M. Tsamenyi, S. Uddin, and D. Wickramasinghe (eds), *Handbook of Accounting and Development* (Edward Elgar 2012) 125–48.

B. Arthur Cockfield, 'The Rise of the OECD as Informal 'World Tax Organization' Through National Responses to E-Commerce Tax Challenges' [2006] 9 Yale J L & Tech 59.

Paul Cordy, et al. 'Characterization, Mapping, and Mitigation of Mercury Vapour Emissions From Artisanal Mining Gold Shops' [2013] Envtl Res 125.

Robert Couzin, 'The OECD Project: Transfer Pricing Meets Permanent Establishment' [2005] 53(2) Can Tax J 401–8.

Ernesto Crivelli, Ruud De Mooij, and Michael Keen, 'Base Erosion, Profit Shifting and Developing Countries' [2015] IMF Working Paper WP/15/118.

Tsilly Dagan, 'The Tax Treaties Myth' [2000] 32 J Int'l L & Pol 939.

Tsilly Dagan, *International Tax Policy: Between Competition and Cooperation* (Cambridge University Press 2018).

Bev Dahlby, 'Globalization and the Future of the Corporate Income Tax' [2002] ATAX Discussion Paper #9, <http://ideas.repec.org/p/nsw/discus/09.html> accessed 31 August 2020.

Philip Daniel and Victor Thuronyi, 'International Tax and Treaty Strategy in Resource-Rich Developing Countries: Experience and Approaches' in Philip Daniel et al. (eds), *International Taxation and the Extractive Industries* (Routledge 2016) 111–32.

Susmita Dasgupta et al., 'Environmental Regulation and Development: A Cross-Country Empirical Analysis' [2001] 29(2) Oxford Dev Stud 173.

Veronika Daurer, 'Tax Treaties and Developing Countries' [2014] 42 (11) Intertax 695–701.

Bruce F. Davie and Bruce F. Duncombe, *Public Finance* (Holt, Rinehart and Winston 1972).

Steven Dean, 'A Constitutional Moment in Cross-Border Taxation' (Working Paper 2020).

Michael P. Devereux and Rachel Griffith, 'Evaluating Tax Policy for Location Decisions' [2003] 10 Int'l Tax & Pub Fin 107.

Peter Dietsch, *Catching Capital: The Ethics of Tax Competition* (Oxford University Press 2015).

Peter Dietsch and Thomas Rixen, 'In Defense of Fiscal Autonomy: A Reply to Risse and Meyer' [2019] 27(4) J Pol Phil 3.

Matthias Dischinger and Nadine Riedel, 'Corporate Taxes and the Location of Intangible Assets within Multinational Firms' [2011] 95(7–8) J Pub Econ 691, 691.

E. Merrick Dodd, Jr., 'For Whom are Corporate Managers Trustees?' [1932] 45 Harv L Rev.

D. Dollar and A. Kraay, 'Growth Is Good for the Poor' [2002] 7 J Econ Growth 195, 219.

D. Dollar, T. Kleineberg, and A. Kraay 'Growth, Inequality, and Social Welfare: Cross-Country Evidence' [2016] World Bank Policy Research Working Paper No. 6842.

Michael Durst, 'Limitations of the BEPS Reforms: Looking Beyond Corporate Taxation for Revenue Gains' [2015] ICTD Working Paper.

Amitava Dutt, 'Direct Foreign Investment, Transnational Corporations and Growth: Some Empirical Evidence and a North–South Model' in Richard Kozul-Wright and Robert Rowthorn (eds), *Transnational Corporations and the Global Economy* (MacMillan Press 1998) 164–91.

Myriam M. Elenge and Christophe De Brouwer, 'Identification of Hazards in the Workplaces of Artisanal Mining in Katanga' [2011] 24(1) Int'l J Occ Med & Env Health 57–66.

Diane Elson and Ruth Pearson, 'Nimble Fingers Make Cheap Workers: An Analysis of Women's Employment in Third World Export Manufacturing' [Spring 1981] 7 Fem Rev 87–107.

M. Shahe Emran and Joseph E. Stiglitz, 'On Selective Indirect Tax Reform in Developing Countries' [2005] 89(4) J Pub Econ 599.

Frank Engelen, 'Some Observations on the Legal Status of the Commentaries on the OECD Model' [2006] 60(3) IBFD Bull 105.

Joachim Englisch and Johannes Becker, 'International Effective Minimum Taxation—The GLOBE Proposal' [2019] 11(4) World Tax J 623–80.

G. Eskeland and A. Harrison, 'Moving to Greener Pastures? Multinationals and the Pollution-Haven Hypothesis' [1997] World Bank Policy Research Department Working Paper No. 174.

Carl Estes, 'Tax Treaties' [1980] 14(3) Int'l Law.

European Commission, 'Transfer Pricing and Developing Countries Final Report' [2011] Euro Comm 9.

Donna Everatt, Terence Tsai, and Bor-shiuan Cheng, *The Acer Group's China Manufacturing Decisions*, Ivey Case Series #9A99M009 (Richard Ivey School of Business, University of Western Ontario 1999).

Alexander Ezenagu, 'Faltering Blocks in the Arguments against Unitary Taxation and the Formulary Apportionment Approach to Income Allocation' [2017] 17 Asper Int'l Bus & Trade L 131–62.

Fair Labor Association, 'Toward Fair Compensation in Global Supply Chains' (Business & Human Rights Gateway 2016).

Tatiana Falcao and Bob Michel, 'Scope and Interpretation of Article 12A: Assessing the Impact of the New Fees for Technical Services Article' [2018] no. 4 Brit Tax Rev 422–40.

Colin Farrelly, 'Taxation and Distributive Justice' [2004] 2 Pol Stud Rev 185.

Colin Farrelly, *Justice, Democracy and Reasonable Agreement* (Palgrave Macmillan 2007).

Fava et al. (eds), *SETAC Workshop Report, A Conceptual Framework for Life Cycle Impact Assessment* (SETAC Press 1993).

William M. Feld, *Lean Manufacturing: Tools, Techniques, and How to Use Them* (CRC Press 2000).

Jonathan Finer, 'World Bank Focused on Fighting Corruption: Graft and Bribery, Once Tolerated, Punished by Blacklisting' Washington Post (4 July 2003).

Nir Fishbien, 'From Switzerland with Love: Surrey's Papers and the Original Intent(s) of Subpart-F' [2018] 38(1) Va Tax Rev.

Valpy Fitzgerald and Tommaso Faccio, 'Sharing the Corporate Tax Base: Equitable Taxing of Multinationals and the Choice of Formulary Apportionment' [2018] 25(2) Transnat'l Corp 67.

Odd-Helge Fjeldstad and Lise Rakner, 'Taxation and Tax Reforms in Developing Countries: Illustrations from Sub-Saharan Africa' (CMI Report 2003: 6).

Clifton Fleming, Robert Peroni, and Stephen Shay, 'Getting Serious about Cross-Border Earnings Stripping: Establishing an Analytical Framework' [2015] 93 N Car L Rev 673.

J. Franze and A. Ciroth 'A Comparison of Cut Roses from Ecuador and the Netherlands' [2011] 16 Int'l J Life Cycle Assess 366–79.

Samuel Freeman, 'Distributive Justice and The Law of Peoples' in Rex Martin and David A. Reidy (eds), *Rawls's Law of Peoples: A Realistic Utopia?* (Blackwell 2006) 243–60.

C. Fuest, T. Hemmelgarn, and F. Ramb, 'How Would the Introduction of an EU-wide Formula Apportionment Affect the Distribution and Size of the Corporate Tax Base? An Analysis Based on German Multinationals' [2007] 14 Int'l Tax & Pub Fin 605.

Clements Fuest et al., 'Profit Shifting and "Aggressive" Tax Planning by Multinational Firms: Issues and Options for Reform' [2013], Discussion Paper No. 13-078, Mannheim: Centre for Economic Research.

Elaine Fultz and Bodhi Pieris, 'Compensation for Employment Injuries in Southern Africa: An Overview of Schemes and Proposals for Reform' [1999] 138(2) Int'l Lab Rev.

William G. Gale and Andrew A. Samwick, 'Effects of Income Tax Changes on Economic Growth' [2016] Brookings <www.brookings.edu>.

Steffen Ganghof, *The Politics of Income Taxation: A Comparative Analysis of Advanced Industrial Countries* (ECPR Press 2006).

Vitor Gaspar et al., 'Fiscal Policy and Development: Human, Social, and Physical Investment for the SDGs' [2019] IMF Staff Discussion Note, SDN/19/03, 9 <www.imf.org/en/Publications/Staff-Discussion-Notes/Issues/2019/01/18/Fiscal-Policy-and-Development-Human-Social-and-Physical-Investments-for-the-SDGs-46444> accessed 31 August 2020.

Philipp Genschel, 'Globalization, Tax Competition and the Welfare State' [2002] 30(2) Pol & Soc 245–75.

Global Living Wage Coalition, 'Living Wage Report: Urban Vietnam' (Global Living Wage Coalition 2016).

Global Living Wage Coalition, 'Living Wage Report: Rural Vietnam' (Global Living Wage Coalition 2017).

Honey Lynn Goldberg, 'Conventions for the Elimination of International Double Taxation: Toward A Developing Country Model' [1983] 15 L Pol'y Int'l Bus 833.

Ian Goldin, 'Will AI Kill Developing World Growth?' BBC News (18 April 2019).
Robert E. Goodin and Christian Barry, 'Benefiting from the Wrongdoing of Others' [2014] 31(4) J Applied Phil 363.
Robert A. Green, 'The Troubled Rule of Nondiscrimination in Taxing Foreign Direct Investment' [1994] 26 L & Pol'y Int'l Bus 113–64.
James Griffin, *On Human Rights* (Oxford University Press 2008).
Dominique Guellec and Bruno van Pottelsberghe, 'Applications, Grants and the Value of Patent' [2000] 69(1) Econ Letters 109.
Sylvain Guignot et al., 'Recycling Construction and Demolition Wastes as Building Materials: A Life Cycle Assessment' [2020] 19(6) J Ind Ecol 1030.
Robert M. Haig, 'The Concept of Income-Economic and Legal Aspects', in the Federal Income Tax 1, 7 (Robert M. Haig ed., 1921), reprinted in Richard A. Musgrave and Carl S. Shoup (eds), [1959] 54 Am Econ Ass'n., Readings in the Economics of Taxation.
Robert Hall and Chad Jones, 'Why Do Some Countries Produce So Much More Output Per Worker Than Others?' [1999] 114(1) Q J Econ 83.
Terence C. Halliday and Gregory Shaffer, 'Introduction' in *Transnational Legal Orders* (Cambridge University 2015) 3–72.
D.-H. Han, M.S. Park, 'Survey of Awareness about Hazardous Chemicals of Residents Living Near Chemical Plants in South Korea' [2018] 56 Ind Health.
Ann Harrison and Andrés Rodríguez-Clare, 'Trade, Foreign Investment, and Industrial Policy for Developing Countries' in Dani Rodrick and Mark R. Rosenzweig (eds), *Handbook of Development Economics* (Vol. 5, Elsevier 2010) 4039–214.
Bashshar Haydar and Gerard Øverland, 'The Normative Implications of Benefiting from Injustice' [2014] 31(4) J Applied Phil 349.
Martin Hearson, 'When Do Developing Countries Negotiate Away Their Corporate Tax Base?' [2018] 30(2) J Int'l Dev 233–55.
Martin Hearson, 'Transnational Expertise and the Expansion of the International Tax Regime: Imposing 'Acceptable' Standards' [2018] 25(5) Rev Int'l Pol Econ 1.
Martin Hearson and Jalia Kangave, 'A Review of Uganda's Tax Treaties and Recommendations for Action' Institute of Development Studies International Centre for Tax and Development Working Paper No. 50 (2016).
Martin Hearson and Wilson Prichard, 'China's Challenge to International Tax Rules and the Implications for Global Economic Governance' [2018] 94(6) Int'l Aff 1287–307.
Dierk Herzer, 'How Does Foreign Direct Investment Really Affect Developing Countries' Growth?' [2012] 20(2) Rev Int'l Econ 396–414.
Jason Hickel, 'Bill Gates Says Poverty Is Decreasing. He Couldn't Be More Wrong' The Guardian (29 January 2019).
Stephen Holmes and Cass R. Sunstein, *The Cost of Rights: Why Liberty Depends on Taxes* (Nova Iorque, W. W. Norton & Company 1999).
IMF, *Rwanda: Letter of Intent, Memorandum of Economic and Financial Policies, and Technical Memorandum of Understanding* (IMF 2005).
IMF, 'Building Fiscal Capacity in Fragile States' [2017] International Monetary Fund.
IMF, *Tax Certainty: IMF/OECD Report for the G20 Finance Ministers* (OECD 2017).
IMF, '*World Economic Outlook, April 2018, Cyclical Upswing, Structural Change* (2018).
International Labour Organization, 'Estimating the Economic Costs of Occupational Injuries and Illnesses in Developing Countries: Essential Information for Decision-Makers' (International Labour Office 2012).
International Labour Organization, *World Employment Social Outlook: Trends 2017* (International Labour Office 2017).

International Organization for Standardization, Environmental Management: Life Cycle Assessment; Principles and Framework (2nd edn, ISO 2006).

R. Itten, Hischier, R., A.S.G. Andrae, et al., 'Digital Transformation—Life Cycle Assessment of Digital Services, Multifunctional Devices and Cloud Computing.' [2020] 25(10) Int'l J Life Cycle Assess 2093–98.

Robert F. Jacobs, 'Enterprise Resource Planning (ERP): A Brief History' [2007] 25(2) J Operations Mgmt 357.

Aaron James, *Fairness in Practice: A Social Contract for a Global Economy* (Oxford University Press 2012).

Aaron James, 'A Theory of Fairness in Trade' [2014] 1(2) Moral Phil & Pol.

Aaron James, 'Fairness in Trade' in David Held and Pietro Maffettone (eds), *Global Political Theory Today* (Polity Press 2016) 213–35.

Beata Smarzynska Javorcik and Shang-Jin Wei, 'Pollution Havens and Foreign Direct Investment: Dirty Secret or Popular Myth?' [2004] 3(2) Contrib Econ Anal & Pol'y 21.

Sunita Jogarajan, 'The Conclusion and Termination of the 'First' Double Taxation Treaty' [2012] 3 Brit Tax Rev 283–306.

Sunita Jogarajan, *Double Taxation and the League of Nations* (Cambridge 2018).

Michael Johnston, 'Why do so Many Anti-Corruption Efforts Fail?' [2012] 67(3) NYU Ann Surv Am L 467.

Rita Kant, 'Textile Dyeing Industry an Environmental Hazard' [2012] 4(1) Nat Sci 22.

Nancy H. Kaufman, 'Fairness and the Taxation of International Income' [1998] 29(2) L & Pol'y Int'l Bus 145–203.

Michael Keen and Peter Mullins, 'International Corporate Taxation and the Extractive Industries: Principles, Practice, Problems' in Philip Daniel et al. (eds), *International Taxation and the Extractive Industries* (Routledge 2016) 11–41.

Michael Keen and Alejandro Simone, 'Is Tax Competition Harming Developing Countries More Than Developed?' [2004] 34(13) Tax Notes Int'l 1317.

Michael Keen and Alejandro Simone, 'Tax Policy in Developing Countries: Some Lessons from the 1990s, and Some Challenges Ahead' in Sanjeev Gupta, Benedict Clements and Gabriela Inchauste (eds), *Helping Countries Develop: The Role of Fiscal Policy* (International Monetary Fund 2004) 302.

Derek K Kellenberg, 'An Empirical Investigation of the Pollution Haven Effect With Strategic Environment and Trade Policy' [2009] 78(2) J Int'l Econ 243.

Oulavanh Keovilignavong and Diana Suhardiman, 'Characterizing Private Investments and Implications for Poverty Reduction and Natural Resource Management in Laos' [2018] 36 Dev Pol'y Rev 341.

M.E. Khan et al., 'Living Wage Report: Dhaka, Bangladesh and Satellite Cities' (Global Living Wage Coalition 2016).

Michael S. Kirsch, 'The Limits of Administrative Guidance in the Interpretation of Tax Treaties' [2009] 87(6) Texas L Rev 1064.

William Klein, 'Income Taxation and Legal Entities' [1972] 20 UCLA L Rev 13, 43.

Walter Klöpffer and Birgit Grahl, *Life Cycle Assessment (LCA): A Guide to Best Practice* (Wiley 2014).

Pierre Kohler, 'Redistributive Policies for Sustainable Development: Looking at the Role of Assets and Equity' [2015] Department of Economic & Social Affairs Working Paper ST/ESA/2015/DWP/139, 8 <www.un.org/development/desa/publications/working-paper/redistributive-policies-for-sustainable-development> accessed 31 August 2020.

Svetislav Kostic, 'In Search of the Digital Nomad: Rethinking the Taxation of Employment Income Under Tax Treaties' [2019] 11(2) World Tax J 189–225.

Nicholas Kristof, 'Where Sweatshops are a Dream' New York Times, 14 January 2009.
Paul Krugman, 'In Praise of Cheap Labor: Bad jobs at Bad Wages Are Better Than No Jobs at All' *Slate*, 21 March 1997.
Chuck C Y Kwok and Solomon Tadesse, 'The MNC as an Agent of Change for Host-Country Institutions: FDI and Corruption' [2006] 37(6) J Int'l Bus Stud 767.
Rebecca M. Kysar, 'Interpreting Tax Treaties' [2015] 101 Iowa L Rev 1387.
Joseph LaDou, 'International Occupational Health' [2003] 206(4–5) Int'l J Hyg & Envtl Health 303.
David Landes, *The Wealth and Poverty of Nations: Why Some are So Rich and Some So Poor* (W.W. Norton & Company 1998).
Philip J. Landrigan et al., 'The Lancet Commission on Pollution and Health' [2017] 391(10119) Lancet Comm 462.
Toma Lankauskienė and Manuela Tvaronavičienė, 'Interrelation of Countries' Developmental Level and Foreign Direct Investments Performance' [2011] 12(3) J Bus Econ & Mgmt 546.
Allan Lanthier, 'The Taxation of Foreign Affiliates' [1995] 43(5) Can Tax J 1603–28.
Michael Lennard, 'Update on the United Nations Tax Committee Developments' [2014] 20(1) Asia-Pac Tax Bull 20.
Michael Lennard, 'Act of Creation: the OECD/G20 Test of "Value Creation" as a Basis for Taxing Rights and Its Relevance to Developing Countries' [2018] 25 Transnat'l Corp 55.
Jinyan Li, 'Global Profit Split: An Evolutionary Approach to International Income Allocation' [2002] 50(3) Can Tax J 823–33.
Jinyan Li, 'Location-Specific Advantages: A Rising Disruptive Factor in Transfer Pricing' [2017] 71(5) BFIT 259.
Ulf Linderfalk and Maria Hilling, 'The Use of OECD Commentaries as Interpretative Aids—The Static/Ambulatory–Approaches Debate Considered from the Perspective of International Law' [2015] 1 Nordic Tax J 34.
John Locke, *Two Treatises of Government* (Cambridge University Press 1988).
Lawrence Lokken, 'What Is This Thing Called Source?' [2011] 37 Int'l Tax J 21.
Bart Los, Marcel P. Timmer, and Gaaitzen J. de Vries, 'How Global Are Global Value Chains? A New Approach to Measure International Fragmentation' [2015] 55(1) J Reg Sci 66–92.
Susan Lund et al., *Globalization in Transition: The Future of Trade and Value Chains*, January 2019, McKinsey Global Institute.
Nora Lustig, 'The Sustainable Development Goals, Domestic Resource Mobilization and the Poor' in Jose Antonio Ocampo and Joseph Stiglitz (eds), *The Welfare State Revisited* (Columbia University Press 2018) 127–46.
Stewart Macaulay, 'Law and the Behavioral Sciences: Is There Any There There?' (1984) 6(2) L & Pol'y 149.
Elaine Croft McKenzie and Pablo Luis Durango-Cohen, 'An Input-Output Approach For the Efficient Design of Sustainable Goods and Services' [2010] 15 Int'l J Life Cycle Assess 946–61.
McKinsey Global Institute, *Globalisation in Transition: The Future of Trade and Value Chains* (McKinsey and Company 2019).
Tarcisio Magalhaes, 'The OECD Multilateral Instrument: Challenge or Opportunity of Multilateralism?' in Johanna Wheeler (ed.), *The Aftermath of BEPS* (IBFD 2020) 161–94.
M. T. Magombeyi, N. M. Odhiambo, and Duncan Watson, 'FDI Inflows and Poverty Reduction in Botswana: An Empirical Investigation' [2018] 6(1) Cogent Econ & Fin 1–15.
Rutsel Silvestre J. Martha, *The Jurisdiction to Tax in International Law* (Kluwer Law and Taxation Publishers 1989).

João Marcus de Melo Rigoni, 'The International Tax Regime in the Twenty-First Century: The Emergence of a Third Stage' [2017] 45(3) Intertax 205–18.

J. Martinez-Alier, 'The Environment as a Luxury Good or "Too Poor to Be Green"?' [2005] 13(1) Ecol Econ 1–10.

Mariana Mazzucato, *The Value of Everything: Making and Taking in the Global Economy* (PublicAffairs 2018).

A. T. Melese, 'Living Wage Report: Non-Metropolitan Urban Ethiopia' (Global Living Wage Coalition 2015).

J. Merk, 'Stitching a Decent Wage Across Borders: The Asia Floor Wage Proposal' [2009] Asia Floor Wage Alliance.

David Miller, *National Responsibility and Global Justice* (Oxford University Press 2007).

David Miller 'National Responsibility and Global Justice' [2008] 11(4) Crit Rev Int'l Soc & Pol Phil 383–99.

David Millon, 'Theories of the Corporation' [1990] Duke L J 201–62.

Edward C. Moore, Jr., 'Corporate Taxation' [1884] 18 Am L Rev 749–77.

M. Moore [2013], 'Obstacles to Increasing Tax Revenues in Low Income Countries' (Working Paper 13/15. Geneva: International Centre for Tax and Development 2013).

Julia C. Morse and Robert O. Keohane, 'Contested Multilateralism' [2014] 9 Rev Int'l Organ 385.

Susan Morse, 'GILTI: The Co-operative Potential of a Unilateral Minimum Tax' [2019] 4 Brit Tax Rev 512.

Mohan Munasinghe, 'Is Environmental Degradation an Inevitable Consequence of Economic Growth: Tunneling Through the Environmental Kuznets Curve' [1999] 29(1) Ecol Econ 89–109.

Richard Musgrave and Peggy Musgrave, 'Inter-Nation Equity' in M. Bird Richard and John, G. Head (eds), *Modern Fiscal Issues: Essays in Honour of Carl S. Shoup* (University of Toronto Press 1972) 63–85.

Richard Musgrave and Peggy Musgrave, *Public Finance in Theory and Practice* (5th edn, McGraw-Hill 1989).

Leif Muten, 'Tax Reform—An International Perspective' in *Vart Economiska Lage [Our Economic Situation]* (1988).

Subramanian Senthilkannan Muthu (ed.), *Social Life Cycle Assessment: An Insight* (Springer 2015).

Athiphat Muthitacharoen and Krislert Samphantharak, 'Tax-Motivated Profit Shifting and Anti-Avoidance Stringency: Firm-Level Evidence from Developing Countries' [2019] Puey Ungphakorn Institute for Economic Research Pier Discussion Papers No. 111, <https://ideas.repec.org/p/pui/dpaper/111.html> accessed 31 August 2020.

Thomas Nagel, 'Poverty and Food: Why Charity is Not Enough' in Henry Shue (ed.), *Food Policy: The Responsibility of The United States in The Life and Death Choices* (1st edn, Free Press 1977) 54–62.

Thomas Nagel, 'The Problem of Global Justice' [2005] 33(2) Phil & Pub Aff 113–47.

National Foreign Trade Council, Inc., 'The NFTC Foreign Income Project: International Tax Policy for the 21st Century, Part One: A Reconsideration of Subpart F' (2001).

Eric Neumayer, 'Pollution Havens: An Analysis of Policy Options for Dealing with an Elusive Phenomenon' [2001] 10(2) J Env & Dev 147.

James Nickel, 'Poverty and Rights' [2005] 55(220) Phil Q 385.

Douglass North, *Institutions, Institutional Change, and Economic Performance* (Cambridge University Press 1990).

Peter Nunnenkamp 'Foreign Direct Investment in Developing Countries: What Policymakers Should Not Do and What Economists Don't Know' [2001] Keil Institute for the World Economy Discussion Papers No. 380 <https://www.econstor.eu/bitstream/10419/2616/1/kd380.pdf> accessed 31 August 2020.

Augustine Nwabuzor, 'Corruption and Development: New Initiatives in Economic Openness and Strengthened Rule of Law' [2005] 59(1–2) J Bus Ethics 121.

OECD, Harmful Tax Competition: An Emerging Global Issue (OECD Publishing 1998).

OECD, *Taxation and Electronic Commerce-Implementing the Ottawa Framework Conditions* (OECD Publishing 2001).

OECD, *A Process for Achieving a Global Level Playing Field* (OECD Global Forum on Taxation, June 2004).

OECD, *Action Plan on Base Erosion and Profit Shifting* (OECD Publishing 2013).

OECD, 'Development Co-operation Report 2014: Mobilising Resources for Sustainable Development' [2014] 93 OECD <www.oecd.org> accessed 31 August 2020.

OECD, *Base Erosion And Profit Shifting (BEPS) Action Plan Report on Addressing the Tax Challenges of the Digital Economy* (OECD Publishing 2015).

OECD, 'Action 3 Final Report: Designing Effective Controlled Foreign Company Rules' (2015).

OECD, 'Strengthening Tax Systems to Mobilise Domestic Resources in the Post-2015 Development Agenda' Element 11 Paper 2 <www.oecd.org/dac/Post%202015%20Domestic%20Resource%20Mobilisation.pdf> accessed 31 August 2020.

OECD, *Development Co-Operation Report 2016: The Sustainable Development Goals as Business Opportunities* 56 (OECD 2016).

OECD, 'Measuring Distance to the SDG Targets: An Assessment of Where OECD Countries Stand' (2017).

OECD, 'OECD Model Tax Convention on Income and on Capital' (2017).

OECD, 'Platform for Collaboration on Tax to Discuss Domestic Resource Mobilisation Challenges on 9 October' (2018) <https://www.oecd.org/tax/platform-for-collaboration-on-tax-to-discuss-domestic-resource-mobilisation-challenges-on-9-october.htm> accessed 31 August 2020.

OECD, *Corporate Tax Statistics*, (1st ed., OECD Publishing 2019).

OECD, 'Global Outlook on Financing for Sustainable Development 2019' (2019).

OECD, 'Brief on the Tax Challenges Arising from Digitalisation: Interim Report' (2018), <www.oecd.org/tax/beps/brief-on-the-tax-challenges-arising-from-digitalisation-interim-report-2018.pdf> accessed 31 August 2020.

OECD, 'Global Anti-Base Erosion Proposal ("GLoBE") Pillar' Two (8 November 2019), <http://www.oecd.org/tax/beps/public-consultation-document-global-anti-base-erosion-proposalpillar-two.pdf>.

Arthur M. Okun, 'Equality and Efficiency: The Big Tradeoff' (Brookings 1974, 2015 ed.).

William Olney, 'A Race to the Bottom, Employment Protection and Foreign Direct Investment' [2013] 91(2) J Int'l Econ 191.

Elisabeth Owens, *The Foreign Tax Credit* (Harvard University Press 1961).

Elisabeth Owens, 'United States Income Tax Treaties: Their Role in Relieving Double Taxation' [1963] 17 Rutgers L Rev 428.

Oxford Poverty and Human Development Initiative [2020], 'Global Multidimensional Poverty Index 2020' <http://hdr.undp.org/sites/default/files/2020_mpi_report_en.pdf>.

Ivan O. Ozai, 'Tax Competition and the Ethics of Burden Sharing' [2018] 42(1) Fordham Int'l L J 61.

Ivan O. Ozai, 'Inter-Nation Equity Revisited' [2020] 12 Colum J Tax L 58–88.

Insop Pak, 'International Finance and State Sovereignty: Global Governance in the International Tax Regime' [2004] 10 Ann Surv Int'l & Comp L 165.

Thomas C. Pearson, 'Preparing Multinational Companies for Transfer Pricing Audits of Intangibles' [2006] 2(2) Int'l L & Mgmt Rev 159.

Eugenio Pellicer et al. 'A Method to Estimate Occupational Health and Safety Costs in Construction Projects.' [2014] 18(7) KSCE J Civ Engin 1955–65.

Claire Peng, 'A Rethink of Location-Specific Advantages with an Analysis of the Chinese Approach' [2017] 24(6) Int'l Transfer Pricing J 482–502.

Sol Picciotto, 'Is the International Tax System Fit for Purpose, Especially for Developing Countries?' [2013] ICTD Working Paper 13.

Sol Picciotto, 'Problems of Transfer Pricing and Possibilities for Simplification' [2018] ICTD Working Paper.

Steven Poelhekke and Frederick Van Den Ploeg, 'Green Havens and Pollution Havens' [2015] 38(7) World Econ 1159–78.

Lant Prichett, 'The World Bank Progresses on Poverty Lines' (Centre for Global Development 24 October 2017) <https://www.cgdev.org/blog/world-bank-progresses-poverty-lines>.

PWC, 'Life Cycle Assessment and Forest Products: A White Paper' (2010).

Vasujith Ram, 'Conceptualizing the History of Subpart F' [15 October 2018] 161 Tax Notes Int'l 315–34.

Delfina G.G. Ramos, Pedro Arezes, and Paulo Afonso, 'Economic Analysis of Occupational Risk Prevention: A Case Study in a Textile Company' in Steenbergen et al. (eds), *Safety, Reliability, and Risk Analysis: Beyond the Horizon* (Taylor & Francis Group 2014) 1473–78.

John Rawls, *The Law of Peoples, with The Idea of Public Reason Revisited* (Harvard University Press 1999).

Melissa Redmiles and Jason Wenrich, 'A History of Controlled Foreign Corporations and the Foreign Tax Credit' IRS Pub (undated).

Ana B. Reis, 'On the Welfare Effects of Foreign Investment' [2001] 54(2) J Int'l Econ 411.

Markus Reitzig, 'What Determines Patent Value?: Insights from the Semiconductor Industry' [2003] 32 Res Pol 13.

E. Jansen van Rensburg, 'The Application and Interpretation by South African Courts of General Renvoi Clauses in South African Double Taxation Agreements' [2019] PER 1.

Martha I. Riaño-Casallas and Emile Tompa, 'Cost-Benefit Analysis of Investment in Occupational Health and Safety in Colombian Companies' [2018] 61(11) Am J Ind Med 893–900.

Mathias Risse, 'How Does the Global Order Harm the Poor?' [2005] 33(4) Phil & Pub Aff 349.

Mathias Risse, *On Global Justice* (Princeton University Press 2012).

Thomas Rixen, *The Political Economy of International Tax Governance* (Palgrave Macmillan 2008).

Christina D. Romer and David H. Romer, 'The Macroeconomic Effects of Tax Changes: Estimates Based on a New Measure of Fiscal Shocks' [2010] 100 Am Econ Rev 763.

Adam Rosenzweig, 'Defining a Country's 'Fair Share' of Taxes' [2015] 42 Fla St L Rev 373.

Marco Runkel and Guttorm Schjelderup, 'The Choice of Apportionment Factors under Formula Apportionment' [2007] CESifo Working Paper Series No. 2072.

Choifor I. Saahdong, 'Indirect Tax Reforms and Revenue Mobilization in Cameroon' (Master's thesis, University of Oslo 2008).

Kerri Sadiq, 'The Inherent International Tax Regime and Its Constraints on Australia's Sovereignty' [2012] 31 U Queensland L J 131.

Helen I. Safa, 'Runaway Shops and Female Employment: The Search for Cheap Labor' [1981] Signs J Women Cult & Soc 7(2): 418–33.

S. Sagar, 'How "Limited" Is Limited Force of Attraction? An Analysis of the Relevant Case Law and the Potential Implications of the OECD/G20 BEPS Initiative' [2017] 71 Bull Int'l Taxn March/April 180–213.

Karl Sauvant, 'Attracting Foreign Direct Investment and Benefiting from it: Challenges for the Least Developed Countries' [2015] 7(2) Transn'l Corp Rev 125–27.

Wanchat Sawaengsak et al., 'Development of a Social Impact Assessment Method and Application to a Case Study of Sugarcane, Sugar, and Ethanol in Thailand' [2019] 24 Int'l J Life Cycle Assess 2054.

Asad Sayeed and Kabeer Dawani, 'Living Wage Report: Urban and Rural Pakistan' (Global Living Wage Coalition 2017).

Georg van Schanz, Der Einkommensbegriff und die Einkommensteuergesetze [1896] 13 Finanz-Archiv 1–87.

Guido Schmidt-Traub, 'Investment Needs to Achieve the Sustainable Development Goals—Understanding the Billions and Trillions' [2015] SDSN Working Paper Version 2 <http://unsdsn.org/wp-content/uploads/2015/09/151112-SDG-Financing-Needs.pdf> accessed 31 August 2020.

Guido Schmidt-Traub and Jeffrey D. Sachs, 'Financing Sustainable Development: Implementing the SDGs through Effective Investment Strategies and Partnerships' [2015] SDSN Working Paper.

Edwin R. A. Seligman, *Double Taxation and International Fiscal Cooperation* (The Macmillan Co 1928).

Senate Finance Committee release, 'Grassley Announces Bill to Rein in Corporate Expatriation' Congressional News Releases (Washington 2002) TNT 71-29.

Bradley Setzler and Felix Tintelnot, 'The Effects of Foreign Multinationals on Workers and Firms in the United States' [2019] NBER Working Paper No. 26149.

Stephen E. Shay, J. Clifton Fleming, Jr., and Robert J. Peroni, The David R. Tillinghast Lecture: 'What's Source Got to Do with It?'—Source Rules and International Taxation' [2002] 56 Tax L Rev 81.

Henry C. Simons, *Personal Income Taxation: The Definition of Income as a Problem of Fiscal Policy* (University of Chicago Press 1938).

Franziska Sixdorf and Sebastian Leitsch, 'Taxation of Technical Services under the New Article 12A of the UN Model – Improved Taxation or a Step in the Wrong Direction?' [2017] 57(6) Euro Tax'n 234.

Henry Shue, *Basic Rights* (Princeton University Press 1980).

Joel Slemrod, 'Location, (Real) Location, (Tax) Location: An Essay on Mobility's Place in Optimal Taxation' [2010] 63 Nat'l Tax J.

Issouf Soumaré, 'Does FDI Improve Economic Development in North African Countries?' [2015] 47(51) Applied Econ 5510.

Lee-Ann Steenkamp, 'The Use of the OECD Model Tax Convention as an Interpretative Aid: The Static Vs Ambulatory Approach Debate Considered from a South African Perspective' [2017] 10(2) J Econ & Fin Sci 195–205.

R. Stefanini, G. Borghesi, A. Ronzano et al., 'Plastic or Glass: A New Environmental Assessment with a Marine Litter Indicator for the Comparison of Pasteurized Milk Bottles' [2021] 26(4) Int'l J Life Cycle Assess 767–84.

Will Steffen et al., 'Planetary Boundaries: Guiding Human Development on a Changing Planet' [2015] 347(6223) Science.

Joseph Stiglitz, 'Capital Market Liberalization, Economic Growth, and Instability, World Development' [2000] 28(6) World Dev 1075–86.

Andrew Sumner, 'Is Foreign Direct Investment Good for the Poor? A Review and Stocktake [2015] 15 Dev Pr 269.

Jukka Takala et al., 'Global Estimates of the Burden of Injury and Illness at Work in 2012' [2014] 11(5) J Occ & Envtl Hyg 326.

Kok-Chor Tan, *Justice without Borders: Cosmopolitanism, Nationalism, and Patriotism* (Cambridge University Press 2004).

Vito Tanzi, 'Globalization, Technological Developments, and the Work of Fiscal Termites' [2001] 26 Brook J Int'l L.

C. John Taylor, 'Some Distinctive Features of Australian Tax Treaty Practice: An Examination of Their Origins and Interpretation' [2011] 9(3) J Tax Res 294.

David R. Tillinghast, 'An Old Timer's Comment on Notice 98-11' Tax Notes, 30 March 1998.

David R. Tillinghast, 'Commentaries to the OECD Model Convention: Ubiquitous, Often Controversial; But Could They Possibly Be Legally Binding?' [2006] 35 Tax Mgmt Int'l J 580.

Afton Titus and Tracy Gutuza, 'The Relationship between Tax Incentives and Human Rights Obligations in the Drive to Attract Foreign Direct Investment: Are African Developing Countries Getting it Right?' [2018] 1 Acta Jur. 149–82.

Trade and Development Board Intergovernmental Group of Experts on Financing for Development, 'Financing for Development: Issues in Domestic Public Resource Mobilization and International Development Cooperation' [2017] <unctad.org/meetings/en/SessionalDocuments/IGE_FfD_1st_session_Agreed_Policy%20_Recommendations.pdf>.

United Nations, 'United Nations Model Double Taxation Convention between Developed and Developing Countries' (United Nations Pub. 1980).

United Nations, 'Transforming Our World: The 2030 Agenda for Sustainable Development' (United Nations 2015).

United Nations, 'Addis Ababa Action Agenda: Monitoring Commitments and Actions' (United Nations 2016).

United Nations, 'Model Double Tax Convention between Developed and Developing Countries' (United Nations 2017).

United Nations, 'Practical Manual on Transfer Pricing' (United Nations 2017).

United Nations, 'Inter-agency Task Force on Financing for Development, Financing for Development: Progress and Prospects' (2018).

United Nations, *Handbook on Selected Issues for the Taxation of the Extractive Industries for Developing Countries* (United Nations 2018).

United Nations 'Extraction Fuels Rights Violations and Racial Subordination—UN Expert' (*OHCHR*, 8 July 2019).

United Nations, Tax Treatments for Payments for Digital Services (2019).

United Nations Conference on Trade and Development [UNCTAD], World Investment Report 2014: Investing in the SDGs: An Action Plan (2014).

Office of the United Nations High Commissioner for Human Rights, 'The Other Infrastructure Gap: Sustainability, Human Rights and Environmental Perspectives Executive Summary' (2018) 7 <www.ohchr.org/Documents/Publications/InfrastructureGapSummary.pdf> accessed 31 August 2020.

UNEP, 'Guidelines for Social Life Cycle Assessment of Products' [2009] 57 (affirming that social life cycle assessments are very costly and time-consuming); PWC [2010].

Krishna Vadlamannati and Ronald Davies, 'A Race to the Bottom in Labour Standards? An Empirical Investigation' [2013] 103 J Dev Econ 1.

John Vail Farr and Isaac Faber, *Engineering Economics of Life Cycle Cost Analysis* (Taylor & Francis 2018).

Laura Valentini, *Justice in a Globalized World* (Oxford University Press 2011).

Cyrus Vance, 'Human Rights and Foreign Policy' (1977) 7 Ga J Int'l & Comp L 223.

Jorge Enrique Velandia Vargas et al., 'Life Cycle Assessment of Electric Vehicles and Buses in Brazil: Effects of Local Manufacturing, Mass Reduction, and Energy Consumption Evolution' [2019] 24 Int'l J Life Cycle Assess 1878.

Alberto Vega, 'International Governance Through Soft Law: The Case of The OECD Transfer Pricing Guidelines' [2012] Working Paper of the Max Planck Institute for Tax Law and Public Finance No. 2012-05.

Jos Verbeek, Marjo Pulliainen, and Eila Kankaanpää, 'A Systematic Review of Occupational Safety and Health Business Cases' [2009] 35(6) Scand J Work Env & Health 403–12.

Klaus Vogel, 'The Influence of the OECD Commentaries on Tax Treaty Interpretation' Bulletin 2000.

Ingo Walter, 'Environmentally Induced Industrial Relocation to Developing Countries' in Seymour Rubin and Thomas Graham (eds), *Environment and Trade: The Relation of International Trade and Environmental Policy* (Frances Pinter 1982) 22–45.

David Ward, 'The Role of Commentaries on the OECD Model in the Tax Treaty Interpretation Process' [2006] 60(3) BFIT.

David Ward et al., 'The Other Income Article of Income Tax Treaties' [1990] 38(2) Can Tax J 233–69.

Marilyn Waring, *If Women Counted: A New Feminist Economics* (Harper & Row 1988).

Marilyn Waring, *Counting for Nothing: What Men Value and What Women are Worth* (Heritage 1999).

Joann Weiner, 'Formulary Apportionment and Group Taxation in the European Union: Insights from the United States and Canada' [2005] Working Paper No. 8.

Joann Weiner, 'An Economist's View of Income Allocation under the Arm's Length Standard and under Formulary Apportionment' [2009–2010] The State and Local Taxpayer. Symposium Edition 25–56.

Martin Weiss, 'Recent Developments in the German Tax Treatment of CFCs' European Taxation, September 2015.

Bret Wells and Cym Lowell, 'Income Tax Treaty Policy in the 21st Century: Residence vs. Source' [2013] 5(1) Colum J Tax L 1–39.

David Wheeler, 'Beyond Pollution Havens, Global Environmental Politics' [2002] 2(2) Global Envtl Pol 1.

WHO, 'Closing the Gap in a Generation: Health Equity Through Action on the Social Determinants of Health: Commission on Social Determinants of Health Final Report' World Health Organization 73 (WHO Commission on Social Determinants of Health & World Health Organization eds. (2008).

Thomas O. Wiedmann et al., 'The Material Footprint of Nations' [2015] 112(20) Proc Nat'l Acad Sci USA 6271–76 <https://doi.org/10.1073/pnas.1220362110> accessed 31 August 2020.

David Woodward, 'Incrementum ad Absurdum: Global Growth, Inequality and Poverty Eradication in a Carbon-Constrained World' [2015] 4 World Soc & Econ Rev 43–62.

The World Bank, 'The Cost of Air Pollution: Strengthening the Economic Case for Action' (WBG 2016).

The World Bank, 'Conference Report: Taxation and the Sustainable Development Goals' (23 April 2019) (World Bank Group 2018).

The World Bank, 'Domestic Resource Mobilization' (The World Bank 2018).

World Bank, 'Poverty and Shared Prosperity 2018: Piecing Together the Poverty Puzzle' (World Bank 2018) 69–70 <https://www.worldbank.org/en/research/brief/poverty-and-shared-prosperity-2018-piecing-together-the-poverty-puzzle-frequently-asked-questions> accessed 31 August 2020.

Caleb Yong, 'Rawls's Duty of Assistance: Transitional not Humanitarian or Sufficientarian' [2012] Nuffield College Working Papers Series in Politics <www.nuffield.ox.ac.uk/politics/papers/2012/Yong_working%20paper_2012_05.pdf> accessed 31 August 2020.

Gabriel Zucman, *Taxing Multinational Corporations in the 21st Century* (Economics for Inclusive Prosperity 2019) <https://econfip.org/policy-brief/taxing-multinational-corporations-in-the-21st-century/> accessed 31 August 2020.

Tarcísio Diniz Magalhães, 'What Is Really Wrong with Global Tax Governance and How to Properly Fix It' [2018] 10(4) World Tax J 499–536.

Tarcísio Diniz Magalhães and Ivan Ozai, 'A Different Unified Approach to Global Tax Policy: Addressing the Challenges of Underdevelopment' [2021] 4(1) Nord J L & Soc 1–31.

Tarcísio Diniz Magalhães, 'International Tax Law Between Loyalty, Exit, and Voice' [2021] 44(1) Dal L J 49–69.

Index

For the benefit of digital users, indexed terms that span two pages (e.g., 52–53) may, on occasion, appear on only one of those pages.